THE PHILOSOPHY
OF SYMBIOSIS

KISHO KUROKAWA

THE PHILOSOPHY OF SYMBIOSIS

AD ACADEMY EDITIONS

Author's note
I would like to express my gratitude to a number of people involved in this project. First of all, to Hans Dirk Köhler of VCH who supported the realisation of this paperback edition, my office staff for their work and and Jeffrey Hunter for translating. Warm thanks are also due to the staff at Academy Editions, Maggie Toy and Natasha Robertson.

Back Cover: Kisho Kurokawa. Photograph from *The Kensetsu Tsushin Shinbun*

Many new theories have been added to this text, originally published in Kisho Kurokawa's *Intercultural Architecture: The Philosophy of Symbiosis*, Academy Editions, 1991, to create this accessible version of Kurokawa's provocative thesis.

Published in Great Britain in 1994 by
ACADEMY EDITIONS
An imprint of the Academy Group Ltd

ACADEMY GROUP LTD
Editorial Offices
42 Leinster Gardens London W2 3AN

ERNST & SOHN
Hohenzollerndamm 170, 10713 Berlin
Members of the VCH Publishing Group

ISBN 1 85490 304 7

Distributed to the trade in the United States of America by
ST MARTIN'S PRESS
175 Fifth Avenue, New York, NY 10010
Printed in Italy by Tipografia Umbra

CONTENTS

INTRODUCTION

The world is changing rapidly. Some think of the end of the Cold War, the defeat of socialism and the triumph of capitalism, as the greatest changes of today. But it is my belief that the change we are witnessing is not simply change in the political sphere but a broad wave of change sweeping simultaneously through every field of human activity: economy, government, society, science, philosophy, art and culture. And it is a change not in volume but in essence, a structural change rather than a fluctuating rate of growth and decline.

The world is moving towards a new order for the twenty-first century. In this book I discuss this paradigm shift to the evolving new world order from several perspectives: 1) the shift from Eurocentricism to the symbiosis of diverse cultures, from Logoscentrism and dualism towards pluralism, towards a symbiosis of plurality of values; 2) from anthropocentrism to ecology, the symbiosis of diverse species; 3) a shift from industrial society to information society; 4) a shift from universalism to an age of the symbiosis of diverse elements; 5) a shift from the age of the machine to the age of life principle.

The ambition of this book is to suggest that symbiosis is the keyword for predicting and interpreting, from these various perspectives, the new world order that will appear in the twenty-first century.

The subjects of architecture and urban planning are raised from time to time in the book to make the discussion easier to follow. Yet I did not write the book for architects or urban planners; my intent was to stimulate ideas and debate among all who have an interest in the new world order and the new world that is fast approaching.

The 'philosophy of symbiosis' that I have articulated has

had a wide influence in Japan, and it has become a keyword of the new age in many areas, including government, business, art and culture, science and philosophy. Since the publication of the English translation of the work, symbiosis has also received much attention from abroad.

President Hirakawa of Keidanren, which leads the Japanese business world, has formed a Committee on Symbiosis and is investigating symbiosis as major economic policy; a Japan-Great Britain Symbiosis Committee has also been formed. Symbiosis was also discussed in the Japan-US Trade Structural Impediments Initiative. An increasing number of private organisations are also now calling for the symbiosis of people and nature, development and preservation, men and women.

The new parties that have split from the Liberal Democratic Party also call for symbiosis, and a growing number of prefectural governors are sympathetic to the philosophy of symbiosis.

More and more people overseas are also offering new ideas sympathetic to symbiosis in such fields as biology, chemistry, philosophy and physics.

Another important point is the fact that the roots of the concept of symbiosis are to be found in Buddhist philosophy and traditional Japanese culture. We can identify a strong current of tradition in the history of Japanese culture for seeing people and nature, past and future, the part and the whole, art and science, different cultures, economics and culture as existing in symbiosis.

In that sense, symbiosis is a key concept in understanding Japanese culture.

It is my hope that this paperback edition will bring these ideas to a wider audience of readers and provoke thought and discussion among many, in Japan and elsewhere.

PROLOGUE
WHY THE PHILOSOPHY OF SYMBIOSIS?

Co-operating While Competing

A great conceptual revolution is under way across the world, but is taking place so quietly that it has gone largely undetected. It is not the birth of a new ideology, like capitalism or communism; nor is it the advent of a new philosophy to replace that of Kant or Descartes. Yet the new currents of thought that are arising around the world will have a greater effect on us than any ideology or systematic philosophy. They are unarguably changing our way of life and our ideas of what it is to be human. This great, invisible change I identify as the philosophy of symbiosis.

Criticism of Japan – 'Japan bashing' – has been popular recently. American congressmen and representatives smashing a Toyota product with sledge-hammers is perhaps the quintessential image of Japan bashing. But the same impulse can be easily observed in Japan itself, where, as the proverb states, 'The nail that sticks out is hammered down'. Japanese society inherited a long tradition of human relations cast in a feudal mode, which dictates that those with special talents, with unique personalities, or those who achieve sudden success are attacked and ostracised by their peers. In an isolationist or protectionist era, when it is sufficient to guard the status quo and shun all external influences, individuality and achievement are despised as destabilising factors, and they are feared for the bad effects they may have on the established order. The fact that most Americans engaged in Japan bashing are protectionists further testifies to the truth of this claim.

The elimination of the spirit of protectionism, both in trade and in the form of group loyalties that exclude all outsiders, is a universal struggle and a universal goal. But to pursue that goal also means that we are plunging into an age of confrontation: between benefit and harm, between personalities and between cultures. It will no longer do to simply hammer down the nail that sticks out. We can no longer solve anything by attacking those who are unique or extraordinary. We are living at the start of an age of symbiosis, in which we will recognise each other's differing personalities and cultures while competing, and in which we will co-operate while we oppose and criticise each other.

Will the traditional Japanese reverence for harmony, the emotional and spiritual commitment to consensus, function effectively in this age of symbiosis? If we define harmony and consensus as undercutting all individuality and exceptional ability, as forcing all to bend to the will of the group, then that tradition will find itself at sea in the age of symbiosis. Nor is there much hope for a harmony that is served by cowering before the strong and failing to put forth one's own position forcefully.

When the positions or standards of cultural value are in disagreement, it is not necessary for one side to defeat the other and force his values on his opponent. They can instead search for common ground, even while remaining in mutual opposition. The success of this approach depends upon whether one has any desire to understand one's opponent. Even two cultures so different from each other that understanding is impossible will find that the sincere desire to understand the other makes co-operation possible.

The intermediate space and sacred zones that I will discuss here are necessary conditions for the establishment of symbiosis.

Whether it be the relationships between federations and peoples, nations and their minorities, or the EC and the individual countries that make it up, the symbiosis of part and whole, the issue of the individual and common rules, will become major themes of discussion and great changes will take place around the world.

The age when strong countries made all the rules, when they forced their ideologies on all other nations, is coming to an end. The nation and the city will gradually achieve an equal status, and cities will become increasingly autonomous, engaging in their own foreign relations, trade and cultural exchange. The minority peoples will also become equal in status to nations and federations, and parallel to such federations, they, too, will engage in their own foreign relations, trade and cultural exchanges.

This is the tide of the age of symbiosis.

This type of symbiosis, which includes opposition and competition, is often seen in the world of living things. This is one reason that I selected the term 'symbiosis' rather than coexistence, harmony, or peace.

The Age of the 'Death of God' and the Icon

One of the great revolutions of the modern age has been the 'death of God'. Up to now, society has taught us that all humankind is equal before God. For those with religious faith, God was the absolute and, at the same time, the one who instructed humanity in its proper course. Even after the masses ceased to believe in an absolute God, mass society created substitutes for the deity: heroes and ideal human beings, or 'superstars'.

There comes a time when each of us notices that his life has not proceeded exactly as he had wished. To compensate for this disappointment, he may transfer unrealised dreams to a hero, an athlete, a superstar or an idol of some sort. At the same time, this ideal image, or icon, becomes his goal. Society until now has been composed of this God, this ideal, this icon, on the one hand and, on the other, the great body of humankind – Heidegger's *das Mann*. But in the present age, God, the ideal and the icon are dead. We have lost the icon as our goal, we have lost our heroes and our superstars. Though stars may still be born, they soon fall to earth, and they are consumed in the blink of an eye.

A society that still has a goal, still has an icon, is a society supported by the concept of progress. Progress is defined as approaching closer to that society's goals, to the human ideal, the social ideal, to the heroes and the stars. For most of the nations of the world, Western society and Western culture have continued to be the ideal and goal. As a result, developing countries have made every effort to approach, even if little by little, the ideal that the West represents. Progress has been identified with Westernisation.

Societies that cherish this ideal refuse utterly to recognise the value or meaning of other cultures. For them, modernisation is Westernisation. It is the conquest of one culture by another.

Japan, in particular, from the time of the Meiji Restoration in 1868, consciously chose this path. With progress as its rallying cry, the nation has spared no pains in its grinding efforts to modernise. Years ago, Tokyo, and especially the Ginza area, was regarded as a major symbol of this belief. Enraptured by the icon of the Ginza, towns across the archipelago dubbed the main streets of their shopping arcades as the local Ginza, and little Ginzas sprouted all over Japan as quickly and thickly as bamboo shoots after rain.

And so, is it that Japan set out in pursuit of Western society and, eventually, surpassed it? This would be a ridiculous point to argue as it is impossible for a society to either overtake or not overtake another society of a completely different nature. We cannot speak of superiority or inferiority among cultures. Each of the different cultural spheres in the world treads a different path; it is not as if they were all on one large athletic field, racing against each other.

Recently in Japan we often hear the claim that it has overtaken the West and no longer has any goal to aim for. This is a great mistake. True, the philosophy of society up to now, with its faith in the ideal, the icon, has crumbled. Without an ideal, the concept of progress becomes meaningless; but now that superstars have faded, it has become possible for each of us to play the role of hero.

A Mirror Society

The film stars of the old days, whose names were synonyms for the ideals of female and male beauty, have passed from the scene and today's stars are on an ordinary human scale. When we see everyday-acting entertainers on our living-room television screens, we might believe we are stars too. Since an absolute and other God, a star as an image of human perfection, no longer exists, we must provide a dwelling for God and for stars within ourselves. This is the beginning of a mirror society in which we define ourselves through the activity of observing others, where others are a mirror in which we see ourselves. Since we cannot find peace of mind in God, we are forced to find it in looking at others. The present is an age when we are all greatly concerned with those around us.

Modern society offers great opportunities for each of us to emphasise our individuality and create a unique identity. We have taken the first step into an age of discrimination which values signs and symbols; the possibility that many unique individuals may flourish in symbiosis, that we may see the birth of a symbiotic society that respects every different cultural sphere is on the horizon.

I have purposefully used the word 'possibility' because the road is not an easy one. A mirror society easily degenerates into a conformist, absolutist society. This danger is particularly strong in Japan, where the strictures of the feudal village – which rejected nonconformists and those of exceptional talent – remain strongly entrenched in people's minds. A mirror society is in danger of becoming conformist to avoid being ostracised.

When one corporation succeeds in a certain venture, the rest follow in a thundering herd. Many Japanese businessmen, on the pretext of socialising, go out drinking night after night with their colleagues to communicate the message: 'I am just like you. We're the same sort. No need to worry that I have any special talent, any real individuality'. They are preserving the peace of the village. And by the same token, they are jealous and spiteful of anyone who does show special talent, anyone who succeeds.

The danger of a backward-looking mirror society spans the world of the university, business, government and the arts. Those who dare to violate the strictures of conformity are denounced by their colleagues and have the value of their achievements challenged. This is the accepted practice in Japan.

The age of heroes and superstars is finished. Recognising and evaluating the individual worth of others is a fundamentally different activity from the process of creating heroes and superstars. From the fair and proper evaluation of different cultures, different talents and different personalities is born the critical spirit, and a society of symbiosis is created.

The End of Universality

In the age of symbiosis the ideals of universality and equality, which have passed unchallenged, will cease to apply. Until now, the most widely accepted form of universality has been technology. It was widely believed that technology, which brought wealth and happiness to the masses, would unify and homogenise the entire world, regardless of the differences in development or culture among nations. Cars, nuclear power plants, and the glass and steel of modern architecture were supposed to make people in the deserts of the Middle East, the tropical cities of Southeast Asia and the loess plains of China happy, and make them the same.

We no longer believe this is true: technology does not take root when it is cut off from culture and tradition. The transfer of technology requires sophistication: adaptation to region, to unique situations and to custom. When the technology of one culture is introduced into another with a different

13

lifestyle, it is often difficult to ensure that the technology will take root. Even if in the future, atomic fusion is perfected and becomes economically viable, is it necessarily a good idea for such power plants to spread across the globe as the universal means of power generation? Probably not. If the per capita income of the Chinese were to reach the level of the Japanese, would it be a good idea for China to become a mass automobile society? Probably not. Each cultural sphere should cultivate its unique technological systems to create its own distinctive lifestyle.

The twenty-first century will be one in which fusion, fission, steam and water-generated electrical plants will exist in symbiosis. This will not be because some regions are too poor to introduce nuclear fusion generators, but because different people will select different technologies to create their own distinctive lifestyles.

The Mix-and-Match Age: Jekyll and Hyde

In contrast to the first half of the twentieth century, during which the concept of progress implied improvements in the quality of materials and standard of living, in the future, creativity will be the concept that expresses the richness of our standard of living. Though we will no longer have a unified goal towards which we progress, people will make the discovery of fluid, mix-and-match goals their aim. While Paris fashion reigns as the model of style, other designers need merely imitate it to create their own fashions. But in an age of mix-and-match, fashions from different periods, sexes and uses are combined and juxtaposed. Unlike an age fond of hierarchy, when conventions of time, place and occasion reign, in the mix-and-match age we can find delight in reading the sensibility that has dictated the choices in each new combination.

This will be an age where people can pursue many different activities at the same time. It will be a time of a broad and flexible 'Jekyll and Hyde' sensibility that can freely juxtapose the sacred with the profane, a Paris mode with farmer's overalls; a creativity that can, through subtle combinations, bring us novelty. It will, in other words, be the age when a richly-creative, schizophrenic personality reigns supreme. Sincerity and insincerity will live side by side, the distinction between work and play will fade, formal and casual will lose their meaning in fashion – such will be the lifestyle.

Whether it will be more enjoyable to live in this new age of symbiosis remains to be seen. The world will be a harder place though it will be 'hard' in a way different from our interpretation of that word. The age of the individual, an age of pluralism and diversification, during which each person will express his individuality and be responsible for making his own choices, will bring the joy of discovering what is different and unique. Each of us will need to make continual efforts to acquire the skills that will allow us that pleasure. Unless we cultivate our sensibilities, it will be difficult to make new discoveries or to be creative. Compared to an age of conformism when we could be lazy, we have no choice but to take the first steps on a path that may be difficult but which leads to a richly creative life.

FROM THE AGE OF MACHINE PRINCIPLE TO THE AGE OF LIFE PRINCIPLE

The Twentieth Century as the Age of the Machine

Thirty-three years have passed since I began my creative work as an architect. My work over those thirty-three years has consistently raised a challenge to the age of the machine and heralded the arrival of the architecture of the age of life.

Industrial society was the ideal of modern architecture. The steam engine, the train, the automobile and the aeroplane freed humanity from labour and permitted it to begin its journey into the realm of unknown. The Model T Ford made the possession of an automobile, until then the privilege of the rich, available to the masses. The main supporters of industrial society were the members of the middle class, who benefited the most from the age of the machine.

Le Corbusier declared that the home was a machine for living, and Sergi Eisenstein called the cinema a machine. Marinetti, the Italian Futurist, said that a poem is a machine.[1] Le Corbusier was fond of placing the latest-model automobile in front of his completed works, and the Futurist city of Antonio Sant'Elia was an expression of the dynamism of the machine. Not only for artists and the architects but for the general public as well, the machine was a longed for saviour that would blaze the trail for humanity's future.

The age of the machine valued models, norms and ideals. The success of the Model T offers abundant proof of this. By mass-producing a selected model of a product, the masses could be provided with a homogeneous satisfaction, an equally distributed happiness, and as the machine seemed to promise the rosiest of futures, no one thought to doubt it. In this manner, the middle class shaped itself into the ideal market for the machines it mass produced. As a natural result of this evolution, architects saw their clients gradually change from royalty and the extremely wealthy to the growing middle class.

The international architecture that became the prototype of modern architecture was also an expression of the models and norms of the age of the machine. The International Style of modern architecture was created by the capitalists who manufactured those products and the middle class that used them.

We must not allow ourselves to forget that the models, norms and ideals of the age of the machine were supported by the universality that represents the spirit of European civilisation; from Greece and Rome these standards have been fundamental concepts of Western thought. The 'Catholic' of the Roman Catholic Church means, in fact, 'universal'.

The age of the machine was the age of the European spirit, the age of universality. We can say, then, that the twentieth century, the age of the machine, has been an age of Eurocentrism and Logoscentrism. Logoscentrism posits that there is one ultimate truth for the whole world, and that it can be demonstrated with human intelligence. This attitude results in a society that honours science and technology, over art, religion, and culture (fields to which feelings and sensitivities contribute) to an inferior position.

The extraordinary strides we have made in science and technology, in economic development and increased productivity, are the results of this emphasis on our powers of reason. The twentieth century, the age of the machine gave birth to Eurocentrism and two great ideologies of the century, communism and capitalism. There can be no doubt that the twentieth century has been a struggle of European civilisation and the spirit that created it to dominate the world. If there were indeed a single truth, it would only be right for it to be spread throughout the globe, and that assumption, the rivalry of capitalism and communism and the pattern of thought that identifies becoming Europeanised with progress, must also be recognised as true and right.

The great reform that took place in Japan from the end of the Edo period (1600-1868) through the Meiji period (1968-1912) as we modernised and internationalised was modelled on Western civilisation. It was an attempt to absorb that civilisation and to approach it as closely and as quickly as possible. It had no other goal than to measure progress by degrees of Europeanisation. Japanese architects of the time debated ardently about which style of Western style to adopt. The well-known Western-style buildings of the period that survive today: Tokyo Station, the Bank of Japan, the old Supreme Court and the Yokohama Seikin Bank, were all products of the policy of modernisation in nineteenth-century Japan. Western food and Western clothing enjoyed a vogue. Modernisation was pursued in every field by adopting Western modes and models in the educational system, the economy, government policies, the constitution, and in the legal system.

This worship of the West, and the inferiority complex that is the other side of the same coin, persists in large measure in postwar Japan, and for the architects of the generations of Togo Murano, Seiichi Shirai, Kunio Maekawa and Kenzo Tange, Western architecture was an absolute, almost sacred ideal. When Murano received a new commission, he always began working by travelling to Europe and sketching design details of the works of famous Western architects. This tendency continues today with Arata Isozaki and a younger generation of architects, who, in a truly strange and inexplicable twist of fate, prize knowledge of Western architecture yet have an aversion to discussion of their own architectural tradition.[2]

Rostow, an American economist whose ideas were influential during the period of Japan's high growth in the 1960s, advocated a theory of stages of economic development. He argued that the economies of the developing countries would pass through stages of maturity and offshore economic activity to a period of high-level mass consumption. Rostow's economic theories are comparable to Darwin's theory of the evolution of species. In the age of the machine, when economic achievement is valued most highly, the cultures of nations with developing economies come to be looked on as developing cultures, as archaic impediments to modernisation. Architects from Japan or other non-Western countries who wish to be on the cutting edge distance themselves from their own history and tradition, or else reject them altogether.[3]

The architecture of the twentieth century, the age of the machine, was based on this view of progress. Yet this architecture was also the architecture of the age of humanism. This same Logoscentrism that so values the existence of reason regarded human beings as the sole possessors of that faculty. It ranked human beings next to divinity and it discounted the value of the lives of other animals, plants and living things. The world revolved around human existence, as the expression, 'A human life is more valuable than the entire world' clearly reveals. Based on this anthropocentrism and Logoscentrism, the pollution of the air, rivers and seas, the destruction of forests, and the extinction of animals and plants were regarded as unavoidable events in the development of the technology and the economic activity necessary to support human society and its cities and buildings, which were regarded as eternal.

The idea of 'architecture for architecture's sake' that we hear from Hans Hollein and Arata Isozaki has much in common with this Logoscentrism. The architecture with a capital 'A' that Isozaki advocates, architecture as form and Noam Chomsky's deep linguistic structure and universal grammar are all examples of Logoscentrism and the universality that characterises the age of the machine.[4]

Humanism played an important role in the medieval period when it liberated humankind from the age of God. But in the age of the machine, the human race has allowed itself to succumb to the delusion that, with machines in its employ, it has attained the role of God and can now rule both the world and the entire universe. Today, humanism has become identical with human superiority and Logoscentrism. This human superiority in the age of the machine is counterproductive in the age of life, with its emphasis on the environment and ecology.

Aesthetically speaking, the ideals of the age of the machine were economy, simplicity, precision, purity, multiplicity of function, abstraction and clarity. The architecture of the machine as envisioned by Le Corbusier required the purity that we can see in his paintings. It had to exemplify a norm, just as the Parthenon did. And it had to possess the clarity of the harsh Mediterranean sun, which divides all into light and shade. The Parthenon is the definitive and eternal monument to the European spirit.

When Bruno Taut and Walter Gropius visited Japan and praised the Ise Shrine and Katsura Detached Palace as exemplifications of the norms of modern architecture, they were praising the simplicity of straight lines, the abstraction free of ornament that they saw there. (Of course, they focused only on those aspects of these works that reflected their own modernist convictions.)

Some argue that the formal aspects of modern architecture should be regarded as high-tech architecture (analogical, formal quotations from the machine as high technology). The forms of Russian Constructivism, the Pompidou Centre of Richard Rogers and Renzo Piano, and Norman Foster's Hong Kong Shanghai Bank all seem at first glance to be representative works of the age of machine, but in fact they are not old. While the architecture of the twentieth century has multiple functions, is simple, economically efficient and expresses the Logoscentrism of the European spirit, the works mentioned above are not defined by structural rationality and efficiency to economic demands. In them, the image of the machine exists as the building's surface; it is autonomous, and it constitutes decoration and represents an experiment in the transition period from the age of the machine to the future.[5]

I have said that abstraction was one of the characteristics of the aesthetic of the age of the machine. Abstraction is common to all the arts of the period: modern architecture, modern painting, modern sculpture, modern literature and modern philosophy.

When Le Corbusier discusses purism in art, he says that the world is composed of such abstract forms as cones, cylinders and cubes. The simplicity so favoured by modern architecture was also a method for achieving this abstraction. The goal of industrialism – increasing production by simplification of the process – and the simplicity and clarity aimed for in modern architecture were regarded as the triumph of reason, in contrast to the plurality and variety of life. Modern architecture purposely sought to banish all historical expressions, decoration, topos and regionalism because it was believed that abstraction was perfect expression of the spirit of the age of the machine.

Yet geometrical forms are not the exclusive possessions of modern architecture. In ancient cultures, geometrical forms – the pyramids of Egypt, the circle and square of the ancient Chinese *Huanazi*, the keyhole-shaped tomb mounds of China and Japan, and the conical Tower of Babel – were thought of as mystical forms that expressed the ultimate being of the universe. The French architect Claude-Nicolas Ledoux frequently employed geometrical forms in his works. Yet the circles and orbs that he used were more expressions of symbolism and mysticism than 'pure' abstractions. Abstraction certainly is one of the products of modern architecture and the modern spirit, but modern architecture does not enjoy exclusive possession of the cone, the circle, the sphere, or the cube. I would like to develop this idea further, in the section on architecture of the age of life.[6]

I have said that the age of machine is the age of the European spirit, and I would now like to enlarge on this. Edmund Husserl, in his 'Die Krisis der Europaischen Wissenschaften und die Transcendentale Phanomenolofie', *Philosophia, i (1936)*, defines the twentieth century as the age of objective rationality. The fundamental nature of the natural science, geometry, physics and psychology in the age of modern rationality, is to seek to objectivise the world, based on the conviction that a single truth underlies all reality. These sciences seek to reduce (or analyse) reality to the measurable, thereby creating a world norm based on a unified world view. This is remarkably similar to the process through which a machine is reduced to its parts and standardised products are distributed universally throughout the world.[7]

This view of the world, this objective rationality and modern rationalism was created and perpetuated by Galileo and his theories, Newton and Lavoisier's physics, Euclid's geometry and Darwin's biology.[8] Common to all of these rational sciences is what is called the Bourbakian system or the axiomatic method, based on the assumption that an ultimate existence and objective methods of measurement exist. This objective rationalism represents the orthodox current of European thought. It is the main current of thought in which we find Plato, Aristotle, Descartes, Hegel and the Cartesian linguists Chomsky and Habermas.[9] The universalism of the Catholic Church, which is the backbone of European Christianity, operates in a similar fashion. At the start of all is a single ideal existence: God. The dualism that lies at the base of this stream of thought is the principle of the machine that makes reductionism and analysis possible. The entire world is perceived as sets of opposites: the part and the whole, the flesh and the spirit, science and art, good and evil, life and death, humanity and nature, and finally intellect and feeling. The principle of majority rule, one of the basic tenets of democracy, is also a dualistic choice between yes and no. The most advanced technology of dualism is the computer. The principle by which thought can be simulated through the repeated choice between 1 and 0 at superhuman speeds must surely be the apogee of the fruits of dualism. In this dualistic world, ambiguous existences, vague zones and multivalent zones are rejected. Contradictory elements, the symbiosis of opposing existences and mixed states have been treated as chaotic or irrational.

The architecture and arts of the age of the machine have employed analysis, structuring and organisation to achieve a universal synthesis. This closely resembles the process of creating a machine, in which parts are assembled to perform a certain function. Ambiguity, the intervention of foreign elements, accident and multivalent elements cannot be permitted in a machine. Instructions must not be literary or poetic, they must be denotation. Indeed introduction, connection, clarification and co-ordination are important. The finished products are precisely defined, syntagmatic; in other words, linear connections are the norm.

Schools must be school-like, hospitals like hospitals, offices like offices and homes like homes. But is there really any objective standard for a school that defines what is school like? In fact, the differences among hospitals – hospitals for the aged, psychiatric hospitals, emergency facilities, examination and diagnostic facilities – may be more marked than the difference between a hospital and a school. In the real world, there is no abstract 'humanity' with a capital 'H', humanity includes men, women, adults, children, Mr A and Mrs B.

The twentieth-century age of Modernism, is wrestling with these many contradictions as it nears its end. The fact that the end of the age of the machine is approaching simultaneously with the end of Eurocentrism, of Logoscentrism, and of industrial society, has aroused unrest throughout the world.

Will the curtain on the twenty-first century be raised by revolutions in all of these realms? Will the new age begin with the rejection of all of the machine, the age of the European spirit? I don't think so. The new century will carry with it the burden of the previous century, which will exist in symbiosis with a new philosophy, a new technology.

The Architecture of the Age of Life
In contrast to the age of the machine, I call the twenty-first

century the age of life. As I said earlier, my work over those thirty-three years has consistently raised a challenge to the age of the machine and heralded the arrival of architecture of the age of life. I founded the Metabolism movement in 1959. I consciously selected the terms and key concepts of metabolism and metamorphosis because they were the vocabulary of life principles.

Machines do not grow, change, or metabolise of their own accord. 'Metabolism' was indeed an excellent choice for a key word to announce the beginning of the age of life.

The astonishing plurality of life stands in sharp contrast to machine-age concepts such as homogeneity and universality. As a result of the combination of individual cells and the genetic information transmitted by the spiral configurations of DNA, each individual life is unique.

We are now questioning Darwin's theory of evolution. We must challenge the claim that the human species exists at the peak of an evolutionary climb and that the economic prosperity and technological culture fashioned by our reason may rightly serve as the means of natural selection for other living beings. Labelling stages of development, such as undeveloped nations, semi-developed nations and developed nations, represents a notion of progress that is similar to Darwin's theory of evolution. As I mentioned previously, the American economist Rostow's theory of stages of economic development was supported by the concept of progress in the age of the machine. The economic and technological advancements of this age, when universality prevailed, are now the subjects of intense reflection and revision.

In the age of life, it is the very plurality of life that possesses a superior and rich value. The rising interest in the environment and the new importance given to ecology aim at preserving the diversity of life.

Life is the creation of meaning. The life of the individual and the diversity each species possesses is linked to the diversity of all of the various human cultures, languages, traditions and arts that exist on the earth. In the coming age, the machine-age ideal of universality will be exchanged for a symbiosis of different cultures.

A new response to diversity is being demanded of the economic and technological sectors of society as well. We must make the creation of a new multipurpose culture, of a symbiosis of heterogeneous cultures, the goal of our economies and technologies. We must move from an age of economic assistance offered by the developed countries to the developing countries, and of the forced introduction of the cultures of the advanced nations to the 'less developed nations' to aid aimed at the creation of a 'developing'. The idea of technology transfer, too, is another manifestation of the domination of the advanced countries, an extension of the 'universalism' of the age of the machine. In the age of life it will be necessary to transform the technologies of the advanced nations and discover ways for them to exist in symbiosis historically existing traditional technologies of other regions. Instead of nuclear fission and fusion reactors becoming universal power sources, technology will have to be adapted in ways appropriate to each region.

In India, even today, dried cow dung supplies most of the energy for cooking fires. The Indians regard cows as sacred beasts, and the use of cow dung for fuel is an inseparable part of Indian culture and life. As Indian energy policy, would it not be best to combine the use of atomic energy, hydroelectric power, and cow dung in the most efficient combination? This type of transformation of technology so that it exists in symbiosis with the traditional technologies and culture is necessary. Such multifaceted responses from the economy and form technology are what we must expect in the age of life.

The intercultural architecture that I advocate is the architecture of this type of the age of life. Intercultural architecture is a hybrid architecture, in which elements of different cultures exist in symbiosis, an architecture that exists in symbiosis with the environment through the symbiosis of tradition and the most advanced technology. Eisenman's concept of 'softness' is intriguing in this context.

If the architecture of the age of the machine expressed function, the architecture of the age of life expresses meaning. The plurality of life is the plurality of genes. Differences are precisely the proof of life's existence; and it is these differences which create meaning.

The operation of the human organism is fundamentally the same for each individual, despite minor differences in capabilities. But the exterior of the body – in other words, our external appearance – is autonomous with these operations. All the feelings that we experience – love, passion, trust, friendship, refinement, dignity, hate, like and dislike – are greatly influenced by external attributions such as appearances, skin colour (white, black, brown or yellow), baldness, height and many other physical traits.

The age of the machine had come into existence with the background of the industrial society while the age of life was brought in with the background of the informationalised society.

In Japan, non-manufacturing industries already account for more than seventy per cent of the GNP. Such non-manufacturing industries as banking, broadcasting, publishing, computer software research, education, design, art, and the service and distribution sectors do not produce goods per se; they produce added value.

Information society and the information industries are based on the production of distinctions and of meaning. People buy clothes based on the added value of their design. A fair percentage of the pianos manufactured are never played; they sit in the living room, keyboards untouched. Such pianos are not purchased to express their function as musical instruments but as symbols that communicate that the purchaser enjoys music, or has the wealth to buy a piano and put it in his living room. In industrial society, this phenomenon is regarded negatively. But in information society these untouched pianos have every reason to exist, since they produce a meaning of their own. This is what Baudrillard advocated of the simulacrum.

Post-modern architecture grasps acutely the transition from industrial society to informational society. The post-modern is now regarded with importance in the fields of physics, science, mathematics and philosophy. It is unfortunate that in architecture the post-modern has been defined in an extremely narrow fashion, as a particular historical style. If the age of the post-modern has gone back to the past age of the historicism, not proceeding into the age of civilisation, there will be no future for the post-modern architecture. The failure of post-modern architecture in this narrow sense also demonstrates that any attempt to return to the modern architecture of the age of the machine will also be without a future.

Just as the plurality of life is created by heredity, architecture acquires plurality through the inheritance of its historical tradition. This inheritance takes place on many levels, and there is no single common method by which it occurs. The Japanese style of architecture called *Sukiya* employs a method in which historical forms are followed but new techniques and materials are introduced to produce gradual change. The *Sukiya* architecture of Sen no Rikyu, Furuta Oribe, Kobori Enshu, and, in more recent times, Isoya Yoshida and Togo Murano are all examples of this method. My *Sukiya* architecture, which I call Hanasuki, is another example of this symbiosis of past and present. In Europe, Palladio's architecture is, like Japan's *Sukiya*, another example of the inheritance of tradition.

A second method of inheriting tradition is to dissect fragments of historical forms and place them freely throughout works of contemporary architecture, the method of recombining. Following this method, the meaning that the historical forms once held is lost, and in their recombination they acquire a new, multivalent significance. This method is fundamentally different from that of recreating historical architecture.

Yet another method of inheriting the architectural past is to express the invisible ideas, aesthetics, lifestyles and historical mind-sets that lay behind historical symbols and forms. Following this method, the visible historical symbols and forms are manipulated intellectually, creating a mode of expression characterised by abstraction, irony, wit, twists, gaps, sophistication and metaphor. To read these historical mind-sets in the midst of contemporary architecture requires broad knowledge and a sharp sense of humour. Which method of inheriting the historical tradition is selected depends upon the situation in which the work is set. One important point of focus in the transformation from the age of the machine to the age of life is the conversion from standpoints of Eurocentrism and Logocentrism to the symbiosis of different cultures and to ecology.

What Robert Venturi, the father of Post-Modernism, Michael Graves, and Arata Isozaki all have in common is that they not only lean too far in the direction of the historical, but their work exists as an extension of Eurocentrism. Nor should we ignore that all are subtly influenced by the inferiority complex towards Europe that is common to Japan and the United States alike.

The prejudices of the humanism which was born from Logocentrism, by which human beings look down on all other forms of life, prescribe that human beings are not more than a part of the plurality of life on the planet; they are a separate form of existence. This means there is a close relationship between the age of life and the ecology. The architecture of the age of life will be an architecture open to regional contexts, urban contexts, and nature and the environment. It will move towards a symbiosis of nature and human beings, of the environment and architecture.

In the age of life, the movement will be from dualism to the philosophy of symbiosis. Symbiosis is essentially different from harmony, compromise, amalgamation, or eclecticism. Symbiosis is made possible by recognising reverence for the sacred zone between different cultures, opposing factors, different elements, between the extremes of dualistic opposition. The sacred zone of another's individuality, or a region's cultural tradition is an unknown region, though we respect that sacred zone. If our respective sacred zones are too all-encompassing, efforts must be made to achieve extended dialogue, mutual exchange, and to discover other positive contributing factors. The belief that all aspects of a particular people's lives are an inviolable sacred zone, an exclusive type of nationalism or a closed regionalism, is not conducive to achieving symbiosis.

The second condition necessary to achieve symbiosis is the presence of intermediary space. Intermediary space is important because it allows the two opposing elements of a dualism to abide by common rules, to reach a common understanding. I call this a tentative understanding. Intermediary space does not exist as a definite thing. It is extremely tentative and dynamic. The presence of intermediate space makes possible a vibrant symbiosis that incorporates opposition.

As the mutual penetration and mutual understanding of two opposing elements proceeds, the bounds of the intermediate space are always in motion. This process, because of the presence of intermediate space reveals the life principle itself, in all its ambivalence, multivalence and vagueness. Tolerance, the lack of clear cut boundaries, and the interpenetration of interior and exterior are special features of Japanese art, culture and architecture. The many essays I have written over three decades on such aspects of Japanese culture as: *Ma* (interval in time or space); *Engawa* (verandah); the concept of *Senu hima,* the moment of silence between thinking and acting as described by Zeami in his treatises on the Noh drama; street space; Rikyu grey; permeability equals transparency; lattices; and *Hanasuki* have all been attempts to pursue this idea of intermediary space. The Buddhist thought that runs through the base of all Japanese culture is also a philosophy of symbiosis, with the result that there is a strong natural connection between the architecture of the age of life and Japanese culture. That is why my works have run on a parallel course, with the simultaneous pursuit of the principle of life and Japanese culture.

Intermediate space can occasionally act as a stimulus for metamorphosis. Metamorphosis is one of the special features of the life process. A larva is transformed into a butterfly, an egg into a bird, or a fish. There is no life principle more sudden or extreme. Architecturally speaking, gates, atriums, large-scale and other extraordinary spaces move people because they make them perceive some sort of leap into the extraordinary, a sudden drama that cannot be explained by the function of the space alone. Such intermediary spaces as street space, plazas, parks, waterfronts, street scenes, city walls, city gates, rivers, landmark towers and the urban infrastructures of highways and freeways play a role as stimuli that make possible the existence of individual buildings.

I think it is now clear why, in the thirty-three years since I began my architectural career in 1959, I have chosen metabolism, metamorphosis and symbiosis as key terms and concepts to express the principle of life.

Philosophies to support the establishment of an architecture of the age of life can indeed be found in the history of Western society, but in the face of the tradition of dualism and objective rationalism they are in the extremely small minority. Unlike Plato and Aristotle, who represent the mainstream of ancient Greek thought, Democritus, Critias and Epicurus taught an atomic naturalism of atoms in the world order.[10] Leibniz, Spinoza and Wittgenstein expounded a natural science in which nature is inside us and possesses the power to create us.[11] Heidegger advocated an ontology of a 'culture of hearing' as opposed to the mainstream Western 'culture of sight'. Merleau-Ponty posited an ambivalence of the human body as opposed to Descartes' mind-body dualism. Lévi-

Strauss exposed the relativity of cultural values with his theory of structuralism. Deleuze and Guattari proposed the rhizome as a model for a new order of multiplicity and variety.[12] Baudrillard spoke of autonomy of the facade and the death of the economy. Derrida advocated the deconstruction of Eurocentrism and Logoscentrism. Julia Kristeva imagined a plural 'I' which she called a polylogue. The mathematician David Boehm discovered 'implicated order', which explains phenomena of the natural world previously thought to be random in terms of a non-linear analysis. Mandel invented a fractal geometry. Arthur Koestler conceived of the *Holon,* a symbiosis of part and whole. There was Prigogine's Dissipative Structure. Haken's Synergetics and Adorno's non-identity, which rejects the whole.[13] Foucault urged the deconstruction of modern rationality and departure from the centre. Umberto Eco wrote the exciting *The Name of the Rose* and *Foucault's Pendulum.* Post-Webern serial music composers such as Stockhausen and Boulez, who recently died, made their contribution as well. While the philosophy and science of the age of the machine were based on axioms of a Bourbakian system, the philosophy, science, literature and music of the age of life will all be problematic, and linked to the philosophy of symbiosis that I have advocated these past three decades.[14]

Not only science and philosophy but technology as well is facing a major transformation as the age of life dawns. While the technology of the machine age, of the age modern architecture was a visible technology represented by the steam engine and the automobile, the main players in the technology of the age of life will be communications, bio-technology, genetic engineering, and other invisible technologies. As opposed to the high-tech architecture of the age of the machine, created as a metaphor for the machine, the high-tech architecture of the age of life will be faced with the extremely difficult problem of expressing invisible technologies. The autonomy of the facade will allow for the birth of a new symbolic architecture. The expression of technology will proceed on a parallel course with the autonomy of the facade in architecture of the age of life, while the spirit of the invisible technologies of the age of life will be abstractly or symbolically expressed.

My own architecture will continue to pursue the architecture of the age of life, based on the three key concepts of metabolism, metamorphosis and symbiosis.

SYMBIOSIS IN ECONOMY

It was towards the end of 1978, I remember, that I received a telephone call from my friend Lou Dorfsman, a graphic designer and vice-president of CBS. 'Would you agree to be the chairman of the 1979 Aspen International Design Conference?' he asked.

Aspen, Colorado was originally a silver-mining town, and after the mines were closed, it was redeveloped as a resort. Three famous events are held each year in Aspen: the Aspen Music Festival, the Seminar of the Aspen Research Institute and the Aspen International Design Conference.

The Aspen International Design Conference is not only a meeting of architects and designers; philosophers, business people, government officials, and political figures also participate. This extremely unique conference is held each summer in Aspen.

Six months later, the busy days of preparing for the up-and-coming conference were upon me. I also had devised, by this time, a secret plan of my own. It was to make several of the aspects of Japanese culture, that were usually identified as unique, the themes of the discussion. Among the aspects of life that the Japanese believe are unique to Japan, there are some that are very well understood by the American people, and, on the other hand, aspects that Americans think are precisely the same as their own culture but are, in fact, quite different. Even if there were truly unique aspects of Japanese culture, I thought that by discussing them from a common point of view they would be transformed from an incomprehensible uniqueness to a uniqueness that can be understood for what it is.

After discussing my ideas with Lou Dorfsman, I decided to

make the theme of the conference 'Japan and the Japanese', in search of a path of symbiosis for America and Japan.

Symbiosis with different cultures was a theme that I had presented since the 1960s, and a subject that I will discuss in greater depth later.

The themes I selected for the subcommittee discussions were also rather different: 'Rice', 'Decision by Consensus' 'Isolationism', 'The Hedge', Verandah' and 'The Bullet Train'. (I also decided to express the subjects for discussion in the original Japanese, hence, '*Kome*', '*Ringi*', '*Sakkoku*', and so forth.) These themes were not only keywords for understanding something important about Japan, but also keywords for discovering the way to a symbiosis of American and Japan, I thought.

In the subcommittee discussion of 'Rice', for example, we reached the conclusion that Californian rice was already as delicious as Japan's *koshihikari*, but we also went on to discuss the fact that California rice included none of the cultural elements that adhered to rice produced in Japan: folk crafts, folk songs, festivals, sake-making and farming life. My conviction that for Japan, rice is a 'sacred cow', that rice *is* culture, and my opposition to the complete liberalisation of rice imports from the United States has continued from the Aspen conference to the present day.

In the subcommittee on 'Decision by Consensus', the discussion attempted to evaluate the traditional Japanese decision-making method of working from the bottom of the organisation up, in a democratic, consensus-style fashion rather than the top-down decision-making style of the American corporate world. The subcommittee's conclusion was that even such an apparently different method could well be adopted in the United States.

In the subcommittee on 'Isolationism', an interesting idea was proposed. Instead of regarding Japan during the Tokugawa period (1603-1867) as completely isolated from the rest of the world, perhaps it was possible to see Japan as having adopted during that period a dynamic semi-isolationism, under the shield of which the country was able to actively take in only what it wanted, rejecting the rest.

In the sessions on 'Hedges' and 'Verandahs', the Japanese traditions of the symbiosis of human beings and nature, and of architecture and nature were evaluated.

Sakyo Komatsu, Heisuku Hironaka, Issey Miyake, Tohru Haga, Nagisa Oshima, Masuo Ikeda, Toshi Ichiyanagi, Tadanori Yokoo and Yotaroh Kobayashi all came from Japan to participate in the conference, which ended in success.

Japanese and English were both made official languages of the conference, and at first there was resistance to and criticism of the decision to express the themes of the subcommittee meetings in Japanese only. This was the first time that any conference had been held in the United States in which Japanese was heard with such frequency. After the conference had ended, I was moved when an official of the US government walked up to me, shook my hand, and remarked, 'This conference demonstrated for the first time that English, too, is no more than a regional language. I feel as if the scales had fallen from my eyes. Thank you.' Another participant declared, 'I feel as if I understand at last the way in which the Japanese tradition and contemporary Japanese life are linked. I am convinced that Japan and the United States can live in symbiosis.'

At its closing, the 1979 Aspen International Design Conference left an enormous impact on the more than two thousand American professionals and students who attended it, as well as the Japanese panellists. What we all learned from the conference was that it was possible to build a common stage on which different cultures could meet, as long as they recognised their differences.

After returning to Japan, many of the Japanese panellists sought to continue to discuss the topics raised at the Aspen Conference, and the Japanese Culture Design Conference was founded to provide this opportunity.

The idea was to choose a different location outside Tokyo each year as the site of the Japanese Culture Design Conference.

The first conference was held the following year, in Yokohama, and I took on the roles of organiser and chairman. The main theme was 'Towards the Age of Symbiosis'. From outside Japan, we invited the French critic and urban studies scholar with whom I had been discussing the idea of symbiosis since the 1960s, François Choay; the Polish film director Andrzej Waida; Paolo Soleri, who was building an Eco-City in the Arizona desert; Renzo Piano, the designer of the Georges Pompidou Centre; and the legendary desert poet Alias Adonis. Japanese participants included the members who had participated in the Aspen Conference, plus Takeshi Umehara, Daizo Kusayanagi, Shuji Takashina, Ichiro Haryu, Shichihei Yamamoto, Hideo Kanze, Taichi Sakaiya, Shozaburo Kimura, Hisashi Inoue, Yasushi Akutagawa, Masahiro Shinoda, Junichi Ushiyama, Masao Yamaguchi, Yuusuke Fukada, Kimihiro Masamura, Tadao Ando, and others.

I remain impressed today how many profoundly signifi-cant issues were raised during the discussions at the various symposiums on the symbiosis of nature and humankind and the symbiosis of different cultures.

Paolo Soleri, who was building an experimental city called *Arcosanti* in the Arizona desert, put forth the idea that the symbiosis of humankind and nature was one in which human beings continuously created new things and in doing so, wrought change on an unfeeling, insentient nature.

For sentient human beings to live in symbiosis with insentient nature, human beings had to dedicate themselves eternally to transforming nature. There was no nature in this world that did not undergo change.

In contrast to this viewpoint, Shichihei Yamamoto de-clared that Paolo Soleri's 'symbiosis' was a Western-type symbiosis, and that Japanese could not live in such an artificially symbiotic city.

According to Yamamoto, the symbiosis of the Japanese with nature meant that the Japanese followed nature and merged with nature, and whatever did not follow and merge with nature was 'unnatural'. Symbiosis in this Japanese interpretation, then was an imminent harmony.

The interesting point that differences in cultures were so broadly reflected in the discussion of symbiosis offered a hint for carrying the discussion of symbiosis to a deeper level.

Another stimulating issue was raised by the Arabian poet Alias Adonis, also a logician interested in the semantic theories of Structuralism. He discussed the trend apparent throughout the Third World for Western culture to harm and trivialise local culture, while at the same time traditional cultures repelled any creative reform that contemporary culture offered and political regimes exploited the customs and traditions of the masses to preserve their own hold on power. Symbiosis, he insisted, would be impossible as long as traditional cultures did not liberate themselves from both Western culture and their own tradition.

The issue of obstructions to the arrival of the age of symbiosis raised by Yamamoto and Adonis percolated in my mind until I organised my thoughts on the subject in my 1987 book, *Philosophy of Symbiosis.*

The Roots of the Philosophy of Symbiosis

It is appropriate for me to explain here why I have been championing the philosophy of symbiosis for the past three decades.

I graduated from Tokai Gakuen in Nagoya (Tokai Junior High School and Tokai High School), the alma mater of both the philosopher Takeshi Umehara and the ex-prime minister Toshiki Kaifu. They are old schools, founded a century ago. No doubt because they began as schools established by monks of the Pure Land school of Japanese Buddhism, they are unique in that even today most of the teachers are Pure Land monks.

When I was at Tokai Junior High School, the principal was Dr Benkyo Shiio, a professor of Buddhist philosophy and head of the Shiba Zojoji in Tokyo.

Professor Shiio had founded the Tomo-iki (Symbiotic) Buddhist Group in 1922, and was part of the movement for developing new directions in Buddhist thought. This movement continues to be active today, as the Foundation for Symbiosis.

Professor Shiio was the author of many works, including the *Kyosei Hokku Shu* (*Verses on Symbiosis*), *Kyosei Bukkyo* (*A Buddhism of Symbiosis*), and *Kyosei Kyohon* (*Manual of Symbiosis*), but at the time I had not read any of his books. But the lectures that Professor Shiio gave on Buddhism at that time remain firmly fixed in my mind:

Human beings cannot live without eating meat and vegetables. They cannot survive without inorganic minerals. Not only that, but we are alive because all sorts of life forms (bacteria) live in our digestive organs. Human beings are kept alive by other life forms and by nature itself. And when people die, they become ashes and return to earth, where they in turn are eaten by plants, animals, and other forms of life. This relation of giving life and being given life is the relation of 'symbiosis' (*tomoiki*). And symbiosis is the most basic teaching of Buddhism.

Professor Shiio's message is none other than the message of environmentalism and ecology so important today.

After deciding to become an architect, I studied at Kyoto University. It was there that I encountered Professor Hajime Nakamura's *The Ways of Thinking of Eastern Peoples*.

This is a famous work that seeks to define the differences among various Asian cultures by examining the way in which Buddhism was transformed in India, Tibet, China, Japan, and other Asian nations as it encountered these very different cultures.

It was in this book that I first learned of the Indian Buddhist philosophy of Consciousness-Only. I had an intuition that the

Consciousness-Only school of Buddhism was in fact the source of the philosophy of symbiosis. From that time on, the Consciousness-Only philosophy has not only been important to me as an element in theories of architecture and urban design, but has also served as a guiding theme for my personal life.

My home is on the eleventh floor of an apartment building in Akasaka. It contains a manmade garden and a reproduction of the teahouse by Enshu Kobori that was part of his Fushimi residence.

I have christened this tea room 'Consciousness-Only Retreat'. And my name as a practitioner of the art of the tea ceremony is Yuishikian Kuchu: 'Suspended in Emptiness of the Consciousness-Only Retreat'. I was given this name by the tea master and president of the Hakuhodo Advertising Agency Michio Kondo, in reference to the fact that my tea room is suspended in space, on the eleventh floor.

This, perhaps, helps you to understand the preoccupation I have with the philosophy of Consciousness-Only and the philosophy of symbiosis.

I have no intention of discussing the philosophy of Consciousness-Only in detail here, but a basic concept of the philosophy is the *alaya*, or unconditioned stream of consciousness. The *alaya* consciousness does not distinguish things into dualisms or pairs of opposites, such as good and evil, body and spirit, human beings and nature. Instead, it is an intermediate zone in which such pairs exist together in symbiosis. In an intermediate zone, opposing, contradicting elements exist together, producing an undifferentiated, vague nature. This undifferentiated, vague element exists at all boundaries and peripheries. Because it is undifferentiated, it includes dense and deeply significant shades of meaning.

Since Western culture is based on dualism and antinomial opposition, undifferentiated and ambiguous elements are rejected as irrational, incomprehensible and unscientific.

It goes without saying that economic achievement, science and technology have played an enormous role in the modernisation of Western civilisation, but nothing could have been attained without the dogma of modern rationalism – that opposition and dualism.

But today the world is in a period of a major transition to a new age, and it is not in the least surprising that in an attempt to discover a new order for the further development of economics, science and technology, rationalism is being abandoned and the ambiguous and undifferentiated elements of intermediary zones that had previously been rejected are being re-evaluated in all fields.

It goes without saying that the philosophy of Consciousness-Only, as part of the fabric of Mahayana Buddhism, has broadly influenced Japanese culture and the Japanese people. If I may give just one example, let us look at the traditional Japanese aesthetic – an aesthetic of symbiosis.

I call an aesthetic that seeks to create a rich significance, by causing different elements to exist in symbiosis, *hanasuki*.

In his *Kadensho*, the Noh actor and playwright Zeami wrote, 'When playing a night scene, bring daylight to it, and when playing an old man bring a youthful feeling to it; when you play a demon, do it with gentleness.' Zeami called this process of bringing opposite, different elements together to create a deeply expressive richness *hana*.

It is often said that the Japanese are vague, or that Japanese politicians are so vague that no one knows what on earth they are saying. The aesthetic of symbiosis that I call *hanasuki* is not this kind of vagueness, which can't be pinned down one way or another. It is an ambiguity produced purposefully and creatively, ambiguity as a new essence altogether.

This Buddhist concept of symbiosis and the symbiotic aesthetic of traditional Japanese culture cannot, as Shichihei Yamamoto suggested, be applied in contemporary international society as they are.

But Japan, which has become an international economic power, is now expected to play a major role in the construction of a new world order – whether it wishes to or not.

Contributing money is an important duty for Japan, of course, but I believe it is also important for Japan to participate in the creation of the new world order through Japanese culture and Japanese ideas. Isn't it appropriate for us to apply ourselves to recasting the philosophy of symbiosis we find in Japanese Buddhism and traditional Japanese culture in such a way that it is useful to the contemporary world?

From the Age of the Machine to the Age of Life

The world order is on the verge of a major transformation. The Soviet Union has collapsed, the Cold War is over, American power has declined, and various national groups are declaring their independence – what kind of new world order are these developments leading to?

Why is it that we hear a call for a re-evaluation of Western ethnocentrism and modernism (dualism) from the midst of Western civilisation?

Why is it that the concept of symbiosis has been adopted by all fields of study and endeavour, from physics, biology and geometry to philosophy, art, medicine, economics and architecture? If a symbiotic order is to be the new world order and the philosophy of the twenty-first century, what kind of a order will it be? Perhaps 'the transition from the age of the machine to the age of life' is suitable framework for explaining the new symbiotic order.

In 1959, the largest international design conference was held in Japan for the first time. I helped with the preparations. While discussing what face we should present to the world, I founded the Metabolism movement with several other architects and critics at this time. My thoughts at that time were concerned with how we might face the relentless domination of Western culture. And my conclusion was a declaration of 'the age of life'.

If we were to describe the twentieth century in a phrase, it would be 'the age of the machine'. Humankind placed great hopes and dreams in a future that would be created by machines and technology.

The goal of the age of the machine was industrial society. A single model of a product could be mass-produced in a factory and then distributed around the world, until people the world over were alike and the world was one. This architecture was called the International Style, in which decoration and traditional elements were rejected as un-modern. The Western culture that produced this industrial society was regarded as indisputably superior to all other cultures, and it was spread throughout the world by force.

Once it is accepted that Western culture is the most advanced culture, all 'minor' cultures were inherently un-modern, and every step they took towards Western culture was regarded as progress. The poet Adonis' question whether traditional culture had to be abandoned for the sake of economic progress was the question on the lips of all developing and Third World nations.

Japan chose the way of Westernisation, cutting itself off from the Edo period and categorising all of traditional culture as un-modern. The great transformation of Japan wrought by the determined efforts of the Meiji government resulted in Japan becoming an honours student in the school of Westernisa-tion, until it had achieved such outstanding economic results that it outstripped its teachers. Without that astonishing 'Meiji *perestroika*', Japan as we know it today would not exist.

But the position that Japan finds itself in today is clearly a dangerous one, on the very edge of a precipice. Its teacher, the Western world, is engaged in serious self-criticism, and is beginning to identify new goals for itself. This will leave Japan an honours student without a school, and the fact of the matter is that Japan does not know what to do.

The reason that Western culture stood at the undisputed peak of modern civilisation was because every aspect of that culture – thought, religion, commerce, industry, science, technology and art – were orchestrated like a grand symphony, moving forward in a unified direction.

The rationalism and dualism that dominated from Aristotle through Descartes, Darwin's 'survival of the fittest' theory of evolution, the belief in universalism in the Catholic Church of Christianity, the doctrine of scientific proof, the Bauhaus school, which praised the beauties of industrialisation, the poets and artists who sang paeans to the age of the machine, the capitalist economy with its praise of competition, the industrial products mass-produced in factories and sent to the far corners of the world – all of these were interrelated in creating a grand, easily grasped social goal.

The spirit of the age of the machine is the essence of the law of survival of the fittest, based on free competition; the rule of domination of the weak by the strong; and modern scientific technology and economic law, which reject all ambiguity and difference in favour of speed, efficiency and standardisation.

The spirit of the age of life is symbiosis among differing things, an ever-changing dynamic balance, sudden mutations, metabolism, cycles, growth, the preservation of unique individuality through genetic codes, and multiplicity. These life principles are the goals of the spirit of the age of life. Among them all, symbiosis is the most representative life principle. The transformation from the age of the machine to the age of life is a simultaneous transformation from industrial society to information society.

During the age of the machine, there was competition to create high-quality products cheaply and in quantity, exploiting the merits of industrial scale. Since consumers wanted high-quality objects at low prices, what could be wrong about producing large quantities of high-quality, cheap goods? This was the typical approach of the age of the machine.

At the recent Environmental Summit in Brazil, the Biodiversity Treaty was signed. This is a ground-breaking event, announcing the beginning of the age of life. If you subscribe to Darwin's evolutionary doctrine of 'survival of the fittest', the extinction of species is a natural phenomenon that we can and should do nothing about. Why, then, do we try to protect species on the edge of extinction?

We should see this as the birth of a new value system for the age of life, which regards the existence of a wider variety of life forms as a richer kind of existence.

During the age of the machine, Western culture spread across and dominated the world, producing a homogeneous world. In contrast, the new age will treasure the distinct cultures of minority peoples and aim for the symbiosis of distinct cultures.

In the field of biology, various arguments are calling the abandonment of Darwin's theory of evolution. *Newsweek* recently introduced biologist Lynn Margulis' theory of symbiosis, which is gradually becoming the most widely held opinion in the field, contributing to the demise of Darwin's theory.

The 'Sharing Theory' of the recently deceased Dr Imai attracted attention as a revision of Darwin's theory of evolution. Within a certain species, Dr Imai found a tendency to create a boundary and then live in symbiosis, sharing the essentials of life.

The relations between medium and small-sized companies and giant enterprises, and the relations between the multinationals and their regional partners will also change.

Up to now, the larger the company, the more centralised and efficient management system it was able to create, and capital investment on a large scale contributed to the manufacture of high-quality, low-cost products in large quantities.

Medium and small-scale companies were 'developing companies' that would someday become giant enterprises or would ally themselves to large enterprises as subcontractors. As we can see from the example of the automobile industry, subcontractors are completely absorbed in the centralised management systems of the large enterprises.

In contrast, in the new age, in the age of symbiosis, medium and small-scale companies will exist in symbiosis with giant enterprises, just as local enterprises will with the multinationals.

In an information society, the desire for added value and variety, even in manufactured goods, will force the system towards diversification. Soon, even manufacturing plants will be very different things from the kind of factory we see in Chaplin's *Modern Times*. Today, when non-manufacturing industries account for seventy per cent of Japan's GNP, there is not necessarily any merit in scale for the production of added value. It may well be that the crisis that confronts IBM, which has pursued largeness without looking back, is related to this major change in the nature of our times.

I believe that symbiosis directed towards the new age will begin in a variety of fields. The movement towards symbiosis in every dimension has begun: the symbiosis of humankind and nature, the symbiosis of intellect and emotion, the symbiosis of science and technology and art, the symbiosis of commerce and culture, the symbiosis of public and private, the symbiosis of large enterprises and medium and small-scale enterprises, the symbiosis of different cultures, the symbiosis of work and play, the symbiosis of industry and society, the symbiosis of city and country, the symbiosis of generations, the symbiosis of men and women, the symbiosis of the weak and the strong, the symbiosis of the part (the individual) and the whole (an enterprise or a nation), and many other relations of symbiosis.

Whether it be inside Japan or in international society, a society that makes symbiosis on all these many levels possible represents a hierarchy of symbiosis.

During the age of the machine, when Western culture was in the lead, the type of society aimed for and the kind of culture that should be produced were clearly defined. The leaders of the West were clearly aware that technology, commerce and government were in the service of the creation of such a society, a method to achieve it.

Once I was asked by a French government official why it

was that Japanese government officials and businessmen were unable to discuss culture. He had clearly identified a weakness of present-day Japanese politicians and businessmen.

In the West, people work to obtain the means to enjoy their lives, for the emotion and joy they receive from cultural experiences, not for the sake of work itself. In contrast, most Japanese politicians and businessmen seem to think that personal enjoyment and cultural activities exist only because of commerce, and that once you have attained a certain degree of comfort and leisure, you can enjoy 'hobbies'. For the Japanese, art and culture are not national goals; they are no more than the 'hobbies' of music and art.

When economic development itself becomes the goal, the country becomes an economic machine directed towards eternal expansion, and from the viewpoint of Westerners, something that simply grows larger and larger without any higher purpose or goal is a monster.

The Debate on Symbiosis in the Business World

Recently, discussion of the concept of symbiosis has become popular in the business world as well. For the business world, which was the motivating force behind industrial society, to entertain the concept of symbiosis represents a dramatic conversion, a *perestroika* that Japan has not seen since the heady days of the Meiji Restoration.

But what is most conspicuously lacking in the discussion of symbiosis among business leaders is the conception of a goal appropriate to the symbiotic society of the age of life, which will replace the industrial society of the age of the machine.

In the recent debate on symbiosis, two essays have attracted my attention. One is by Yotaroh Kobayashi, and appeared in the *Sankei Shimbun* under the title, 'The Philosophy of Symbiosis for Japan'. The other is by Akio Morita and was serialised in *Bungei Shunju* under the title 'Japanese-style Business in Crisis'.

Yotaroh Kobayashi offers three points that must be addressed when discussing symbiosis. The first is defining the concrete conditions that must exist to say that industry and consumers are in symbiosis, or that Toyota and Fiat, or Japan and France exist in symbiosis. The second point he raises is that:

> While Japan may talk about symbiosis, it is naive to suppose that Japan's competitors will repay Japan's symbiosis in kind. Japan must take care not to lapse into a one-sided Japan-style symbiosis and it is important for Japan to realise that at times a certain kind of stubbornness will be necessary.

The third point he raises is that 'Symbiosis is not a goal in itself, but a method and necessary condition that a person, an industry, or a nation must employ to be and act as it truly wishes to'. On the other hand, Kobayashi does suggest that since the Japanese ideal is to become a nation with a high standard of living – or 'Standard of Living Giant', *Seikatsu Taikoku*, a newly popular spill off on the term 'Economic Giant' – the philosophy of symbiosis is the necessary means to achieve that goal.

If symbiosis is a method for achieving a goal (an ideal), there is really no need to even use the term symbiosis. 'Adjustment', 'compromise', 'mutual understanding' and 'co-operation' would serve as well and are easier to grasp.

If we regard symbiosis as no more than a means, then, as Tsuneo Iida has said:

> The cartel is the easiest method for getting along with one's competitors. If you cast symbiosis in economic terms, you have a cartel. When the Keidanren starts talking about symbiosis, it must be because they wish to change the method of coming to terms with environmental issues, regional problems, and foreign industry.

In an interview in the *Nihon Keizai Shimbun*, J Dowling, the chairman of the Japan-US Economic Council, expressed his doubts about the idea of symbiosis, remarking that it could be in violation of the US anti-monopoly and anti-trust laws.

The objections raised to symbiosis in business and

industrial circles arise from the existence of a deeply rooted methodology there that is opposed to the idea of symbiosis.

J Dowling later read my *Philosophy of Symbiosis* in English and wrote me a letter about it, from which I quote below:

> Reading your *Philosophy of Symbiosis*, I learned of the intellectually challenging and stimulating concept of symbiosis as a new world order. But the problem is that symbiosis as discussed in Japanese industry is very close to government managed trade and sharing of markets. I am concerned that it is unlikely to encourage new ideas, and that it could well obstruct the growth that new competition should bring.

In contrast, the main argument of Akio Morita's thesis is that the products of Japanese industry, which are high-quality and sell in great numbers, are produced from a different set of circumstances than prevail in non-Japanese industries. Japanese industry should try to approach the conditions that prevail in Western industry, with regard to vacations, salaries, environmental responsibility and contributions to the community, for example. If prices rise as a result, then Japanese industry can sell high-quality products at high prices.

What Japan must do now is aim to move from 'Economic Giant' to 'Standard-of-Living Giant'. It is necessary to change the Japanese economic and social systems as a whole.

I am in agreement with Morita's conclusions, but in his argument he suggests that Japanese industry must compete with foreign industry on its terms, and to do that Japanese business methods must be reformed. The new world order that he is aiming to achieve through economic means is, however, unclear.

Both Kobayashi and Morita affirm the 'Standard-of-Living Giant' that is a policy of the Miyazawa cabinet. I agree that this policy is important, since it represents the first time that Japan has made the improvement of daily life a national goal. But if all that means is merely larger houses, indoor plumbing, and a network of superhighways, that is, the improvement of the standard of living in terms of quantity alone, Japan will remain undistinguished among the nations of the world.

There is also the possibility that nations of the Third World will criticise the idea of symbiosis as a means for Japan and Japan alone to attain a high standard of living.

The idea that the goal of business is more business, that all profit is immediately reinvested for further economic expansion and more profit is now recognised as one of the causes of Japan's 'bubble economy' of recent years. Shouldn't the business world as a whole be engaging now in a serious discussion of a new world order with a society of symbiosis as its goal?

Towards Economic Assistance and Technology Transfer that Encourages Multiplicity

If we recognise the symbiotic world order represented by the Biodiversity Treaty, we cannot avoid the fact that it has called into question the oppressive universality of technology and economic factors that have dominated up to the present day.

As long as the developing nations seek to modernise after the model of Western culture, they have the potential of developing into a future market. Until the entire world has achieved a homogeneous modernisation, Western manufactured goods can continue to be produced in ever-increasing quantities.

It cannot be denied that economic assistance from developed to developing nations has been regarded as advance investment for developing future markets. But all nations do not necessarily follow the Western-style path of modernisation. Precisely because each follows its unique path, diverse cultural identities are created in the world, and so it is we who must drastically revise the universal application of technology and economic assistance regarded up until now as obvious.

The very term 'developing nations' will lose its meaning, and the concept of economic assistance, in which the rich help the poor, must be abandoned. A new kind of economic assistance, which includes the 'developed countries' as well, will become necessary. If we pursue this new way of thinking, we may come to the conclusion that the country Japan should be strategically concentrating its economic assistance on now is the United States.

In order to realise a new symbiotic order, a symbiosis of diverse cultures, money must be used strategically. I will discuss the reasons for this later, but what I mean by a strategy of the age of symbiosis is to protect the American identity by providing economic assistance to the US automobile manufacturing industry.

It is also necessary to change the very essence of technology transfer, through which the developed nations passed their technology without any modification to developing nations. Is it a good idea, for example, to transfer nuclear fission and fusion electricity-generating technology to India and Africa?

As mentioned previously in Chapter I, the main source of fuel for cooking in India is dried cow dung, a practice which is grounded in a culture that regards the cow as a sacred animal. If indeed our goal is to create a symbiosis of diverse cultures, our task is to effect a transformation of technology that will allow electricity and cow dung fuel to exist in symbiosis.

This shows us that in the new age of an order of symbiosis, the economy and technology can no longer evolve separately from culture and tradition. For the world of commerce, which believed up to now that the principles of business and technology had universal application, a new scenario is going to be required for the age of symbiosis.

Since in the age of symbiosis the symbiosis of diverse cultures the world over, including the smallest minorities, will be the goal, we will have to drastically alter the direction of economic assistance and technology transfer in such a way that they will contribute to the preservation of this enormous cultural diversity. And of course, we must dissuade the developing nations from the path of modernisation through industrialisation.

For example, if we build highways in every country of the world and make automobiles the universal mode of transportation, we probably cannot avoid destroying distinct traditional lifestyles. Isn't it possible to combine the most advanced technology of the developed nations with the traditional technology of each 'developing' nation and support instead a creative and distinct development of technology unique to that society?

In order to discuss this in more concrete terms, let me introduce my experience working in the Sahara desert.

I was approached with the project of creating a desert city with a population of tens of thousands. A large reservoir of water was discovered several hundred meters below the desert in the North Sahara, near As-Sarir. The plan was to tap that underground deposit and use it for farming in the desert.

When I first arrived at the site and looked to the horizon, all there was to see was the vast, empty desert. That's when I had an inspiration: wouldn't it be wonderful if we could use the sand all around us as a building material? We would create a recycled city, born from the sands which would someday return to them again.

The grains of desert sand, unlike ordinary sand, are perfectly round. They are also finer than ordinary sand, and they can't be mixed successfully with cement. But after two years of work and with the co-operation of a desert centre located in England, we were able to develop sand bricks using the local desert sands.

We made plans for revising the most advanced mass-produced kitchen sets and toilet facilities to fit the lifestyle of the Bedouin inhabitants.

Because of future maintenance problems for electrical equipment, we decided not to install air conditioning and heating but to rely instead on the traditional 'wind chimneys'.

A wind chimney is a tower attached to a house that helps to

create, by exploiting breezes or temperature gaps, an updraft inside the house. Though the desert surface undergoes drastic changes in temperature, the earth from one to several meters below the ground is stable in temperature. A wind chimney brings cool air up from below the earth when it is forty degrees outside, and when it is cold at night, it warms the floor, acting as a natural and traditional heating and cooling system.

Our experiment in our desert town was not simply bringing in the newest technology and the industrial products of the developed nations unchanged, but transforming the technology and products to exist in symbiosis with the traditions and climate of the region, the lifestyle that is the region's culture.

Simply preserving tradition is a backward-looking approach, and quickly lapses into old-style racialism. On the other hand, introducing the economy and technology of the developed nations into the developing nations without making any changes results in the destruction of the culture and lifestyle of the people and the region.

The technology of the developed nations, and the economies that have been grown from that technology, are unavoidably being pushed to a new transformation for the age of symbiosis that incorporates regional identity and traditional cultures and lifestyles.

The argument that business comes before culture, that cultural support for the arts depends first upon thriving commerce, no longer holds, even for the sake of business growth itself.

A Shared Strategy for Business and Culture
I would like to discuss another experience I had because it is relevant to our discussion of Japanese business.

As everyone knows, excess Japanese capital has poured out into the world, seeking new enterprises in which to invest. I have fielded questions from American and European businessmen and intellectuals regarding Japanese industry, which has bought property in Europe and America and is engaging in many redevelopment projects.

When the oil dollars began to buy buildings around the world and engage 'in redevelopment projects, it was our evaluation that the goal of this investment was a quick return, and that sooner or later the investors would withdraw again. As a result, we agreed to be very cautious about such investments.

We all hoped that the recent Japanese investment outside Japan would be different, but now the emerging consensus is that the Japanese investment is not so different from the oil dollar investment before it.

From the perspective of our friends in Europe and the United States, architecture and urban development are the very core of a country's culture, and as such are part of a long-term general strategy that encompasses business, technology and culture.

François Mitterand's 'Grand Projet' – including the construction of the New Paris Opera, museums, the new Arc de Triomphe, libraries, the Arab Cultural Research Centre, and the renovations and additions to the Louvre – was a grand international strategy to assure that twenty-first-century France would remain an international centre of art and culture.

Looking to the upcoming unity of the EC, the goal of Mitterand's strategy was to make Paris an international cultural centre, and he clearly stated that business and technology were means to achieve this cultural goal.

Nations with powerful economies and advanced technology have a comparable authority, and their political clout is strong. Usually, such nations also increase their military power and take the role of world leader or world policeman. England in the Victorian period, the Prussian Empire, and post-war America are all examples.

But it is no longer true that a nation with a strong economy, advanced technology, and a large military force necessarily commands respect from other nations in the world.

The fear of Japan that is whispered about in the world recently is not a simple phenomenon; its source ranges from jealousy to complete misunderstanding, but especially frequently heard is that others have no idea what kind of nation the Japanese want to create with their money and technology, what kind of world order is their goal. Perhaps Japan has no cultural goals and seeks only to expand its economy and increase its profit. The thought of an infinitely expanding giant economic machine is unsettling.

To become a world leader that can contribute to the construction of a new world order, a nation needs not only power but authority. Power is obtained through economic achievement, technology and military force, but those are not the elements that make up authority. Authority is acquired through culture.

In every country on earth, people look down on the nouveau riche, people who spend all their time hustling after money and have no interest at all in art or culture. You can't expect to have the respect of others simply because you are rich and your hands are covered with gold and diamond rings. The farther such a person goes, in having the Mercedes Benz trademark cast in gold or making an all-gold bathtub, the more he is scorned.

In contrast, the poorest artist or scholar may well possess the authority to move people's hearts. This is the power of intelligence, of culture. The criticism that 'Japan has no face' is another way of saying that though Japan may be wealthy, it has no cultural authority.

The many and diverse regional cultures that exist in the world today may be a bit backward from an economic or technological perspective, but each possesses its unique cultural identity. The symbiosis of different cultures around the world only becomes possible when we respect and value the authority and pride of each of these traditional cultures.

This is no doubt the sense of the Arab poet Adonis' remark that an indispensable condition for symbiosis is the liberation of other cultures from the oppression of Western culture, which hurts their pride.

Sacred Zones, Indispensable for Symbiosis

I believe that a theory of sacred zones is a key concept in discussing the significance of the dawning age of symbiosis in greater depth.

The word 'symbiosis' is probably of little interest to friends, to people without competition or opposition. Symbiosis as a new world order should really be used to describe the relationship we form between two essentially opposing mutually exclusive elements. In this sense, it is completely different from Shichihei Yamamoto's Japanese-style symbiosis as imminent harmony.

The 'harmony' that the Japanese are so fond of is a sort of peaceful compromise that avoids struggle, conflict, and competition. It is a concept that the Japanese probably acquired in the communalism of agricultural society. We also have the term 'coexistence'. How is that different from symbiosis?

During the Cold War, the period of the Iron Curtain, the Soviet Union and the United States turned their backs on each other and competed to dominate the world. I think this can be described as a state in which neither party needs the other.

What I mean by 'symbiosis' is a relationship of mutual need – while competition, opposition and struggle continue. How can mutually opposing, different things exist in symbiosis? The concept of sacred zones is the key. I believe that every country, every culture should have its sacred zones.

As I followed the meeting of the Japan-US Structural Impediments Imperative, it seemed to me that the US position was that as world leader, America's rules should be the world's rules. Everyone should follow the same, common rules, which transcend differences among cultures and peoples. This is a typical form of domination, of the universalism of age.

Certainly, as much as possible commonly held rules are a good idea. No one, I think, would oppose the statement that as much as possible, we should have free competition based on a fair and agreed-upon basis. But on the other hand, the fact that differences remain is not evil, nor is it irrational. The United States certainly does not suggest that Iran, for example, should abandon Islam and Islamic customs.

Protecting the diversity of life means protecting the diversity of culture, and supporting that diversity. A symbiotic order is an order in which we recognise others' differences and their sacred zones, and compete on that basis. Economic activity can be statistically measured, but the same standards cannot be applied to culture, religion, or a lifestyle. These things are judged by quality. That is why we cannot rank cultures in a hierarchy of superior and inferior.

I think that for Japan, the emperor system, rice cultivation, and the Sumo rank of yokozuna (grand champion) Kabuki and the tea ceremony (with its *sukiya*-style architecture) are sacred zones.

Though the emperor system may be regarded as merely a symbolic rank today, I believe it plays an immeasurable role in stabilising Japanese society. That is the reason that the US Occupation made positive efforts to preserve the system after the war.

I have mentioned rice earlier, and as long as rice is discussed purely as a foodstuff, I think it is only natural to completely liberalise the market and allow the free import of US-produced rice.

But though it may be true that Japanese agriculture is gradually becoming a part-time occupation and the nation is increasingly urbanised, rice production is shrouded in the very roots of Japanese culture in farming villages, festivals, folk songs, sake production, and the other aspects of rice as culture. The forestry industry, now in crisis, is supported by agricultural labour during fall and winter, as is lacquer work and other traditional crafts. This 'culture of rice' does not come with rice grown in California, which is a foodstuff pure and simple.

If sumo were simply a sport, no one would disagree that everything in it should be decided on the basis of matches won and lost. But from its inception sumo has been closely linked to the emperor system, and it has a strong traditional and ceremonial aspect. If we ascribe a special significance to the grand champion, who carries out many of those ceremonies, there is nothing wrong with regarding his rank as a sacred zone. This is not racial discrimination by any interpretation.

The idea of sacred zones is fundamentally distinct from the doctrine of protectionism in trade.

It is important to note that America has its sacred zones as well. Having adopted a dominant, universalist posture, it is hard for the United States to admit that it has its own sacred zones; so, for the sake of building the new symbiotic order, Japan should come out and say to the US that it is all right to have sacred zones. Once Japan has helped America defend its sacred zones, Japan will be able to declare its own sacred zones.

In my opinion, the automobile industry, baseball and Hollywood are all sacred zones for the United States. American culture as we know it would not exist without the automobile industry, baseball, space and aeronautics industries and Hollywood. All are deeply rooted in the American lifestyle and are sources of pride for Americans.

If we think solely from the perspective of economics, there is no reason why Japanese companies shouldn't buy Hollywood studios, become owners of major-league teams, or crush the US auto industry. Japanese companies could insist that they were invited to buy out American interests, or that US consumers prefer Japanese cars.

According to M&A, one of the rules of American business is that a company can be sold at any time, and the Japanese buyers thus see no problem with their acquisitions, even thinking, with some justification, that the Americans should be grateful to find a buyer. But US business leaders and the American people are two different things. The rules of business and technology are not just that but should also be seen as connected to a people's lifestyle and feelings.

The feelings of the American people are deeply hurt. In addition to the need to bring Japanese industry closer to that in the West and to change the Japanese economic and social system as a whole, we need to recognise the cultural imperative not to invade the sacred zones of other cultures. When we do business abroad, we must make efforts to preserve the unique local culture, participate in the cultural life of the cities, and strengthen the links between business and culture.

Even if two parties recognise each other's sacred zones, if they share no common rules, there is no way they can exist in symbiosis. But if they share at least a certain amount of rules, and if they have any desire at all to understand each other, they can use that common ground to open a dialogue and the construction of a symbiotic relationship becomes possible.

The size of the arena of shared rules is never fixed. It is better to think of it as always changing, in response to the changing strengths of both parties and global conditions.

Symbiosis is a dynamically changing relationship. At times Japanese business style should be followed, and at other times the other nation's business style should be adopted. Through a process of trial and error, the arena of shared rules can be enlarged.

That is why Japanese companies should not become the sole owners or operators of foreign companies. Whenever possible, they should expand co-operative ventures with the companies of other countries. Yet the reason Japanese companies prefer to completely buy out a company is that they regard it as a loss of face unless they have complete and sole control.

But through trial and error and repeated dialogue, and to

deepen mutual understanding, we must change direction from outright purchase to participatory investment, from sole operation to joint operation, from buying completed buildings to building a symbiotic relationship through participation in long-term urban redevelopment programmes.

In any ease, the new symbiotic order that is beginning is different from the free competition we have known until now, and it is without a doubt a goal that requires painstaking effort and one that is fraught with difficulties to overcome.

TRANSCENDING MODERNISM

For half a century, beginning in the 1920s, the following three elements have characterised what we know as the modern world: 1) universalism based on industrialisation; 2) a division of labour based on function; and 3) elimination of classes. Industrial products such as watches, automobiles and aeroplanes were great luxuries when first invented, but our industrial society now provides these things in great quantity and at reasonable prices to the masses, fulfilling its great dream of producing the blessings of a material civilisation and eliminating the gap between rich and poor. As a result, today almost all of us can buy anything from a watch to a personal computer with our pocket money.

This great wave of industrialisation gave birth to the International Style. This is the Modern architecture we are all so familiar with, the great boxes of steel, glass and concrete. The International Style liberated architecture from past modes through the use of new materials and revolutionary technologies, creating a universal architectural model that spread to all countries and cultures. For me, the International Style resembles Esperanto since it sought to create a common architectural language for all humanity.

But this universal model is in fact based on the values and ethos of Western civilisation. Again, the resemblance to Esperanto is clear, for Esperanto was a universal language based on Western languages. Modernisation turned out to be industrialisation, based on the value system of the West; and the developing nations, in their pursuit of modernisation through industrialisation, have all quite naturally pursued Westernisation with equal keenness.

By ignoring the climate and traditional culture of the site, the International Style imposes a single style throughout the world. As part of the process of modernisation unfolding in the People's Republic of China, an all-glass hotel called the Changcheng Fandian has been constructed in Beijing. But with Beijing's climate – cold in winter and hot in summer – the operating costs of an all-glass multistorey structure are enormous. Such local maintenance problems are typical of buildings in the International Style. It is not enough to carry the latest in building technology into a developing country and put together a building from it; if replacement parts and proper repair services aren't available, the new building will soon be severely crippled: elevators stop running and spare parts cannot be found.

When Toyota decided to sell its cars in the United States, it began by establishing a customer-service network of several hundred outlets; for without a proper maintenance system, sophisticated technology is soon reduced to utter uselessness. When high technologies are introduced into developing countries, they must be adapted to the culture and climate of the site. The need for a symbiosis between technology and the cultural tradition must be appreciated.

It is time, too, to correct the mistaken Western conception that universalism is divinely ordained; we should abandon Esperanto-style thinking. Internationalism can be achieved by deepening our understanding of our own language while engaging in exchange with other languages. If Yukio Mishima or Yasunari Kawabata had written their classics *The Temple of the Golden Pavilion* or *Snow Country* in Esperanto, they could not have created the literary depth that they achieved in Japanese. It is precisely because they wrote in their richly suggestive vernacular that they achieved literary success. But need we conclude that a literature that could only have been written in Japanese can only be understood and appreciated in Japan? Quite the contrary. People around the world are reading Mishima and Kawabata, Tanizaki, Abe Kobo and Oe Kenzaburo – in translation. Through translation, literature of quality in Japanese becomes literature of international quality.

I must make perfectly clear, however, that in rejecting the universalism and internationalism that presupposed the superiority of the West, I do not advocate a static traditionalism or narrow racialism. I believe instead that the coming age will be a time when the different regions of the world will re-examine their own traditions. On the international level, each region will confront the values and standards of other regions and, while mutually influencing each other, each will produce its own distinctive culture. Rather than internationalism, I call this interculturalism.

The Weakness of a Purebred Culture

As a culture matures, it becomes more and more centripetal, and conservative forces aimed at preserving its purity come strongly into play. It rejects all dissonant, opposing and heterogeneous elements and constructs its own distinct hierarchy. In this process, the culture's identity is sharpened and refined. Such a refined, highly distinctive culture – a purebred culture as it were – is surprisingly unstable, and this is particularly so when it has grown tremendously. Unlike a 'mongrel culture', which contains many heterogeneous elements, a purebred culture is unable to adapt to changes in its environment. One of the reasons European culture is undeniably on the wane is that since the time of the Greeks and Romans, Europeans have been excessively concerned with preserving the orthodoxy of their culture, excluding all the surrounding cultures of the Islamic world and Asia.

The weakness of the pure-blooded and the strength of the mongrel can be seen in business organisations as well. If a company limits itself to one product and concentrates entirely on strategies for its production and sale, it will acquire very sophisticated skills and know-how concerning that product. If that product is automobiles, for example, the company is capable of becoming an unchallenged giant in that industry.

But if, due to external circumstances, the automotive industry as a whole falls upon hard times, the company will collapse – victim of the transportation revolution, an upset in the balance of petroleum supply and demand, or trade friction.

In the past, coal-mining was the leading industry in many outlying regions, but now it is disappearing and taking the coal-mining towns with it. The textile industry is on its way out as a major Japanese industry. A look at the present state of the national railways system, the petrochemical industry, steel and shipbuilding shows how technologies that are organised centripetally around a single product are susceptible to the passage of time and, for all their size and strength, deteriorate easily when conditions change.

To acquire the necessary flexibility and adaptability, many industries today are sub-dividing and diversifying. The companies Toray and Kanebo are excellent examples: originally textile manufacturers, their main products are now cosmetics, clothing, sporting goods and pharmaceuticals. The break-up and privatisation of the Japanese National Railways is another example of the benefits of diversification.

The Age of the Minor

The mongrel has the flexibility to incorporate heterogeneous, even opposing elements. Such an organisation is youthful; but as it ages, it begins to reject the heterogeneous. The key to youth and life lies in whether the mainstream of a culture can still incorporate non-mainstream elements. The re-evaluation of the so-called minor elements that is much talked about among French philosophers of the new school can be taken as a warning to contemporary society of the truth of this fact. The subtitle of *Kafka* by Gilles Deleuze and Felix Guattari is *Pour une Littérature Mineure* (Towards a Minor Literature), indicating the importance of minor traditions in the authors' minds.[1] They frequently speak of 'Literature with a capital L'. The source of this idea is probably Jacques Lacan's '*Autre* (the Other, the subject) with a Capital A'.[2]

Because the absolute subject contains plurality and free space within itself, we must respect minorities and heretics and allow a state of tension between the part and the whole. The key concept behind these authors' attempts to re-evaluate minor literature is that a 'simple conglomeration of individuals cannot be called a group. A group first comes into existence when heterogeneous elements assemble and exist at the same time'. In other words, to create a group it is necessary for elements that exist as extremes at a given time, the minor elements, to be incorporated into the purified mainstream.

Deleuze and Guattari make frequent reference to the concepts of links and the rhizome, models of systems that are not organised in either a vertical or a horizontal hierarchy, but display intersection and fluidity.

Liberation from all dialectic, dualism and binomial opposition is what these authors seek. In order to transcend dualism, they offer the new terms (insisting that they are not systematised sufficiently to rank as *concepts*) rhizome, multiplicity and machine. The rhizome is the antithesis of the tree, which, for them, is a model for the hierarchy of dualism. First there is the central trunk, from which branches sprout in order. This hierarchy is firmly established; a branch, for example, never sprouts a trunk. A rhizome, by contrast, is an interwoven complex that defies division: an intertwining of many heterogeneous things, out of order, without a centre. It is always dynamic and changing, producing bulbs here and there as it mingles and twists back on itself.

Deleuze and Guattari distinguish their machine from an unmoving rigid mechanism. Their machine is an assemblage of various independent and heterogeneous elements with a living, fluid existence.

I believe that the advent of an information society will provide us with the chance to deconstruct and rebuild the social 'tree' structure of our present rigid industrial society. If we are not careful, however, the network of our information society may take shape as an ever greater 'trunk', or central-ised structure. The test in the years ahead will be whether we can create a fluid and living rhizome instead.

Incorporating 'Noise' into our Lifestyle

René Girard in his book *Mensonge Romantique et Vérité Romanesque* (1961), says that when one structure is com-pleted it begins to close itself off.[3] The completion or realisation of a culture, society or nation is followed by this closing, as it becomes more and more difficult to incorporate things from outside.

The same is true for a human individual. After building a personal life by entering adulthood and marrying, a person's defensive instincts begin naturally to operate. He selects and rejects information accordingly, and builds a closed structure around himself. This structure is his lifestyle, his personality, or his society. In other words, as a person matures he tends to close himself off and, in the interest of avoiding danger, avoids intercourse with those heterogeneous elements that are actually necessary to achieve further maturity. But accord-ing to Girard, the fundamental nature of human thought processes is differentiation, which is born of crisis, or what Girard calls 'the theatrical factor'.

In order to preserve both our physical and spiritual youth and continue to receive proof that we are alive it is necessary to incorporate heterogeneous elements – 'noise' – into our lifestyle.

Girard's theory of the scapegoat is another way of saying the same thing. According to Girard, the creation of a scapegoat – that is, the elimination of heterogeneous ele-ments from the hierarchy, or structure of authority – is a means of preserving that hierarchy. For that reason, heteroge-neous elements ('noise') that shake the structure of authority, or stability, are most important.

In the second volume of his work *L'Espirit du Temps*, the French sociologist Edgar Morin discusses the concepts of crisis and event and writes of 'order from noise'. The economist Jacques Attali, too, has written on this topic in his article 'L'Ordre par le Bruit' ('Order from Noise') that appeared in the special 1976 issue of *Communication* on the topic of crisis.[4]

Crisis and 'noise' as defined by Morin are elements that stand in opposition to, or are heterogeneous to a system. This is not a heterogeneity that can be quoted, absorbed and harmonised in a peaceful fashion, but refers to the event or process that upsets the hierarchy and makes it feel endangered, forcing it into a new level or a different dimension. 'Noise', in this sense, is related to a critique of Claude Lévi-Strauss' theory of Structuralism.[5]

Lévi-Strauss examined myths and family structures of peoples in various cultures and illuminated the connections and relations between them. In other words, he organised them. But his model rejected the unknown factors and elements that remained outside of his organised structures or were difficult to organise into structures; in other words, 'noise'.

To exclude 'noise' from a society or culture is to send that society or culture on its path of decline. By refusing to be bound by a single standard of values, by cleverly incorporating elements from other cultures into one's own, one makes possible a reconfirmation of one's culture. This will be the internationalism of the new age.

Japan is a small nation situated next to a large one, China. The Japanese have always cultivated the ability to survive by incorporating elements of Chinese civilisation into their own. On the other hand, its farming villages were governed by a rigid communalism, and those who did not obey the rules of the village, or who were unique, were labelled strange or mad and, to maintain the village order, were driven away. Outsiders were allowed to join the village unit only after the most careful consideration. One of the reasons Japan has survived to the present is this dual structure, the fine balance the

Japanese have maintained between a hermeticism that preserves the social order and an openness to new elements.

That wonderful sense of balance can be seen in the rapid swings of the country between an open and closed nation in the years before the complete opening up of the Meiji era. Though Japan was technically closed to the outside world for several centuries, trade and communication with other countries continued. Chinese publications – many of them translations into Chinese of European works – provided the Japanese with sufficient acquaintance with the West, and trade routes were never completely closed.

Japan's problems began, rather, after the country was officially opened to the world, from the Meiji era on. The race to modernise in the form of a complete Westernisation resulted in efforts to reject Japanese culture up to that time. This is not the same as incorporating Western culture into the Japanese as 'noise'. Since Meiji times, study abroad in the United States or Europe has been regarded as crucial for a complete education. Western food, architecture and clothing have become the norm, and the Japanese have lived by a Western standard of values.

This tendency to look exclusively to the West is still with us. To be recognised abroad or to be active abroad means to the Japanese Europe and America. There is still no awareness of recognition or activity in the broader world that includes the regions of Islamic culture, China, Southeast Asia, Australia, Eastern Europe and the Soviet Union.

Japan must adopt new government policies that place the Islamic world, China, the countries of Asia and Eastern Europe on a par with the West. Yet we must guard against letting the new importance we give to the many regions of the globe lapse into a provincial regionalism. Some advocate an insular regionalism, insisting on carrying out all projects solely with the resources of the region involved, refusing foreign capital investment and the help of outside specialists, but this type of isolationism can only result in decline.

We would do well to remember the case of Kyoto. While preserving Japan's ancient cultural traditions, the city was a pioneer in a major public works project to supply industrial water and was the first Japanese city to have streetcars. It reached out to talented people from other cities in Japan and abroad to achieve these things. Kyoto is able to preserve its traditions today precisely because it took such positive and liberal steps and embraced the future with open arms. This is exactly what we mean by incorporating 'noise' into the established order.

This concept of 'noise' has something in common with Yamaguchi Masao's concept of the periphery.[6] A culture that focuses its interest on the centre may intensify its own purity, but its outlying regions are fated to decline. Let us direct our attention to the heterogeneous elements around us, the strange, suspicious and quirky, idiosyncratic things. Let us be alert to them, and cultivate a broad magnanimity. Unless we say goodbye to our distinct brand of communalism – the lifestyle of the farm village – that leads us to ostracise anyone with individual or special talent, Japan has no future.

Time-sharing and the Rabbit Hutch
The second guiding principle of the modern age is division of labour based on function. The social policy of segregation by function reaches its extreme form in the analysis and distribution of industry and architectural and urban space by function. The social rule of 'time, place and occasion' is another form of division by function. Houses contain bedrooms, which are used for sleeping; dining rooms for eating; living rooms for entertainment; and halls to connect these separate facilities: this is the way of Modernism. And since according to that way of thinking, the sole function of the bedroom is sleeping and the sole function of the dining room is eating, every home must have a considerable amount of space.

Japanese houses have been described as rabbit hutches. They are indeed small, but this has a distinct advantage.

Because of the versatility of tatami-floored rooms, Japanese houses have escaped a thoroughgoing division of space by function. The multipurpose tatami-floored room becomes a bedroom when you pull the futon mattresses out of the closet and spread them on the matting. When you place a low table in the centre of the room, it becomes a dining room. Set floor cushions here and there and you have a room to receive guests. Place a flower arrangement and hang a scroll in the tokonoma, and you have a tea room. By changing the signs – the décor – one room takes on many different meanings. This multipurpose space makes time sharing possible and in this way we triumph over the limitations of a relatively small space.

This strategy of time-sharing shows a way to transform the densely overpopulated city of Tokyo. The central business district of Tokyo is nearly a hundred per cent utilised during the day, but from midnight to dawn it is a ghost town. Surely lockers and other systems could be devised that would make it possible for two businesses to use the same building around the clock. Hotels, for example, have nearly doubled their guest turnover and their profit by transforming themselves from mere places to sleep in to centres for banquets, conferences, business meetings, places to nap during the day, and even sites for romantic assignations, 'love hotels'. Once we cease to regard a place or thing as wedded to a single function and adopt a flexible, time-sharing system, we increase efficiency and require far fewer facilities to meet a wide variety of needs. By restoring even a small degree of plurality to our present classification and segregation by function, we can create new riches and a new life-style.

The startling rise in property prices in Tokyo in recent years is a major problem, and will be the undoing of the Japanese economy unless it is checked. In Chapter XIII I present a plan for the complete reconstruction of the city that I believe is necessary. Rather than redevelopment of the present city by tearing this down and rebuilding that, I propose the construction of an island in Tokyo Bay that will restore the proper balance between demand for land and its supply. This plan involves cleaning up Tokyo Bay and preserving Tokyo's historic Shitamachi area, while restoring the old forests of Musashino in the city's western suburbs and building looping canals as fire breaks, in a symbiosis of development and restoration.

If the problems of land costs and the threat of fire were solved, I believe that Tokyo could be the most fascinating and futuristic city on earth. One reason is that Tokyo is already a time-sharing city. There can be no denying that houses in Tokyo are small; but the city itself provides every sort of 'second home' conceivable, for even the most arcane tastes. Tokyoites may not be able to invite their friends or colleagues to their home for a party or dinner after work, but the city is filled with fine restaurants, bars and clubs where they can entertain their friends. A Tokyoite may not have a games room in his home, but he does not lack for mah-jong, pachinko and billiard parlours, computer-game centres and sing-along clubs. He may not have his own tennis court or pool, but there is no shortage of sports clubs, golf courses, driving ranges and tennis courts in the city.

These facilities take the place of your own private living room, games room, your own pool and tennis court; they are your second homes. Since they provide space efficiently, by the hour or other period of time, they are time-sharing second homes. Considered from this point of view, it is precisely because of this time-sharing system that Tokyo offers cuisine from nearly every country on earth and such a tremendous variety of entertainment spaces. We can see how a group (or a wealthy individual) could purchase or rent a one-room apartment in the city and make it into an actual second home – a study, a hobby room or a place to entertain guests – while building the family home in the suburbs, where land prices are more reasonable.

What is lost to Functionalism and Dualism

Application of Modernism's division by function has not been restricted to the home but has extended to urban space in general. In the Athens Declaration of the CIAM (Congrès International d'Architecture Moderne) conference in 1933, the city was analysed and divided into areas for work, living and recreation, with transportation facilities connecting these different functions.[7] The present systems of land-use planning and zoning, dividing the city into colour-coded functional areas, are based on this way of thinking. But not everyone has assented to this functionalism, promulgated by Le Corbusier.[8]

Jan Mukarovsky, a member of the 1930s structuralist group in Prague, criticised Le Corbusier's simple functionalism as follows: 'The existence of the whole is the source of the life-energy of all individual functions, and no human action is limited to a simple function'.[9] But with the increasing industrialisation of our society, segregation based on simple functionalism has spread around the world. The segregation of functions is, above all, easy to grasp; like explaining a machine by describing its parts. In addition, functionalism was a convenient weapon for dismantling the academism and feudal elements that remained so strongly rooted early in this century. The lions of Modernism rejected the state of the city of their day, where pluralistic functions accumulated over the ages existed in an overlapping state, as anti-modern. They made the purification of functions, open green spaces and fresh air their slogans and embraced Le Corbusier's 'shining city' as the vital new breeze of Modernism that would sweep away the confusion of the past. The image of the city of the future as a place of multistorey buildings and huge empty plazas, which has spread to Brasilia and Chandigarh and all modern cities of the world, dates from that time.

This principle is evident in the zoning system that segregates residential from industrial areas, and in the segregation of race and class (for example that seen in Chinatown and

Harlem, New York) and the designation of the city centre as a business district and the suburbs as residential districts. Social welfare policy is conceived along the same lines. The handicapped and the elderly are accommodated in special segregated facilities away from the centre of the city and treated as wards of the state, cut off from normal human relations with the community and the family. It is crucial to retrieve and reclaim what has been sacrificed in a wide range of spheres to these principles of Modernism and Modern architecture, segregation and dualism. The whole of existence, the essentially indivisible chaos of life, the complementary nature of functions, the intermediary zone that has been lost through segregation, the ambiguity lost through clarity – all of these elements are missing from Modernism and Modern architecture.

The Pyramid Model of Aristotle, Descartes and Kant

Of course, the simple functionalism by which each part and each space has a single function is not just a product of Modernism; it is the very basis of Western Rationalism, and can be traced back to the ancient Greek philosophy of architecture.

In his *Metaphysics*, Aristotle declared that 'the primary features of beauty are *taxis*, *symmetria* and *horismmenon*, and they can be expressed mathematically'. *Taxis* is order or hierarchy. The word *symmetria* derives from *syn*, meaning common, and *metreo*, meaning measurement; therefore it means dividing an object into equal measures or quantities. *Horismmenon* means a limit. The philosophy of ancient Greece was to lift man from chaos through the exercise of reason in categorising, analysing, defining and limiting phenomena.

The categorisation and analysis of nature by the faculty of reason is a central attitude of Western culture in every age. The religious, mythological dualism which postulates good and evil gods, a good god of light and the evil material world, the creator god and his creation, is derived from this.

Similarly, the philosophy of Descartes, which divides all of finite existence, dependent upon God's will, into spirit and matter, and the philosophy of Kant, who distinguishes the thing itself from phenomena, freedom from necessity, are based on Western analytical dualism. This same philosophy has permeated the social structures, the cities and the architecture of all industrialised nations. But how great is our loss as a result! The relentless pendulum swing between humanity and technology, science and religion, good and evil, the part and the whole that has afflicted modern society is a direct result of this unrelenting binomial opposition.

Dynamic Pluralism that Incorporates Binomial Opposition
The dualism – binomial opposition, the analytic method – that has played such an important role in Western modernisation is deeply entrenched in our ways of thinking and living. As a result, when we wish to refute dualism, we inevitably fall into the contradiction of creating a new binomial opposition. In discussing the concept of symbiosis, too, we are most often forced to produce a binomial opposition in our attempt to transcend all dualism. This is without doubt the greatest weakness of the concept of symbiosis.

Maurice Merleau-Ponty's philosophy is often described as a philosophy of multivalence or ambiguity.[10] Alphonse De Waelhens, in his foreword to Merleau-Ponty's *The Structure of Behaviour (La Structure du Comportement*, 1941), compares Sartre and Merleau-Ponty: 'In the end, Sartre strengthened the Cartesian dualism of mind and matter, while Merleau-Ponty remained endlessly concerned with the subtle connections between the two.'[11] One paradigm Merleau-Ponty considered was the case of a man confined to a prison cell: the prisoner's perception (mind) of a meal placed outside the cell changes drastically depending on whether his body (matter) can pass through the bars. The state of the body is the basis for the state of the mind (*cogito*); or the mind can project itself out of the body and be out of synchronisation with it.

Critics of Merleau-Ponty – Lacan, for example – claim that to divide being into matter and mind and set them up as two opposing entities is already to fall into the Cartesian dualism. By the same reasoning, as long as the arguments for the concept of symbiosis against dualism resort to creating oppositions (symbiosis versus dualism), there can be no escape from it.

The concept of symbiosis is basically a dynamic pluralism. It does not seek to reconcile binomial opposites through dialectic, nor does it follow Merleau-Ponty in searching for a unified principle that transcends two opposing elements. At times it is a binomial opposition; at times Merleau-Ponty's unified principle; and it can also be neither. It can only be described as a dynamic, pluralistic principle that can take many different forms.

Post-Modernism that Assimilates Binomial Opposition

Man is flesh, man is spirit, man is a unity of flesh and spirit. Man is something that is neither flesh nor spirit; as, for example, the consciousness referred to in the Buddhist philosophy of Consciousness Only, referred to as the *alaya* consciousness.[12] The 'neither flesh nor spirit' here is an intermediary space, a central concept of the philosophy of symbiosis. The intermediary space that is neither assimilates both flesh and spirit, the two elements of the binomial opposition; it is not a third element itself.

In intermediary space, we can postulate two elements in combinations of differing proportions; for example, flesh and spirit, in ratios varying from 10:1 to 1:10. In other words, an infinite number of elements in a plural system can be postulated. But, in fact, the concept of intermediary space is easier to understand if we abandon these opposing elements and describe it instead as the creation of dynamic relations between an infinite number of freely combined proportions of flesh and spirit.

Deleuze and Guattari's concept of the rhizome contains

this element of dynamic relationships. In the past, new ideas and revolutionary philosophies have established their value and truth by refuting all previous philosophies. By creating a new binomial opposition, they discredit and refute their predecessors. But the philosophy of symbiosis, while refuting its opposing element (philosophy, theory, or social system), which had previously been the mainstream, also assimilates it. Modernism, for example, is the element that the philosophy of symbiosis must oppose most of all. But rather than completely rejecting Modernism, symbiosis must simultaneously assimilate it.

Post-Modern architecture, in the narrower sense of the term (we might also call it 'historicist' architecture), which made its appearance as a rejection of Modern architecture, has fallen into the same old binomial opposition or pattern of dualism. Modern architecture, with its emphasis on function, rationality and efficiency, must be criticised at the present moment. But a new horizon will only be opened up by a dynamic, free philosophy that assimilates Modern architecture while criticising it.

Asserting Japan's Identity in a Nomadic World

The philosophy of symbiosis is dynamic, free and light; it is the philosophy of the nomads of the new age.

In a society of settlers, people live at fixed sites within a certain territory and create boundaries and neutral zones to avoid conflict. In such a society of mutually closed groups, peace means not violating the boundaries of others or interfering in their internal rules. This is a world of coexisting protectionist societies.

But today we live in the society of *homo movens*, which has learned the value of movement, exchange and discovery. Our world transcends differences in ideology, culture and levels of economic and technological development. A society of symbiosis is a pluralistic world where each person can display his own individuality, where many different cultural spheres exist together. In this situation, the expression of a unique national character, a people's identity, becomes extremely important.

Imagine that in a part of the world peopled by nomadic tribes, an unknown band suddenly appears in the middle of the desert. The members give no sign of their intentions. Without a doubt, they would be driven away as a band of brigands or demons. In the nomad's world, it is crucial to clearly indicate who you are, why you have come, and that you mean no harm. Japan today is like a band of silent black-robed horsemen that suddenly appears in the desert. There is nothing more unsettling than a silent group that simply stands there, smiling slightly. The group may even seem to be demonic. One of the reasons for 'Japan-bashing' is the unsettling effect of Japanese behaviour.

The Japanese tradition of prizing silence and regarding clever speakers as lacking in substance has produced a nation of slow, silent craftsmen and silent, hairsplitting researchers and academicians. It has gone so far that an artist or scholar in Japan who is articulate is regarded as a performer, and his achievements suspect. We must put an end to this. Japan's educational system is far behind in teaching young people to express themselves clearly and to explain themselves and their views. Ambiguity is, indeed, a special and important characteristic of Japanese culture; but the inability to express oneself has nothing to do with the ambiguity I speak of.

Japan must present her culture more clearly to the peoples of the world and make the goals of the Japanese nation clear: this is an urgent necessity. Our goal is a world in which the many different cultures recognise one another's values, compete with each other, and while opposing each other in their unique identities also live in symbiosis.

Leaving the Pendulum Phenomenon Behind
European history has been marked by extreme swings of the pendulum between rationalism and non-rationalism. Since the Industrial Revolution, with its philosophy of mass produc-

tion, the sudden appearance in England of William Morris' Arts and Crafts Movement emphasised the importance of craftsmanship and handwork.[13] The universal popularity of Art Nouveau and *Jugendstil* design at the end of the nineteenth century employing curving lines of plants and other natural forms, was part of a reaction against the Industrial Revolution, another pendulum swing. Antonio Gaudí is regarded as having conceived of the structure of architecture in an extremely rational manner, yet his architecture shares much with Art Nouveau and *Jugendstil* and was in its own way a reaction against, or pendulum swing back from, the Industrial Revolution.

At the beginning of the twentieth century however, architects such as Peter Behrens, Tony Garnier and Auguste Perret advocated rationalism, and swung the pendulum back to that extreme with the Bauhaus and Modern Architecture movements.[14]

This pendulum phenomenon was imported into Japan. The Japanese who advocated rapid growth in the 1960s were suddenly opposed to rapid growth and technology in the 1970s. Japanese journalism performed a sudden about-face and unleashed a zero-growth campaign, printing daily articles and editorials labelling all technology evil. The simple, ordinary life, lived at an easy rhythm, became the approved lifestyle. In the 1980s, Japan became ever more directly involved in international society, and rapid growth was no longer a subject of debate; it became difficult even to maintain the current rates of growth, faced with the vicious circle of oil price shocks, the emerging NICs economies, the high yen, trade friction, reduced government budgets and a cooling of domestic demand. Now the most advanced technologies, such as biotechnology, new media, computer communications and superconductors, are looked to in hope for a revival of the economy.

What we see here are two extremes: an extreme faith in the virtues of technology and, at the same time, an extreme rejection of the value of technology. This dualistic, pendulum phenomenon only confuses and unsettles our thinking; it produces few positive results. And the swings of the pendulum seem to be wider in younger, less mature nations. When chauffeured by a bad driver, we are rocked back and forth by his sudden acceleration and braking; a good driver makes these transitions smoothly and effortlessly. Indeed, to continue this analogy, truly accomplished racers have even mastered the technique of pressing the accelerator and the brake at the same time.

The time has come for us to transcend dualism and leave these extreme swings of the pendulum behind us. Since human beings are by nature an ambiguous form of existence, incorporating contradictions and oppositions, we have no grounds for disdaining or finding fault with that which is intermediate, which cannot be divided into opposing dualisms. On the contrary, I am convinced that this intermediary zone will prove to be a fertile field of human creativity as we face the future.

Centralised Authority in Industrial Society

The last characteristic principle of the modern age, the elimination of social class, is based on a pyramid hierarchy in which part and whole are clearly distinguished and the whole is valued above the part. In architectural terms this takes shape as: 1) the superiority of the structure to the interior; 2) the superiority of the infrastructure to the substructure; and 3) the superiority of public space to private space. All of these are examples of the whole taking precedence over the part, resting on a higher level than the part in a pyramid-type hierarchy. Since housing is a part of the city, it is only planned after the public spaces and facilities, the squares and roadways that make up the city's infrastructure, are in place. Housing is secondary and subsidiary.

The same can be said with regard to works of architecture and the various spaces of which they consist. The part is always subsidiary to the whole, in a hierarchy of levels. Nor is this way of thinking restricted to architecture or urban planning. Industrial society subscribes to a strategy of the concentration of efforts in the name of efficiency, with the corollary of priority to big science, big technology and big industry. The components that make up these areas of human activity are subsidiary to the whole, as an industrial hierarchy of sorts is created. This structure of industrial centralisation has merely replaced the old structure of feudal centralisation. Modernism's hierarchy of levels, its insistence on the superiority of the macrostructure, reigns at the expense of plurality and the variety of the parts, their humanity and subtlety of perception. As we move into the information age, the modern industrial structure will radically change. Small and medium-sized manufacturers will outstrip their huge rivals and the service industries rather than manufacturing will lead the industrial world. The present pyramidal hierarchy, in which large enterprises form the superstructure and parcel out work to medium and small enterprises, will be replaced by an entirely new industrial network.

The Holon: Equality of the Part and the Whole

There is considerable interest across a wide range of fields in a non-dualistic view of the part and the whole, or philosophy of symbiosis. One articulation of this view was offered by Arthur Koestler, who formulated the concept of the *holon*.[15] Koestler has coined the term *holon* by combining the Greek root *holos*, meaning whole, and the suffix *on*, for 'part' or 'particle'. The word simultaneously signifies the part and the whole. Koestler is a critic of reductionism, which reduces a phenomenon to its parts for analysis. In that process, he insists, the essence of the phenomenon – the harmonious sum of its parts – is inevitably lost, and the thing falsified. In his essay, 'The Tree and the Candle', in *Unity Through Diversity*, Koestler describes the properties of the holon using two examples. A burning candle serves as a metaphor for the concept of an open system, since the candle, while retaining its own basic form, takes oxygen from the atmosphere around it and in turn releases moisture, carbon dioxide, water and heat. He cites a tree as a living example of levels of hierarchy, an intermediate structure because it represents the whole system for all units smaller than itself but at the same time it is only another unit in an even larger system, the forest.

Koestler points out that biological and social structures as well as human activities and linguistic systems all exhibit these two properties of openness and hierarchy. He calls this the open hierarchy, which he regards as the fundamental characteristic of the *holon*.

Tokyo: Holon of Three Hundred Cities

In my book *Toshigaku Nyumon*, I called Tokyo a conglomeration of three hundred cities. I think that all cities should actually be considered conglomerations of smaller cities. We are accustomed to thinking of a city as a single, unified entity simply because it is an independent administrative unit with prescribed boundaries. But the simple act of tracing an administrative boundary does not make a city single and unified. In fact, the smaller cities that make it up each possess their own histories, and physically they merge and separate, changing shape to match the local topography. If we realise that the greater city is made up of independent areas, each with its own identity, linked to the others in fluid relationships, it is clear how Tokyo is a conglomeration of three hundred cities. When we have accepted this way of looking at things, we see that the smaller parts that form the larger city need not be subjugated to the whole in a 'tree' hierarchy, but that the parts and the city (the whole) form a *holon*.

A few years ago, I chaired a planning committee to establish a code for scenic views in the city of Nagoya. The unique thing about the regulations we proposed was that we did not urge the creation of a unified view for the entire city but suggested instead that scenic views be designated in more than a hundred places throughout Nagoya. These locations were chosen as representing the cultural and natural life of the city, its inhabitants, and its environments; we called them Autonomous Scenic Zones. Each was a unique expression of the life of Nagoya City, and we allowed them to retain this uniqueness and variety. The concept was revolutionary when compared with the typical modernist approach, which would be to establish universal standards and then apply them uniformly to all individual cases. Our work in Nagoya produced another *holon*, of the individual Autonomous Scenic Zones and the city as a whole.

A Revolutionary Concept: the State and the City-State

The philosophy of the *holon* can also be applied to the relationship between the state and other self-governing bodies. When Prime Minister Masayoshi Ohira was still alive, I sat on his policy research council and had many opportunities to discuss various ideas with him. One day in a discussion of relationships among the state, the prefectures and the cities, the prime minister said suddenly, 'Mr Kurokawa, why not eliminate the prefectures entirely and just get by with the state and its cities? In place of the prefectures, we could have a general communications processing agency.' The prime minister's ideal was to increase the autonomy of Japan's cities, in the direction of city-states. Our report was entitled 'A Plan for a National Garden City-State'. Rather than a nation centred around garden cities, we meant a garden city-state at a national level. From the standpoint of the hallowed concept of the subordination of self-governing bodies such as cities to the state, this view of the state and the city-state as equal entities is indeed revolutionary and *holonic*.

The philosophy of *holonism* is bound to exert a strong influence on theories of industrial and business organisation as well as on architecture and artistic creation. The top-down method where a general framework is followed by a part-by-part breakdown of the components fails to give sufficient consideration to the final details. On the other hand, there is no guarantee that the whole will reach successful completion if we proceed from the bottom up, by piling detail upon detail to build the totality. The truly creative and *holonic* approach is to give equal weight and consideration to both top-down and bottom-up approaches.

In my own designs, I begin with extremely general, macro considerations, such as the urban planning, the surrounding environment, and various social factors. At the same time, I begin to imagine and sketch very specific parts and details: the shape of the door handles and their feel in my hand, the curve of the hand rails on the stairs, carpet patterns, the furniture and the textures of the walls. This parallel approach, working on the whole and the details simultaneously leads to a *holonic* style of architecture. Non-Japanese architects and architectural critics have described my work as a combination of bold spatial structure and eloquent, handcrafted details. This evaluation pleases me, particularly because it shows an appreciation of the *holonic* relationship I have striven to create between the parts and the whole.

Koestler's essay, 'Janus', is named after the two-faced god of Roman mythology who, on the one hand, forces humanity into the various levels of the hierarchy but, on the other, urges it onto a transcendent and whole reality. For in Koestler's part and whole there is the drive towards the symbiosis of man and God. Koestler also postulates three levels of reality: sensual awareness, followed by conceptual awareness, and finally the mystical awareness of 'oceanic feeling', a world that transcends both sense perceptions and concepts. Koestler claims that this oceanic feeling is similar to the synchronicity described by Carl Jung and Wolfgang Pauli. I interpret the idea of synchronicity to mean the symbiosis of past, present and future; Koestler, however, while referring to Jung and Pauli's synchronicity, enlarges it to mean the symbiosis of body and spirit, consciousness and the unconscious, and man and God.

Towards a Merging of Mysticism and Science

Recently, the continuity between religion and science has also become apparent. As the physicist David Bohm has proclaimed, 'Even life can be made from matter'.[16] An extremely interesting discussion between Bohm and René Weber, was included in Weber's book *The Holographic Paradigm and Other Paradoxes*. In their conversation, entitled 'The Physicist and the Mystic – Is a Dialogue Between Them Possible?' they noted how, up to the present, physics has applied itself to discovering the unity of part and part, yet no trace of the unity of the part and the whole has been uncovered. For the first time, physics is broaching this issue.

We see here that the same problem that attracted Koestler is drawing the attention of the science of physics. Quoting Einstein's remark that 'the most beautiful of all things is God', Bohm and Weber claim that mysticism, once the province of religion and art, is beginning to evolve a point of contact with science and physics. A new dynamism that transcends the dualistic categorisation of science and religion as distinct fields is making itself felt. The defeat of Modernism is a great common theme of our age; but Japan has the additional task of freeing itself from the ideology of Westernisation. To Japan's great advantage, it has a tradition of Buddhist thought that articulates a philosophy of symbiosis which transcends the limits of dualism. This tradition, cultivated over long centuries, is inherent in Japan's culture and way of life.

An Identity of Opposites

Suzuki Daisetz's philosophy of the identity of opposites is the fundamental principle by which the part and the whole, or contradictory opposites, are revealed as existing in relation to each other.[17] The *Vajracchedika Sutra* contains a verse which can be translated, 'A is non-A, therefore it is called A'. And this is the source of the philosophy of the identity of opposites:

> The oriental individuum is not an independent individual as in the West. It contains no self-existent core, but exists

by virtue of emptiness (*sunyata*), which transcends the individuum. Though the individuum and that which transcends the individuum are contradictory, they exist together without the loss of the individuum's identity. 'Identity' (*soku*) means that two things are not different. 'Non' means that two things are not the same.

The identity of opposites creates an ambiguity of meaning, a floating multivalence, through simultaneous affirmation and rejection on a conceptual level. The entities A and non-A are in fact a single entity. Since two contradictory entities are a single entity, Suzuki Daisetz calls the mutually embracing relationship of the part and the whole the philosophy of the identity of opposites. Human beings exist as a part of the universe; at the same time, the universe is enfolded in the consciousness of human beings. Zen teaches that the universe and humanity are mutually inclusive, and it is easy to find other expressions of this antidualism or non-dualism in Asian thought.

In the world of the oriental individuum, where the part and the whole are accorded the same value and the individual and the meta-individual exist together, neither losing their own nature nor contradicting each other, there is no pyramidal hierarchy in which the part is subjugated in its unity with the whole.

The Edo philosopher Miura Baien devised a sympathetic philosophy of the unification of opposites, which he set forth in a trilogy: the discourses on metaphysics, corollaries and morality.[18] It has been shown that Miura Baien invented the dialectic a half century before Hegel.[19] More important than any comparison with Hegel however, is the recognition of Baien's inspirations in Asian thought, particularly Indian philosophy. His philosophy is typical of the Asian tradition in that it resolves dualism into monism and represents a symbiosis of analysis and unification, the part and the whole. In his dialectical analysis, Miura Baien's philosophy indeed seems close to Hegel's but it is clear from the name he used, the unification of opposites, that he ultimately sought a unified, whole world. We can interpret his thought as a philosophy of apprehending all seeming opposites as a single totality, a philosophy of the symbiosis of part and whole. We do not know whether Miura Baien ever studied the Buddhist philosophy of Consciousness Only, but his thought bears a close resemblance to it. I am convinced that the philosophy of Consciousness Only will be the source for the thought of the twenty-first century. While Western thought has reached the dead end of dualism, Buddhism and its philosophy of Consciousness Only offers Japan a means to assume the intellectual leadership of the future.

Sacred Zones for Each Nation, Each People

In 1979, the Aspen International Design Conference was held in Aspen, Colorado. The theme of the conference was 'Japan and the Japanese, and the CBS vice-president Lou Dorfsman and I were joint chairman of the conference. I suggested 'Rice' as an important sub theme of this conference.

The thrust of my argument was that California rice was indeed food, but for the Japanese 'rice' is not merely food; it is their culture. Since that conference, for more than ten years, I have continued to argue that rice is culture, and I have opposed the liberalisation of foreign rice imports into Japan.

I can sum up my reason for this view in a phrase: the concept of sacred zones. I have said again and again that the philosophy of symbiosis destroys all dualisms. Yet in doing so it in no way resembles the 'coexistence' of the United States and the Soviet Union during the Cold War period, nor can it be compared to the synthesis of thesis and antithesis as described in the European philosophy of dialectical materialism. And of course it is not the haphazard mingling or the temporary compromise of different things.

The most important features of the philosophy of symbiosis are the concepts of intermediate spaces and sacred zones.

I will discuss intermediate spaces in another section of this work, and for our present purposes, an outline of the essence of the idea will suffice. Intermediate space is the zone tentatively established between two opposing elements; it is a third zone which belongs to neither. When such an intermediate space is placed between two clearly opposing, radically separated, rationalised extremes, the ambiguous elements that were purposefully excluded in the process of creating the binomial opposition and its rationalisation, the non-rational elements, can be recouped.

There are many intermediate spaces in our world, zones which have been forgotten, discarded, ignored, or dismissed because they do not belong to the two main, opposing currents.

Many of the concepts that I have investigated as premises of the philosophy of symbiosis can be grouped under the heading of intermediate space: street space; the concept of ambiguity, ambivalence and multivalence; Rikyu grey; *ma*, or interval, as intermediate space and several others.

Intermediate zones are created when two different, opposing things continue to exist as they are pro forma, yet each extends some part of itself into the third, intermediate space. Even if each opposing element only offers, for example, ten per cent of itself to the intermediate zone, a third, partly shared region is created. This is not a theory of domination, in which the stronger of the two opposing elements rules over the weaker. Rather, it is an attempt to discover common elements and rules without erasing the opposition between the elements.

The concept of intermediate space poses a challenge to authoritarianism, to universalism, and to revolutionism.

The most fundamental principle of the philosophy of symbiosis is that there is always an intermediate space, always something shared between extremes: cultures however different, ideologies however opposing. This is what distinguishes the philosophy of symbiosis from co-existence and compromise, from dualism, from dialectical materialism, and from tripartite philosophical models.

The philosophy of symbiosis also possesses a fundamentally new idea: sacred zones. As I noted earlier, I continue to oppose the liberalisation of rice imports to Japan, and one of my reasons is linked to this idea of sacred zones. Each country, people, culture, company, and individual has its own sacred zones.

Up to now, the sacred zones of religion and cultural tradition have been called tabus. The cow is sacred in India; the pig is tabu in Islamic culture, so pork is not eaten. The failure to observe tabus was condemned with a harshness approaching a sentence of death, yet no one ever thought of inquiring in a systematic fashion into the reasons for its hold over us.

In modern times, such tabus and sacred zones have been declared irrational and unscientific and are considered signs of a lack of development. They have been excised from our lives with the sharp knives of science and economics.

The rules of the dominant countries have become the universal rules, and the sacred zones of weak countries have been declared irrational or 'non-tariff trade barriers'.

Symbiosis Means Recognising Each Other's Sacred Zone

In the forum of the Structural Impediments Initiative (SII), a Japan-US institutional framework, Japanese customs such as intragroup trading, consensus price setting and rice-growing policy are coming under attack from the United States as incompatible with international rules. The philosophy of symbiosis, on the other hand, seeks to recognise the respective sacred zones of different cultures.

As times change, these sacred zones may disappear or alter. Therefore, each country must proclaim the most important and the most essential of its sacred zones today.

Sacred zones are linked to the lifestyle and national pride of a country. They have strong roots in cultural traditions intimately linked to religion and language. To return to the example of rice, America's California-grown rice has been improved in quality and taste. Some varieties are far better tasting than the average rice available in Japan. When we consider that Californian rice costs a fraction of the price of Japanese rice, it's only normal to wonder why it shouldn't be imported. But this argument treats California rice and Japanese rice as if they were both only a foodstuff.

If all the rice in California were suddenly to disappear, California would be little changed by it, nor would the American lifestyle or national pride be damaged. But what would happen if rice growing was to disappear from Japan? The traditional Japanese countryside scenery, with its groves surrounding large homes and shrines, its forested village hills, its paddies, and its fields – the most typical Japanese landscapes would all disappear. Japanese sake, a work of art in itself, would disappear, as would many crafts, folk songs and festivals, and the regional cultural traditions transmitted with those festivals would all perish.

Even though inhabitants of farm villages are gradually taking outside part-time and full-time jobs, the villages remain refuges where the ancient skills of craftsmen are preserved. When the harvest is in, the farmers turn their hands to different tasks, to forestry, to lacquer work, and other crafts.

The villagers teach their children what they must know to carry on the traditions of the major summer and autumn festivals. Such village performing arts as Kagura dancing, Kurokawa Noh and the puppet plays of Awaji have been kept alive in this way.

If rice culture were to disappear from Japan, a large part of the Japanese cultural heritage would disappear with it. This is the reason that I have opposed liberalisation of rice imports for well over a decade. The Japanese government and bureaucracy, and the farmer's associations, too, argue that Japan must protect its supply of foodstuffs by being agriculturally self-sufficient. But as long as Japan argues with America on the premise that rice is food, Japan has no hope of winning.

Rice growing should be declared as one of the sacred zones of Japanese culture, and as such isn't a suitable area for trade friction. In conjunction with this, respect for the sacred zones of US culture must be declared.

A New International Horizon Created by Sacred Zones and Intermediate Space

The present emperor system, with the emperor as a symbolic presence, is a perfect manifestation of Japanese history and the pride of the Japanese people. The worlds of Kabuki and the tea ceremony, with their hereditary lineages; *sukiya* architecture, with its traditional techniques; and Sumo, which is not so much a sport as a meeting of the emperor system and rice culture – these are all typical sacred zones of Japanese culture.

By its very definition, a sacred zone cannot be scientifically analysed, it cannot be governed by international rules. It is instead ineffable, a mystical region. Such sacred zones are, of course, found not only in Japan but in every country.

After World War II, the American movies dazzled the Japanese with American cars and the lifestyle built around the automobile. They saw and heard the glory of American civilisation in its musicals and jazz. Baseball was the very essence of America.

Because America and Europe are the champions of modernism, the leaders of universalism, rationalism and dualism, they are extremely reluctant to admit that sacred zones exist in their own cultures; embarrassed perhaps to acknowledge such non-rational elements in their cultures.

The Japanese government and leaders of Japanese industry have no idea how insulted and threatened Americans feel when Japanese companies wield their economic might and buy Hollywood studios or major league baseball teams. If the automobile industry was simply another industry, the law of the marketplace would be the arbiter of success. But the automobile used to be the very essence of the culture of Europe and America, as well as a symbol of its future potential. The car society and lifestyle are the deepest source of self-esteem for Americans. The space and aeronautics industry, too, is another symbol of the future of American society.

If the Japanese government and industry tramp into these scared zones with mud-covered feet, like some rural parvenus, they are bound to deeply insult Europeans and Americans.

In modern times, we have been educated to think based on the scientific method, poisoned as it is by rationalism and dualism. As a result, we tend to think that if we cannot understand others one hundred per cent, it is because we haven't tried hard enough. The human race has suffered greatly because of this belief that we must understand each other completely.

It is one of the great illusions of our age that we believe we can understand each other completely – whether we are lovers, husband and wife, or child and parent. Human relations should be based on discovering and respecting each person's identity in his or her sacred zone. This is the establishment of a symbiotic relationship.

The difference between creating symbiotic relationships between different cultures, between binomial oppositions (such as science and religion, the spirit and the flesh, man and nature, the individual and the group, the city and the state, federalism and tribalism, tradition and advanced technology, socialism and capitalism, and so forth) and such concepts and methods as compromise, harmony, coexistence and synthesis (the *aufheben* of the dialectic) can be summarised as follows.

Symbiosis makes positive steps to recognise the ineffable areas of the two elements of a binomial opposition or of two different cultures, and each side or element respects the sacred zone of the other. The sacred zone is respected precisely because it encompasses the ineffable.

Next, the philosophy of symbiosis creates an intermediate zone between the two opposing elements. The intermediate space is a common, shared element tentatively established between the two. This intermediate space may, in the future, be forcefully appropriated or rejected by one of the two. In that sense, the intermediate space is dynamic, vague, tentative, ambivalent and multivalent.

However, symbiosis does not completely deny universalism, common rules, or the world order of Modernism.

Symbiosis rests on the assumption that between every pair of opposing elements, there are common elements, common rules and universal values. While the universalism of Modernism demanded one hundred per cent shared elements and mutual understanding, symbiosis recognises a portion of shared; this is the prophesy I have made throughout my life for the twenty-first century.

What is the basic difference between a machine and life?

Intermediate space in the forms of waste, play and ambiguity exists in the living organism. The existence of sacred zones and intermediate space is the very proof of life, of the living being.

With the concepts of sacred zones and intermediate space as its source, the philosophy of symbiosis is clearly distinct from all previous philosophies. It opens our eyes to the horizon of a new world.

EDO, THE PRETEXT FOR
THE AGE OF SYMBIOSIS

Much has been published on the rich and varied culture of Edo as the flowering of classical Japanese life. In the early 1960s, I predicted that Edo would be widely reappraised, and I studied the city from a variety of perspectives. I have emphasised the importance of Edo's Shitamachi, or central, 'downtown' area; the value of streets and alleys as opposed to squares; the city's *sukiya*-style architecture in relation to its population density; the automatons of the Edo period; the philosophy of Miura Baien. I have collected and studied the woodblock prints of the last years of the Edo period, with special attention to the typically Edo-period colour known as Rikyu grey.[1]

In 1981 I designed the Arts of Edo Exhibition at the Royal Academy of Arts, and in my introductory talk at Oxford University, I suggested that 'the Edo period – or more broadly, the three-century span of purely Japanese culture from the mid-sixteenth to the mid-nineteenth century – holds the roots of all that is Japan today'. The major Japanese art traditions that survive today – the way of tea (*sado*), flower arrangement (*ikebana*), the Noh and Kabuki dramas, *sukiya*-style architecture – all can be traced back to the latter half of the sixteenth century and all gained popular acceptance in the Edo period. They flourished until the 'reforms' of the Meiji era brought a wholesale rejection of everything associated with the past. Certainly the new government, but also the populace, sought to disassociate itself from the feudal past in the push towards Westernisation, even if that meant depreciating 'pre-Modern' life and culture.

With the opening of Japan to the West, Japanese architecture suddenly started copying Western architecture outright;

Japanese people took to wearing Western clothes. This seems to support the view that modern Japan began from the Meiji era. We often hear that Japan rose from being a backward country to an advanced industrial state in a little over a hundred years, and that the leaders of developing nations should look to Japan as a model for their next hundred years of growth. Such explanations, however, overlook a number of important facts.

As is gradually becoming clear, the Edo period saw grand achievements in mass culture and was far more 'modern' than has been appreciated. Ronald Dore notes in *Education in Tokugawa Japan* that by the end of the Edo period (1868), forty-three per cent of boys and ten per cent of girls between the ages of six and thirteen attended school – higher percentages than in England at the time. Edo was the largest city in the world, with a population of well over a million. In scientific scholarship, Yamagata Banto proposed a steady-state theory of the solar system in his *Instead of Dreams* (*Yume no Shiro*, 1820), while Shizuku Tadao translated John Keill's commentaries on Newton's *Principia* only very shortly after they had reached France.[2] By the early nineteenth century, cartographer Ino Tadataka (1785-1818) had drawn accurate maps of the Japanese islands.[3] Moreover, in the 1770s, philosopher Miura Baien had set forth his dialectical system in three *Discourses on Metaphysics*, *Corollaries* and *Morality*, predating Hegel's dialectic by fifty years. Most importantly, however, Edo society had already attained its own unique modernity, quite distinct from Europe. No doubt the speed with which Japan was able to assimilate Western ideas and practices in the Meiji era, like a blotter absorbing ink, related to the basically modern character of mature Edo society.

Indeed, it is in Japan's own unique and mature modern society of the Edo period that we should search for Japan's cultural roots.

An Urban Centre of Popular Culture

Edo Japan was a predominantly popular culture. In the eighth century, the total population of Japan was five million; a thousand years later, immediately prior to the Edo period, that figure had only just reached ten million. One hundred years into the Edo period the population had tripled, reaching thirty million by the time of shogun Tokugawa Yoshimune (1716-45). This in itself made for accelerated urbanisation.

The city of Edo, the world's largest metropolis, was home to the world's first mass popular culture. The vast shrine and temple complexes of earlier ages gave way to the popular architecture of *sukiya*-style tea rooms, Kabuki, Noh and Joruri theatres, as well as vernacular masterpieces in the forms of farmhouses and merchant town houses.[4] As papermaking and woodblock printmaking techniques developed, a vast popular literature burst forth in the form of romances, humour, erotica and several varieties of picture books named after the colour of their covers – 'blue books', folios and 'yellow covers' for adults, and 'red books' and 'black books' for children. Bookshops sprang up all over Edo.

High Population Density and Non-verbal Communication

The second special feature of Edo was its extremely high population density, which resulted in the cultivation of subtle sensitivities. The average family had six members and lived in a home with a frontage of only two *ken* (about 3.6 metres). Under those circumstances, it was impossible for a married couple to have a private bedroom. Even in my own childhood I remember that my parents slept in the same room with one child, and my grandparents slept in an adjoining room with the other children. This was the norm in Japan.

In Tokyo today, with some 250 people per hectare, we speak of a high population density. But there were 688 people per hectare in old Edo. In a city that crowded, one loud voice can annoy scores of people. In Japanese we say 'The eyes are as eloquent as the lips', and we speak of 'probing another's stomach'. Silent communication of the eyes and the 'stomach' – which is the Chinese and Japanese metaphorical equivalent of the heart or breast in the West – was a corollary of Edo's high population density.

In such a densely populated society, the slightest change in feeling or expression, gesture or attitude, can have an impact on interpersonal relationships; consequently a subtle and refined sensitivity is fostered. It was this sensitivity that produced the subtle psychological dramas of the Kabuki theatre's *sewamono*, or domestic plays. The heightened sensitivity to materials that characterises *sukiya*-style architecture can also be traced back to these roots. From another perspective, feudal society with its rigid class distinctions, densely populated cities, and tight web of human relationships, did not permit the individual to expand his frame of reference and open his world out to broader horizons. Instead an intense in-turning was fostered, a concentration on and refinement of the internal world, which found expression in the human emotions of love, hate, duty, in an extreme sensitivity to the changes of the four seasons, and a love of plants and animals.

In modern city planning, high population density is regarded as undesirable. The ideal is thought to be single-family dwellings spread out at a very low density among spacious parks and greenery. Yet I am convinced that it is far more natural for human beings to live together in relatively dense population environments.

What are the best examples of the modern ideal of low-density urban populations? Take Canberra and Los Angeles – the people of those cities are definitely not satisfied with their living environments. In Canberra, houses dot the open landscape at wide intervals. Is fruitful human interaction possible when you have to get in your car and drive to your nearest neighbour's home? And the high crime rate of Los Angeles, where there is no way of knowing what has happened at one's next-door neighbour's house, makes it difficult to claim that these low-population-density communities are good urban environments.

The Edo Rowhouse: an Urban Model

Another trait of the Edo urban environment was its mixed, hybrid, pluralistic nature. The comic monologues of this period regale us with tales of colourful characters who lived in the rowhouses, or *nagaya*, so characteristic of the city: the landlord, a wise old sort, now retired; the stranger with a mysterious background; the quiet young couple, actually the daughter of a feudal lord and the head clerk of a great merchant, who have eloped together and are in hiding; the quack doctor; the hardworking carpenter with a large brood of children; and many other interesting characters shared the same lodgings in the typical Edo *nagaya*.

The Edo period is often thought of as a time of strict social castes, with little opportunity for people to move between them. But though externally these castes may have defined people's lives, internally a completely different principle was at work. The samurai class, for example, was actually very poor. The merchants, who were officially the lowest class, were in contrast relatively well off. Many of the merchant class were also leaders of the intellectual world, particularly in the study of Western science ('Dutch Learning' or *Rangaku*). As a result, samurai had to swallow their pride and ask to be accepted as the disciples and pupils of these merchants. In other words, though an external class structure divided the populace into samurai, farmers, craftsmen and merchants, other divisions cut across these groups: an economic class system, an intellectual class system, and an artistic class system. Social position was defined by the overlapping combination of all these relationships. There was nothing strange about a samurai setting up shop as an umbrella maker next door to a carpenter's shop, for example.

In fact, the present is, if anything, more class conscious than the Edo period as far as housing is concerned. When a public housing project is designed now, care is taken that all of the units should have a nearly equal amount of living space. Rent is calculated from the price of land and building costs in the so-called cost-price system. These uniform conditions ensure that the people who move into the housing project are very similar in social class. For example, if the rent is just about right for a couple in their thirties with one child, the housing project is very likely to fill up with thousands or tens of thousands of couples in their thirties with a single child. The children that move in will all go to school at about the same time, and their fathers will all be at about the same step on the ladder of worldly success. The social environment of this housing project becomes, as a result, tremendously competitive. Which is more humane, the modern housing project or the Edo-period *nagaya*, populated by people of all ages, classes and professions?

The separation of the social classes in modern society results in the exclusion of the weak from the social situation. The modern housing project is not a suitable place for the elderly or the handicapped to live. To avoid this unfortunate situation, I have always insisted that in designing public housing it is important to begin with a breakdown of the percentages of the different types of projected inhabitants, ensuring that a wide variety of people will be able to live together in the project. We must start by determining the ideal percentages of couples in their thirties, forties and sixties, handicapped people, and all other groups. Only on this basis can the real design and planning begin.

For over twenty years I have continued to insist that if homes for the elderly are to be built at all, they should be located next to day care centres. Then the elderly residents have a chance to play with the children, just as if they were their own grandchildren. The generations need places which enable them to come into contact with each other. Some people think that because the elderly are not very active, homes for them should be located in quiet places out in the midst of nature. This way of thinking reflects the coldness of modern society's functionalism and segregation, which regards efficiency above all else. On the outskirts of San Francisco I visited a retirement community built quite some time ago as part of a survey I was conducting. The entire town was designed with the needs of the elderly in mind: because many older people have trouble walking, the land is flat and houses are all single-storey dwellings. And because they tend to wake early, the dining hall opens at five am for breakfast and the games room opens at six.

At first glance it really does seem to be a town designed entirely for the elderly. But after breakfast, almost the entire population of the community gathers in the games room to play cards. This is indeed a strange sight. It speaks of a society so harsh that there is no place in it for the elderly, who must be segregated from the real world. In the week I spent interviewing the people of this town, I learned that some sixty per cent of the residents regarded the move there as a mistake. Living in an ordinary city has its inconveniences and can be noisy, but at least there they could see their grandchildren and other younger people. The consensus of the residents of this retirement community was that they should have stayed where they were. Unfortunately, in most cases the move had exhausted their life savings, and they were unable to return to the real world.

The segregation of modern urban planning creates inhuman living environments like this. In cities the world over, there is a conspicuous segregation by economic class. The high-density communities of Edo, in which different generations and classes lived together in symbiosis, offer us an important hint for urban planning of the future.

An Art of Symbiosis of Abstraction and Realism
The third characteristic of Edo-period culture is the importance of fantasy. The mysterious woodblock-print artist Sharaku for example, draws the features of actors in a frankly

exaggerated fashion, yet his work does not lose its realism.[5] In the *shunga* pornographic prints the male organ may be depicted as almost a metre in length, yet it works in the picture because the same level of realism and stylistic technique in the rest of the print is applied to it. The works of the Rimpa school of painters – Koetsu, Sotatsu, Korin and Kenzan among others – are strongly fictitious in their structure in sharp contrast to the concrete realism of their Western contemporaries.[6]

The combination of abstract and realistic techniques, pioneered in the West by Picasso was already applied most effectively by Japanese artists some four centuries ago. Kabuki costumes and stylised *kumadori* make-up also illustrate the characteristically Japanese combination of abstract and real.[7] The transition from fantasy to abstraction can be seen in other Edo-period arts as well, such as in Kimono patterns, strikingly similar to modern aesthetic tastes in design and artistic conception.

The importance of fantasy in Edo culture can also be seen in its attitude to nature. Edo was known as the city of blossoms – in part a metaphor for the city's brilliant and flourishing culture as the capital of the realm and the seat of the shogunate; but the city was also extraordinary for the amount of greenery and flowers it cultivated. Though Edo lacked the public squares of Paris and the parks of London, the doorways and backyards of people's houses were lined with rows of potted bonsai, and in the summer, morning glory and flowering gourd vines climbed the facades of Edo's buildings. Flower markets were held most days of the week, and peddlers hawked flowers and potted plants throughout the city.

The bonsai of Japan are not natural, but in the tiny tree we read a sign of nature. When the citizens of Edo looked at a bonsai pine they saw a hoary, thousand-year-old tree and heard the salt breezes of the sea shore. I applied the symbolism of the bonsai in my design for the Prince Hotel in Roppongi, placing a camphor tree in the centre of the interior poolside area. The curved shape of the pool is a metaphor for the ocean. It is a small pool, not really large enough to be of much use, but the sides are made of acrylic so people can watch the swimmers and enjoy it as an image of the sea. The single tree set in the centre of the poolside area is like a bonsai, standing as a metaphor for the forest. With that single tree, people can feel the coolness of shade in summer, imagine the soughing of the wind through its branches, and sense the arrival of autumn seeing its fallen leaves.

The feudal lords in residence in Edo had official residences on plots near the shogun's castle assigned to them by the shogunate and they also built private residences further from the castle, incorporating large gardens. *Sukiya*-style architecture also spread among the wealthier commoners, and with this a more highly developed awareness of the garden evolved. Japanese gardens, of course, have a long history, dating from the palace-style gardens of the Heian period and including the sand and stone Zen gardens of the medieval period, but gardens first enjoyed general popularity in the Edo period. Japanese gardens exhibit a high degree of abstraction and fantasy. If you want the ocean in your garden, you dig a pond and read it as the sea; if you want islands, you place a big rock in the pond and view it as an island. Nature in this fashion is man-made and fictitious in the context of the densely populated city of Edo.

Sukiya-style architecture itself, the tea house, built of wood, paper and earth, is nothing more than a fantasy for viewing nature.

The sort of androgyny of present-day pop idols was also quite popular in Edo; this is another example of a culture of fictions. The beauties depicted by the mid-Edo-period woodblock-print artist Suzuki Harunobu are as thin as Twiggy in her heyday.[8] They are rejections of female physicality, androgynous presences which represent the exact opposite of a figure like Marilyn Monroe. In Kabuki, the convention of men playing the roles of women is exploited to present woman as fantasy. The same impulse must have lead the geisha of the Fukugawa district of old Edo to adopt men's names.[9] This type of inversion is a kind of sophistication that is part of the essence of an ambiguous culture. A culture that pursues a straightforward masculinity and femininity – where all men are John Wayne and all women are Marilyn Monroe – is based on a simplistic physicality. This is the aesthetic of the 1960s, when the goal of human life was thought to be material welfare – the aesthetic of Western-style Modernism. In contrast, a fictitiousness that allows men and women to exist in symbiosis is what is now sought after and will continue to be pursued in the future. The feminisation of men, the masculinisation of women and gay culture, are not signs of the collapse of civilisation: they are the pulse of a new aesthetic consciousness being born.

The Intentional Artlessness of *Sukiya*-style Architecture

The fourth trait of Edo culture was its preoccupation with detail. The work of Kobayashi Rekisai, a craftsman who specialised in making tiny models of everyday objects, transmits to us today this Edo fascination with detail.[10] Kobayashi stood in a long line of superb craftsmen, stretching back to the Edo period. Among his many amazing works is a writing box only a few millimetres in size, yet painstakingly decorated with inlaid *maki-e* designs.[11]

There are many other examples at hand: the famous and finely detailed Edo *komon* kimono patterns, miniature books and Buddhist altars constructed as tiny miniatures of Buddhist temples.[12] The architecture of the Edo period is also preoccupied with detail. The carvings that decorate the Toshogu shrine are an obvious example, and Edo castles, exemplified by Himeji Castle, exhibit a far greater wealth of design detail than their Momoyama predecessors.

Sukiya-style architecture, when compared to the palatial *shoin* style that preceded it, makes greater use of natural materials and a simple, even rough design.[13] But aside from the question of sheer amount of decorative detail, *sukiya*-style architecture shows great concern for the details and the proportions of the materials it uses. A naturally bent branch used in a *sukiya*-style work may at first seem to be an artless thing that might be picked up anywhere, but in fact that single branch was painstakingly selected from hundreds of naturally twisted branches, especially chosen to appear artless and natural.

The fifth trait of Edo-period culture was its symbiosis of technology and humanity – what I call the concept of *karakuri*, or the automaton. In contrast to the West, where technology is opposed to humanity, technology in Japan has traditionally been regarded as an extension of humanity, that can exist in symbiosis with humanity. I will come back to this idea later in the book.

A Hybrid Style: Synthesis of East and West
The sixth trait of Edo culture was the development of a hybrid style of architecture. Carpenters of the Edo period freely combined the styles of all previous ages, to create a unique hybrid style. The Hiunkaku, or Flying Cloud Pavilion of the Nishi Honganji temple in Kyoto is a masterpiece of the hybrid style of the early Edo period.[14] The *sukiya*-style is a blend of the residential *shoin* style and the *soan*, or grass hut, style of tea room architecture.[15] The Joan of Oda Uraku is a master-piece of this hybrid tea room architecture.

Another style that gained popularity in the Edo period was the so-called *gongen*, or avatar, style of architecture. The Toshogu shrine is the outstanding example, combining Buddhist and Shinto architectural styles (the name reflects the concept that Shinto deities were avatars of the Buddhas and Bodhisattvas).[16] The secret carpenters' manual known as the 'transmission of Shrine Architecture' (*Jingu Soden*) handed down through the Kenninji lineage of carpenters, contains instructions for linking the main hall and the worship hall of a Shinto shrine with a stone-floored room, a combination of

Buddhist and Shinto architectural styles. Relatively early works such as the tomb of Daitokuin, Sugen'in, Gen'yuin and Joken'in in Ueno, and the tomb of Bunshoin in Chiba can be regarded as precursors of the *gongen* style. By the mid-Edo period, full-blown examples abound: Yushima Tenmangu shrine, Kanda Myojin shrine, Kamakura Hachimangu shrine, Nezu Gongen shrine, Kameido Tanmangu shrine and Tomioka Hachiman shrine.

Japanese culture has always maintained a skilful synthesis of different inputs, and a hybrid style of architecture is hardly anomalous in Japanese history. But this hybridisation reached its peak in the Edo period, an era of architectural methodology, when the method of design and construction was given great importance. This tradition culminated in the hybrid Eastern-Western architecture from the late Edo through the Meiji period: the Tsukiji Hotel, the First National Bank of Tokyo, the Mitsuigumi Headquarters at Nihombashi and the foreign merchants' houses in Yokohama are all representative works of this style. Contemporary master carpenters incorporated Western styles into their work, producing buildings with a naive yet creative blending of East and West.

The arch of the gate of the Tsukiji Hotel, for example, suggests Islamic architecture. The building itself is a dramatic combination of diverse and hybrid elements: crisscross lath and plaster outer walls, bell-shaped and round windows in the tower, a hipped Western-style roof, a weathercock and the red-lacquered sash and frame construction. At the same time, it clearly surpasses any of the imitations of Western architecture produced in Japan from the mid-Meiji period on. This is because it was designed before Japan had adopted Western values as its own; the beauty of the Tsukiji Hotel is the product of the collision of two different cultures and their symbiotic synthesis.

Unfortunately, due to the Meiji government's determined policy of Westernisation, the value of this hybrid architecture was not recognised, and was destroyed. With the Meiji era, the symbiotic culture of the Edo period was rejected as backward and chaotic; the age of modernisation and the 'pure' Westernisation of Japan began.

For over twenty years I have been working to re-create these works of hybrid architecture, most of which have been lost to us. The richest source of documentation is in woodblock prints of the period, the so-called Yokohama prints and 'Civilisation' (*kaika*) prints.[17] From the last years of the Edo period on into early Meiji, prints illustrating foreigners and their customs were popular. These lively prints depicted the new 'civilisation and enlightenment' that the government aimed for, and showed such scenes as Western ships, steam locomotives, foreign dress and accessories and foreigners disporting in the brothels and gay quarters. The hybrid architecture of the age was also a popular subject, and many buildings are shown in prints.

Yokohama and Civilisation prints were produced for a period of about twenty years, spanning the last decade of the Edo period and the first decade of Meiji. Some eighty per cent were created in the years from 1860 to 1865. In 1868, the last year of the old regime and the first year of Meiji, Tokyo's harbour was opened to foreign ships, and popular interest began to move from Yokohama to Tokyo. In general, the Yokohama prints depicted scenes in and around Yokohama, and the Civilisation prints showed scenes of Tokyo.

It is my ambition to re-create the plans for these works of East-West hybrid architecture depicted in the woodblock prints but otherwise lost to posterity. I believe we can discover the tremendous dynamism of a Japanese aesthetic of symbiosis in the process of re-creating these works, as well as the true path that Post-Modern architecture should take as it transcends the limits of Modernism.

From Centralisation and Decentralisation to Centralisation and Decentralisation

The seventh special characteristic of Edo culture was the

symbiosis of part and whole under the system of the centralised shogunate and decentralised fief governments. The shogunate determined all national policy; it was a centralised administrative system with an enormous amount of power. But from the mid-Edo period on, the shogunate, in financial difficulties partly because of the enormous expense incurred in the construction of the Toshogu shrine, encouraged each of the fiefs to develop its own economy. The Satsuma fief in Kyushu developed cut glass wares, Nagasaki encouraged the manufacture of blown glass; Ako was known for its salt production and Kanazawa for its Kutani ceramics and Wajima lacquerware. Wakayama also produced lacquerware, and Ibaraki *yuki tsumugi* cloth; Oita manufactured a special kind of tatami matting and Tosa supplied camphor. All of these were fief-run local industries.

In intellectual circles too, each fief had its own educational system of village schools and fief academies. In addition, specialised private institutes were established to teach Western studies, neo-Confucianism, military strategy, the art of poetry and various practical skills. The crown of these local systems was the Shoheiko academy in Edo, the official academy of the shogunate. But since the Meiji Restoration, Japan's educational system has gradually become more and more centralised and standardised.

The re-evaluation of Japan's educational system initiated during the Nakasone administration suggested reforms to reintroduce more freedom and individuality, but in fact we could learn much along these lines by looking back at the educational system during the Edo period.

The shogunate's policy of requiring the feudal lords to commute back and forth from their fiefs to Edo contributed greatly to the development of communication and transportation networks linking Edo to the fiefs; but still the fiefs were not absorbed into the central government and each retained its own independence and vitality. This precedent can guide us today: it teaches us that we are not forced to make a choice between centralisation and decentralisation; we can have both, in the ideal model offered by Edo.

The cities of the Federal Republic of Germany are a European example of the success of decentralisation. Since the capital of the republic was moved to Bonn, the cities of Germany have been decentralised to an almost ideal degree. Frankfurt, Hamburg, Düsseldorf, Cologne, Bonn, Munich and Stuttgart are all cities between one million and three million inhabitants; no huge megalopolis like Tokyo dominates. Each region has its own universities and newspapers, independent and individual in character. The country itself is a federal republic, and historically the individual states have always been strongly independent.

Yet others argue that Berlin, one of the great world cities in the 1920s, should be restored as the capital of West Germany; that without the culture of a great city, their country cannot be an international centre. In France, on the other hand, everything is concentrated in Paris, yet the French value each of the regions of their country for its unique culture and atmosphere, its local wine and its more relaxed pace of life. While all Frenchmen are proud of their great capital, the other regions of France exist in symbiosis with the centre.

In this context, the current criticism in Japan concerning the concentration of the country's energies and resources on Tokyo seems to be exaggerated. Our goal should be to ensure that the great cities and other regions of the country all develop independently, in a simultaneously centralised and decentralised fashion. That is why the model of the shogunate and the fiefs is such an apt one as we face the future.

HANASUKI
THE AESTHETIC OF SYMBIOSIS

A Re-creation of Kobori Enshu's Yuishikian

In my own home, I enjoy a life in which the most advanced technology exists in symbiosis with tradition. My apartment is perched on the eleventh floor. Next to my study, where my IBM 5560 sits, I have constructed a traditional Japanese tea room, which I have named Yuishikian – the Hut of Consciousness Only.[1] My personal computer is part of a communication network designed by a friend, Richard Farson, president of the Western Behavioral Sciences Institute in La Jolla, California. It is directly linked over the Venus P satellite network to some fifty men and women in the worlds of scholarship, politics and finance. Yuishikian, on the other hand, is my place to retreat and think, and to receive and entertain guests and friends from Japan and abroad with the hospitality of the tea ceremony.

Yuishikian is the re-creation of a particular tea room that once existed but has disappeared, a symbol that represents a formative, crucial and yet forgotten model of Japanese aesthetics. This model is profoundly linked to the basic principles of the Japanese aesthetic, *wabi* and *sabi*.[2] But this will be discussed in greater detail further on; I will first of all describe the tea room that served as the model for my Yuishikian.

This particular tea room was in Takimotobo, a residence for Buddhist monks, constructed at the Iwashimizu Hachimangu shrine in Kyoto by the scholar-monk Shokado Shojo.[3] Shojo's tea room was, in turn, a reconstruction of an earlier tea room, the Kan'unken, built in the first decades of the seventeenth century, but destroyed by fire in 1773.[4] Shojo studied the tea ceremony under the great tea-master Kobori Enshu, and his

Kan'unken was an exact duplicate of Enshu's Shosuitei, the tea room in his Fushimi residence.[5] Both consist of four mats and a *daime*-sized mat.[6] My Yuishikian, then, is a re-creation of Kobori Enshu's most representative tea room, the Shosuitei at Kobori's Fushimi residence. I spent seventeen years reproducing this tea room. Why did it take so long?

Originally, tea rooms were constructed of materials that could be found easily and near at hand. Rare and expensive materials were avoided. A log or branch from a nearby grove of trees, and a stone by the roadside, were collected and incorporated into the final design. As a result, the tea room seems not to have been designed but built through a process of natural accretion. But of course the aesthetic perceptions of the tea masters were operating in the selection process. Their ability to discover the beauty of such commonplace objects, unremarkable to the average person, was crucial. And they possessed the skill to incorporate these objects into the design of a tea room. Though the tea rooms contemporary with Kan'unken and Shosuitei did not employ rare or luxurious materials, obviously many problems arise when one tries faithfully to reproduce the same tea room some three hundred years later.

Tea room plans provide a detailed account of the original structures. In the eighteenth-century plans I was working from, not only are the materials and dimensions noted, but the way in which the natural timbers bend and twist, and the details of finishing the materials are all clearly recorded. Yet when one actually attempts an accurate reconstruction, one finds that crucial information is still missing. The challenge is to acquire that information in the process of the construction.

To clarify the missing details I studied diaries and accounts of tea ceremonies held in this tea room. In his *Matsuya Kaiki*, (1741),[7] Matsuya Hisayoshi describes a tea ceremony that he attended at Enshu's Shosuitei. In addition to a detailed account of the tea utensils and the food and sweets served, he also describes the tea room. His remarks gave certain details not provided by the extant plans of the tea room.

I knew from the plan that the tea room had a basketwork ceiling with a bamboo frame, but the material from which the ceiling was woven was not identified. According to *Matsuya Kaiki*, it was made of reeds. The plan told me that the tokonoma post was made of *kunogi*. It took some time to identify this wood. Was it a sort of tree that no longer existed? Or was it now known by a different name? Was *kuno* an orthographical mistake for *kuri*, or chestnut? I considered various possibilities, but in the end an acquaintance in Kyoto who is familiar with ancient manuscripts told me that *kunogi* was a dialect variation of *kunugi* – a kind of oak.

According to the plan, the back and sides of the tokonoma were papered with antique paper, but what sort of paper? I looked for a model to the Joan tea room.[8] This was designed by Oda Uraku and its tokonoma was papered with the leaves of old almanacs.[9] Searching for almanacs from the early decades of the seventeenth century, I frequented rare book and antique shops. It took over ten years to acquire enough paper for my tokonoma walls. In one place in the tea room, a gently curving log is called for, and I had to pester my carpenter to go searching in the mountains for just the right one; it took more than ten years to find it.

The height at which a flower container is hung from a decorative hook or nail in the tea room is quite important as well, but this was not indicated in the plan, and it was no mean feat to determine the authentic height. A plan called 'Enshu's Four and One *Daime*-sized Mat Tea Room at Fushimi Roku Jizo', by a certain Ensai (otherwise unknown), tells us that the hook should be three *shaku* two *bu* and five *rin* (about 91cm) from the floor. But when we tried hanging it at this height it seemed inappropriately low. I checked the source again and found that some regarded the note on this plan an orthographic mistake for three *shaku* two *sun* and five *bu* (about 98cm). Still, even this height seemed far too low and so out of harmony with the tea room as a whole that on this particular detail I made an exception and followed the example of the Yuin teahouse,[10] setting the decorative hook at three *shaku* seven *sun* (about 112cm).

Following this process of careful consideration of historical sources and inspection of available materials, and relying on the skills of the mere handful of tea room carpenters to be found in all Japan, it took me seventeen years to complete Yuishikian. And since there is no space in central Tokyo to build a tea room, I constructed it as a rooftop garden to my apartment, harmonising it with the rest of the garden area, so that, when completed, my Yuishikian nested among the apartment buildings of the central city.

Why did I take so much trouble to recreate this particular tea room with such painstaking accuracy? As a symbol of the aesthetic vision I call *hanasuki*.

Wabi Implying both Splendour and Simplicity

I offer the term *hanasuki* in place of *wabisuki* because I believe that *wabi* as a concept has come to be interpreted in too narrow and one-dimensional a fashion. Traditionally, *wabi* has been thought of as silence as opposed to loquacity; darkness as opposed to light; simplicity as opposed to complexity; spareness as opposed to decoration; monochrome as opposed to colour; the grass hut, not the aristocrat's palace. Even in school texts, *wabi* is defined as an aesthetic of nothingness.

But isn't the true and essential Japanese aesthetic one in which silence and loquacity, darkness and light, simplicity and complexity, spareness and decoration, monochrome and polychrome, the grass hut and the aristocrat's palace exist in symbiosis? In *wabi* a superbly decorative principle, a special splendour, is to be found – like the undertaste in fine cuisine, that lingers and perfumes each subtle dish.

Nambo Sokei finds the essence of Takeno Joo's tea ceremony in Fujiwara no Teika's poem in the *Shin Kokin Shu*:[11]

> I gaze afar
> And ask for neither cherry flowers
> Nor crimson leaves;
> The inlet with its grass-thatched huts
> Clustered in the growing autumn dusk.[12]

The blossoms of spring and the red leaves of autumn are a metaphor for the gorgeous daisu-style tea ceremony of the aristocrat's mansion.[13] When we gaze at them deeply, we arrive at a realm where not a single thing exists – the rush-thatched cottage on the shore. Those who do not first know the blossoms and the leaves can never live in the thatched hut. Only because we gaze and gaze at the blossoms and leaves can we spy out the thatched hut. This is to be regarded as the essence of tea.

What Nambo is saying is that only one who knows the splendour and gorgeous beauty of the blossoms of spring and the red leaves of autumn can appreciate the *wabi* of the roughly thatched hut on the lonely beach. This is not an aesthetic of nothingness by any means. It is an aesthetic of a double code, in which we are asked to gaze at the roughly thatched hut while recalling the gorgeous flowers and leaves. It is an ambiguous, symbiotic aesthetic which simultaneously embraces splendour and simplicity.

Murata Juko, who is known for his pursuit of the most severe state of Zen[14] says in *Yamanoue Soji Ki*: 'Juko described his ideal as a splendid steed tethered to a grass hut'.[15] *Wabi* is not simply a grass hut; it is the scene of a beautifully caparisoned, powerful horse tied to a humble, elegantly simple straw hut'. The goal of this aesthetic is an ambiguous code in which two symbols simultaneously contradict and overlap.

The Splendour of *Wabi*

The novelist Tanizaki Jun'ichiro wrote in his essay *In Praise of Shadows (In'ei Raisan)*:

Sometimes a superb piece of black lacquerware, decorated

perhaps with flecks of silver and gold – a box or a desk or a set of shelves – will seem to me unsettlingly garish and altogether vulgar. But render pitch black the void in which they stand, and light them not with the rays of the sun or electricity but rather a single lantern or candle: suddenly those garish objects turn sombre, refined, dignified. Artisans of old, when they finished their works in lacquer and decorated them in sparkling patterns, must surely have had in mind dark rooms and sought to turn to good effect what feeble light there was. Their extravagant use of gold, too, I should imagine, came of understanding how it gleams forth from out of the darkness and reflects the lamplight.[16]

We see here that Tanizaki is by no means simply praising shadows alone. His aesthetic, too, is a double code – the absolute opposition of the gorgeous golden decoration and the shadows of the night. In his dramatic phrase, 'the brocade of the night itself', we detect the lineage of an aesthetic of *wabi* that is very far indeed from a philosophy of nothingness.

The ambiguity of this aesthetic of *wabi* is even clearer when we arrive at the related term, *sabi*, as propounded by the haiku poet Matsuo Basho.[17] Mukai Kyorai, Basho's leading disciple in the art of poetry, described the master's verses as 'unchanging flux'; this symbiosis of 'flux' or impermanence and changeableness with an 'unchanging' quality that transcends the flow of time and achieves eternal existence, lies at the core of Basho's idea of *sabi*.[18]

Kyorai writes in the treatise known as the *Kyorai Sho* that:

Sabi is the colour of a verse; it does not mean a sad and lonely verse. It is like an aged warrior who arrays himself in his gorgeous armour and throws himself into battle. Though he dons brocade robes and serves at a banquet, he is still old. It is the combination of a flower-bearer and a white-haired crone.[19]

In other words, the withered, sad state of old age is not *sabi*. On the contrary, *sabi* is the sight of the old man in his glorious armour, fighting bravely; or seated at a splendid banquet in his fine raiment. The aesthetic of *sabi* is produced in the contradiction of two symbiotically existing elements, the splendid brocades and the old man's quietly elegant appearance.

Thus, the interpretation of these two core principles of traditional Japanese aesthetics, *wabi* and *sabi*, as spare, restrained and anti-decorative concepts is badly skewed. In order to restore the present vulgarised and corrupted version of *wabi* to its original meaning, I have invented a new term: *hanasuki*.

Zeami, who brought the art of the Noh theatre to perfection, wrote in works such as *Fushi Kaden* and *Kakyo* that *hana* – flower – was the life of Noh.[20] The aesthetic of *hana* is one of the symbiosis of heterogeneous elements, of disparate moods or feelings. In *Fushi Kaden* Zeami instructs the actor who portrays a demon to perform in an enjoyable way, combining the qualities of frightfulness and enjoyment. In the role of an old man, the actor should don the mask and costume of an old person and 'portray an old man while still possessing the Flower'.[21] When one performs Noh during the day, he tells us, he must act with the dark energy of night inside himself. Zeami's aesthetic is a characteristically Japanese one of symbiosis that has much in common with the original meaning of *wabi*. Indeed, I am convinced that Zeami's aesthetic of the flower is identical with the true meaning of *wabi*.

Yuishikian as an example of *Hanasuki*

Yuishikian, which I constructed as a symbol of the aesthetic of *hanasuki*, has twelve windows and is an extremely bright tea room. Kobori Enshu favoured tea rooms with many windows: the eight-windowed Konjiin tea room at Nanzenji was a favourite. My twelve windows can be regarded as stage lighting for the host's mat. By opening and closing different windows from season to season, the interior can be illuminated in a variety of ways. If I leave the door to the garden open, that view and all its light become part of the tea room interior as well.

In front of the *daime*-sized host's mat the four long mats are lined up in a row. This simple yet bold layout emphasises the theatricality of the host's mat. The tokonoma is framed by a white juniper post on one side and the *kunugi* oak, with a bark resembling red pine, on the other. The juniper is roughly finished in a square shape by hand chiselling four corners, but leaving the bark on its four sides. The bark has been left on the oak post, which disappears into the upper wall. The combination of materials with such a range of expression produces a great dynamism.

The roof and the placement of the windows add variety to the design, making Yuishikian a highly decorative tea room. But I did not sacrifice the simplicity and calm that are characteristic of tea room architecture. This is what makes Yuishikian a model of *hanasuki*.

Why has the idea of *wabi* become so perverted that we are forced to invent a new term, *hanasuki*, to convey its original meaning? I can offer two answers to this question. The first can be traced to the confrontation between the great tea master Sen no Rikyu and his master, the feudal warlord Toyotomi Hideyoshi (1536-98).[22]

Hideyoshi has been described as either the son of a farmer or the son of a foot soldier. Whichever he may have been, he had no time to acquire learning and cultural polish in the years of his rise from a humble station to the position of ruler of all Japan. Even if he had been blessed with the time and the opportunity, in my opinion he lacked by nature a sensitivity to the arts and learning.

Sen no Rikyu served Hideyoshi as an artist in residence and his teacher in the art of the tea ceremony. In their relationship we can detect the conflict between authority and art, the ruler and the creator. Though Hideyoshi was the supreme ruler of all Japan and brooked no opposition from anyone, in the art of tea Rikyu was his superior. Given Hideyoshi's nature, it is quite likely that he resented this great man of the world of art, a realm even Hideyoshi could not rule. After hearing Rikyu speak on *wabi* tea, which placed great emphasis on simplicity and humility, Hideyoshi asked Rikyu to design a tea room entirely papered in gold leaf, as if to taunt his master. And in fact he actually held a tea ceremony in such a tea room.

I believe that Rikyu was forced to articulate an extreme form of *wabi* as an antidote to Hideyoshi's equally extreme tendency towards ostentation, that he pursued this radical *wabi* as rigorously as a Zen monk pursues the way of enlightenment in the special context of this struggle between the ruler and the artist. These particular circumstances are what led Rikyu to develop *wabi* into an aesthetic of nothingness, of death.

In this contest between political and artistic authority, Rikyu may at first seem the loser: Hideyoshi eventually forced him to commit ritual suicide. But in the struggle, Rikyu refined and distilled his aesthetic ideal until he arrived at the nearly inconceivable extreme of simplicity: a tea room of one-and-a-half mats.

Rikyu was a genius, the great formulator of the aesthetic of *wabi* tea. But a more balanced concept of *wabi*, a *wabi* of *hanasuki*, can be detected in the tea ceremony practised by Rikyu's disciples.

Rikyu's leading disciple was Furuta Oribe.[23] The simple addition of a single mat to Oribe's three-mat tea room, En'an, results in the four-and-a-half mat tea room by Enshu.[24] Furuta's tea room then, is one of the sources of Yuishikian. The deep eaves over the earthen area by the corner entrance, the displaced external post construction, the abundance of windows, including a small floor-level latticework portal staggered with another higher portal and a flower-viewing window – Furuta's design displays a wealth of detailing and testifies to a sensitivity attuned to the symbiotic interplay of simplicity and grandeur, silence and drama: a skylight is cut through the roof of the entrance eaves to offer a view of nearby Mount Atago.

Another important follower of Rikyu was Oda Uraku. His Joan tea room is also a classic example of inventive and original *hanasuki*: a round window is boldly cut through the sleeve wall at the left end of the main facade and a triangular floorboard inset beside the tokonoma brings a fresh new touch to the three-and-a-half-mat plan, not to mention the decorativeness of the arched, cut-out wooden hearth partition, old calendar pages pasted around the base of the walls, and the bright atmosphere created by the row of waist-high windows.

Finally, when we consider Yuishikian's model, the Shosuitei tea room designed by Enshu (Oribe's disciple) we come to the unavoidable conclusion that Rikyu could not have taught only simplicity and spareness.

Bruno Taut at Katsura Detached Palace

The reason that the traditional interpretation of *wabi* has been far too narrow and shallow can be found in Rikyu's articulation of the concept in an extreme form, as an antidote to Hideyoshi's ostentation. I also believe that it can be traced to the encounter of Bruno Taut and Walter Gropius with the Katsura Detached Palace and their well-publicised response to it.[25]

The attention of Japanese architects was first drawn to their own tradition by the remarks of these Europeans, who praised Katsura and the Grand Ise Shrine as models of Modern architecture and then promptly returned home to the West.[26] Japanese architects meekly followed their lead; they accepted the judgement that their native aesthetic tradition was one of nothingness, silence and simplicity. But it is important to note that the judgements Taut and Gropius passed on these works of Japanese architecture were made entirely from within the context of Modern architecture.

The Modern architecture aesthetic was born from industrialisation and mass production; its straight, spare, non-decorative line is that of the mass product. Taut and Gropius read Katsura Palace as an icon, an ideal image of Modern architecture. But they overlooked several important features of the palace: the decorative metalwork of the staggered shelves in the first room of the Chu Shoin; the dramatic checked pattern of the tokonoma of the first room in the Shokintei arbour; the side window of the tokonoma of the second room of the Shin Shoin; the round window in the transom of the Shoiken retainers' quarters and the velvet baseboard wall covering the elegant door-pulls of those same quarters. These details are astonishing in their rich decoration, and they stand out even more sharply, embedded as they are within a space that is so pure and simple.

We can see then how one-dimensional was the appreciation of Katsura Palace by Taut and Gropius. Their rejection of the Toshogu shrine at Nikko as an example of the bad taste of the shoguns is further evidence of their failure to grasp the totality of the Japanese aesthetic tradition.[27] The shrine at Nikko must have seemed to these modernists terribly extreme, while the Grand Ise shrine and Katsura Palace are contemporary works. Yet only when they are placed side by side can Japanese architecture of that age be appreciated in its wholeness. What understanding is there to be gained by totally rejecting one and interpreting the other in a highly selective and clearly self-serving way? Perhaps this is just another manifestation of the doctrine of expediency that is at the core of Modern architecture.

As the sculptor Okamoto Taro has suggested, the Japanese tradition embraces two aesthetic currents that exist together in symbiosis.[28] One is bold and dramatic, the other a simple, non-decorative and extremely refined beauty. He traces the first to the ancient Jomon period and the second to the subsequent Yayoi period.[29] There is nothing strange about the fact that both Toshogu shrine and the Katsura Palace were built in the same Edo period, and there are no grounds for dismissing the former as an embarrassing lapse in taste by the Tokugawa shoguns. The vigorous, even violent decorativeness of Jomon culture finally flowered in the gorgeous castle architecture of the Azuchi-Momoyama period (1568-1600), which has continued to nourish Japanese culture to the present day.

There may be those who believe they have discovered the source of Japan's aesthetic tradition when they visit the temples of Kyoto, with their unadorned, unfinished wood. But we must not forget that when Todaiji and Toshodaiji were first built, their pillars were painted crimson and their rafters glowed vermilion, gold and green.[30] They were a rainbow of rich primary colours. Except for certain Zen monasteries, the temples of Japan were all originally as colourful as the Toshogu shrine is today. I regard the decision not to restore those colours as they faded naturally and to accept their new, quieter, but very different beauty, as an indication of the great range of Japanese aesthetic sensitivity. The reaffirmation of Japan's symbiotic aesthetic is not only of importance as a reinterpretation of traditional Japanese aesthetics, but I believe that this sensitivity of symbiosis has replaced Modernism and will be the aesthetic of the twenty-first century.

RIKYU GREY AND
THE ART OF AMBIGUITY

Unlike concepts, sensations are much harder to identify and explain. But this is only fitting, for by trying to analyse and discuss sensations, we only constrain their spontaneity and betray their inherent naturalness. Yet I want to consider sensation, because rather than simply succumbing to the embrace of a sensation, I believe there is self-discovery in grappling with the discordant impulses it creates in the mind.

If one is going to name a certain sensation, formulate an outline of its features, trace its history or search for the origin of that sensation, it must inspire a profound sympathy, yet awake a certain critical awareness. For me, such a sensation is 'Rikyu grey'. The sensation of Rikyu grey represents an aesthetic of an ambivalent or multiple meaning. My interest in it began seventeen years ago when, with a number of friends, I had started the Metabolism movement and developed a strong dissatisfaction with functional architecture. Function as a criterion in architecture achieved many things, but it also resulted in the articulation and concretisation of space. In the process of providing rationally and clearly articulated spaces, the virtues of nebulous and undifferentiated space that naturally exist between demarcated areas was totally neglected. Spaces which might embrace two or more meanings were eliminated in functional architecture.

During the sixties I became fascinated with the comparison of space in Asian and Western cities and I proposed the hypothesis that Oriental cities have no squares or plazas while Western cities possess no streets. Although Asian cities may have no public squares, their streets carry out the function of these open spaces. On the other hand, Western cities have squares or plazas while their streets are little more than thoroughfares. This essay is an attempt to provide a detailed study of what is meant by this hypothesis.

In Asian cities, street spaces exist between private and public space and between residential and commercial space, possessing the characteristics of both the former and the latter types of space. There is a difference between this type of open space and the Western square which is more clearly defined both in terms of area and function. The Asian street, by contrast, is not so clearly defined, it is harder to tell where it begins or ends, and it generates responses to innumerable variations with time.

In the Indian Vedas, the ideal cities of Dendaka, Nandyavarta, Padmaka and Swastika all share a common layout composed of a straight-line grid pattern of streets. None of these cities have squares or plazas, their basic framework was determined by the 'avenue of the sun' (*Rajapata*) set from the sundial, and 'the avenue of the wind' (*Mahakala*). During the monsoon season, the avenue of the sun overflowed with people; on hot, humid nights they could set up their beds along the avenue of the wind to sleep in the cool under the stars. Public and religious institutions were distributed along these perpendicularly intersecting streets and the multifarious functions of daily life occured here side by side.

The ancient Japanese capital of Heian (Kyoto) had no central square either; shrines, temples and public buildings were built along the lattice-like framework of streets. It was a city without one 'core', but a poly-nuclear one made up of an integrated framework of streets. In the sixteenth century Hideyoshi (1536-98) changed the subdivisions of Kyoto by diagonally dividing into four equal parts the square blocks formed by the streets, until then called *machi*. These new units were called *cho* and each pair of *cho* facing each other were named *machi*. This revision in the division of the city, while it may seem insignificant, had pervasive impact. Units of living space until then enclosed by the streets became units which enveloped the street. Living space then could expand freely in horizontal directions.

Hideyoshi's policy was built upon a long historical process of development from the dismantling of the *za* or tradesmen's guilds, the establishment of the monopoly guilds (*rakuza*), the flowering of popular urban culture and the growth of commerce and urbanisation in Japanese society. His policy turned the street into the core of the community. The homes and shops of these street-oriented communities featured lattice-work facades, bench-like porches (*agedana*), low fences and other structural techniques which exploit the openness of wooden architecture and create continuity with the street outside. Street space became an ambivalent space – a medium in which individual living space and the metropolis converge.

The street is thus an undifferentiated, demarcated area of multiple functions, but these dense and rich spatial qualities of the street were completely ignored in the function-oriented city planning of the West. There instead, the square or plaza developed, an open space of sun and greenery. I have no wish to deny the rationality of functional city planning, but I am more and more certain that we must go back and reassess the advantages of space with an ambivalent or multiple meaning, spaces which have been sacrificed for the sake of functional priorities.

At the risk of being misunderstood, I would like to suggest that the difference between the Western concept of space and the Japanese concept of space is the difference between *spatial confrontation* and *spatial continuity*.

Western architecture emerged from a philosophy of confrontation with nature and the impulse to conquer it. In that sense the stone wall, which sharply divides inside from outside, is extremely significant. The Japanese concept of space reaches out to embrace nature and to achieve unity and harmony with it. Another reason that the complete wall did not develop in Japan was a matter of materials; wood, rather than stone became the primary building material. But more significantly, there was always a conscious effort made to allow inner and outer space to inter-penetrate. The spaces under the eaves, the verandah, corridors, lattice-work dividers and other such details of building are all examples of such intermediating zones. My effort to rediscover the tremendous variety of meaning in these intermediate spaces was inspired by Japan's rich architectural tradition.

The Nature of Rikyu Grey

This study of Rikyu grey was originally published as an essay in a special issue of *The Japan Architect* in September 1977 and republished in the same year as part of a book, *Gurei no bunka* (*The Culture of Grey*).

The term Rikyu grey, as Isamu Kurita has pointed out (see No 339 of *Geijutsu shincho*) has no clear origin; and it is used here as a purely symbolic term expressing the multiple meanings or ambiguity of Japan's open spaces. As I will show, a very similar aesthetic sense is expressed in the sixteenth-century Mannerism movement, in Baroque and in modern 'Camp' in the West.

Masayoshi Nishida has written that Rikyu grey (Rikyu *nezumi*) first appeared in the *Choandoki* (*Annals of Choando*), a book of tea written in 1640 by Kubo Gondaifu Toshinari, priest of the Kasuga Shrine in Nara, which contains the following passage:

After Soeki (Sen no Rikyu) was summoned by Hideyoshi to be his teacher of tea, all ceremonial tea came to follow his style. Soeki disliked that which was ornate or gorgeous and he wrote numerous satirical poems admonishing people to follow the principle of *wabi* (simplicity, rusticity). 'Change your collar cloth,' said he, 'wear a fresh sash of charcoal gray cotton (*sumizome*) cloth and a new pair of socks, carry a new fan. To entertain your guests at dinner, lentil soup and shrimp in vinegar sauce is quite enough to serve'. Ever since, this charcoal grey colour has been extremely popular, and dark grey twilled cotton cloth has been widely imported from China. The dark grey colour of this cotton cloth is what came to be known as Rikyu grey.

Whereas previously grey was generally considered a vile colour conjuring up images of rats or ashes and had never been popular; when it became known as Rikyu grey, it was better appreciated. In the latter part of the Edo period (1600-1868) it gained tremendous popularity, along with brown and indigo (navy) blue as the embodiment of the aesthetic ideal of *iki*. *Iki* in this period is a complex concept but may be simply described as 'richness in sobriety'. As the cult of tea spread beyond the upper classes to be practised in the homes of ordinary people, so did the taste for this grey colour. People took pleasure in naming all manner of colours containing the element of charcoal grey such as Fukagawa grey, silver grey, indigo grey, reddish grey, lavender grey, grape grey, brown grey, dove grey and lentil grey. When various colours are mixed until no trace of any specific colour remains, it is called simply 'grey'. All these colours have chromas of very low intensity and their subtle differences of tone had great appeal in that period. This taste in colours prevailed throughout Edo culture from the Genroku period beginning in 1688 and continuing throughout the eighteenth century.

Toru Haga has written on the An'ei and Tenmei periods (1722-1781) that the patterns in kimono fabric preferred by women included *kabeshijira* or *akebono shibori*. *Akebono shibori* is a faint bluish purple pattern like the essence of morning glories, while *kabeshijira* is a very delicate, finely woven silk pattern that appears pure white but in shifting light reveals a subtle pattern.

Gen Itasaka has described the change in taste during the Edo period as the transition between the styles of wood block print artists Moronobu and Harunobu. Moronobu's women are pleasantly plump, Marilyn Monroe-type beauties with round faces, ample bosoms and hips. Harunobu's women are less sensual, androgynous beauties with slender faces and delicate, willowy figures.

This aesthetic development is of particular interest because it suggests the denial of the generous voluptuousness of Marilyn Monroe-type beauty which symbolised the prosperous growth and material abundance of pre-modern Japan up until Genroku. The An'ei Tenmei aesthetic was rather one of nonsensuality, eccentricity and nonphysicalness, expressing the spirit of the age characterised by a more refined ambiguity and a highly sophisticated rhetoric.

In his book *Beauty in Japan* Masayoshi Nishida explains Rikyu grey as a 'colourless, nonsensual hue produced by combining various colours until they cancel each other out'. In terms of chromatics, *Rikyuiro* is a dark grey-green, or ash colour with a greenish tint; Rikyu grey (*Rikyunezumi*) is grey with a hint of *Rikyuiro*.

Rikyu grey epitomises the confrontation or collision of various contradictory elements and describes a condition in which those elements cancel each other out, thus achieving coexistence and continuity. This condition might also be described as nonsensuality. Perhaps through the aesthetic of Rikyu grey, Sen no Rikyu was deliberately attempting to create a two-dimensional world temporarily frozen in time and space.

In the grey of twilight, the spatial qualities of the city of Kyoto, Japan's traditional community, are at their best. Roof tiles and plaster walls dissolve into shades of grey; they seem to lose all perspective and three-dimensionality. This dramatic effect, in which a three-dimensional world shifts into a two-dimensional, plane world, is impossible to experience in any city in Western Europe. The spatial arrangement of Western cities and of buildings is superbly three-dimensional. The discovery of the principle of perspective in the Renaissance period brought three-dimensional shading to cities and architecture. Towers, monuments and public squares form fixed points of perspective which have become important elements of city spaces in Western Europe, space is experienced from a single point of perspective and these landmarks became indispensable for grasping that space. Western cities thus demonstrate their most dramatic effects under the strong, bright sun which highlights their three-dimensional qualities.

Two-Dimensionalisation of Space

The spatial composition of Katsura Detached Palace is similar to a drawing in a picture scroll in which the point of perspective moves, dissolving building facades and street spaces into plane elements. This is a garden of meandering walks among hills and around a lake, it refuses any single, fixed point of perspective. It is a two-dimensional world created by a moving visual point and in the grey of twilight the most dramatic effect of this two-dimensionality appears. At the very basis of Japanese aesthetic consciousness, be it in painting, music, drama or even in buildings and cities, is this two-dimensionality or frontality. It is a quality of timeless nonsensuality, it is the continuum in which contradictory elements coexist and the quality which dissolves demarcations between disparate dimensions and cancels out ambiguity. Rikyu grey, or the 'philosophy of grey' shares all and is a medium of all these concepts. Needless to say, such concepts epitomise the special qualities imparted to Japanese culture by the pervasive influence of Buddhism. The centrality of Buddhism to the tea ceremony is reflected in the *Nanporoku* in which a disciple of Sen no Rikyu, Nanbo Sokei, master of Shuun'an, at the Nansoji in Sakai, recorded the teachings of his master. Rikyu said:

> You must practise and master tea ceremony in a small hut, first and foremost, according to the teachings of Buddhism. The comfort of a home and the taste of meals are merely worldly concerns, and a house which shelter you from the elements and food sufficient to prevent you from starvation are all you need. This is the teaching of the Buddha and the intent of the tea ceremony. Briny water, gather firewood, boil water, and make tea. Offer the first cup to Buddha, then to others, lastly partake yourself. Arrange

some flowers and burn incense. In all, follow the way of the Buddha. Further details may be found in my humble writings.

Joo (Takeno Joo, 1504-55) said:

Fujiwara Teika captured the spirit of *wabi-cha* in a poem in the *Shin Kokinshu*:

Miwataseba
Hana mo momiji mo
Nakarikeri
Ura no tomaya no
Aki no yugure.

As I look about,
What need is there for cherry flowers
Or crimson leaves?
The inlet with its grass-thatched huts
Clustered in the growing autumn dusk.[1]

According to Joo, here 'cherry flowers and crimson leaves' are analogous to the formal *daisu* ceremony. After gazing long at such flowers and leaves, you come to a hut by the water, the world of nothingness. Those who have not known this gaudy beauty of flowers and leaves will not appreciate such a hut. Only after you have looked at the flowers and leaves are you able to see the truly elegant simplicity of the hut. This for Joo is the very essence of tea.

The image in Teika's poem quoted in this description coincides with what I feel at dusk on the streets of Kyoto or indeed in the twilight in any old Japanese community. The *Nanporoku* goes on to describe Rikyu's ideas about tea ceremony rooms.

As I have said many times, the deepest meaning in tea is to be found in the simple, rustic tea hut. In the most formal *daisu* ceremony, the prescribed rules must be observed because that is customary. In the simple hut, though it conforms to the formal measurements, you can break away from formal measurements, discard technique, revert to

the innocent and empty mind and go beyond customs and
rules, beyond worldly cares.

'Break away from formal measurements'. 'Discard technique'.
'Revert to the innocent and empty mind'. These are notions of
great contrast to the techniques of Western architecture,
which begin with the Order of Greek and Roman tradition and
underlie module building in modern architecture.

The tea room that Rikyu built 'breaking away from formal
measurement' and 'discarding technique' went far beyond the
four-mat room to a one-mat room. He attempted to overcome
the narrowness of physical space by creating a detached,
nonsensual, spiritual space.

Measured by Western standards, the height of the ceiling,
the windows, and the low entrance *nijiri-guchi* are ridicu-
lously small, almost inhuman. Heterogeneous design elements such as circular windows, unplaned alcove support
pillars, various kinds of ceiling materials and openings may
seem to clash with each other yet coexist harmoniously. From
the point of view of the Western sense of order, this is no
doubt quite difficult to understand.

In Japanese architecture, including tea room architecture,
the traditional spatial elements of a design such as ceilings,
alcoves, and walls are each autonomous, that is, they are on
the independent planes of a two dimensional world. The
heterogeneous elements mutually deny any direct three-
dimensional relationship. There are many examples, such as
where the windows in two opposite walls are placed with
total disregard to conformity in size, height or other measurements. This is one technique of encouraging the sense of two-
dimensionality. In any case, Rikyu grey likewise is a medium
in which three-dimensional, cubic, sculptural, substantial
space of single meaning is rendered into plane, one-dimensional, nonsensual space of multiple meaning.

Confrontation and Harmony

Few other examples express the sensation and the aesthetic of

Rikyu grey (or Baroque) better than the interior of the Denkan room of Katsura Detached Palace. From the curved lines and white hues used in the frame of the entrance to the tea room from the *mizuya* (preparation room), to the fit of the rounded edges – all are of different qualities, yet superbly harmonised. They are serene, yet dynamic. It was Baroque in the West which finally broke up the classical order by employing the dramatic element of curved lines; but I consider the interior of the Denkan more typical of Baroque aesthetic than even the Jesuit Chapel by della Porta, which is considered the archetype of early Baroque.

There are other examples of the ways heterogeneous elements can be handled, such as in the garden benches of the Katsura Detached Palace. Naturally curved timbers are used for supports and pillars and are set in conformity with autonomous criteria, without influencing structural components in any way. In other words, they create dramatic spaces where confrontation and harmony coexist.

The Toshogu Shrine is usually given as an example of 'Japanese Baroque' but it does not apply to the aspect of Baroque (or Mannerism) in the same sense as Rikyu grey. The quality of Baroque is represented by the mutual resistance and harmony of movement and drift, stillness and movement, straight lines and curved lines. A further example of this type of the Hiunkaku (Fleeting Cloud Pavilion) is the Nishi-Honganji Temple, a structure said to be the only remaining part of the Jurakudai Palace. This asymmetrical three-storey structure demonstrates an amazing heterogeneity of straight and curved lines which coexist in an overall appearance of great tranquillity. This again, is precisely the same sensation as Rikyu grey, as well as a further example of early Baroque aesthetics.

The first time I incorporated the aesthetic of Rikyu grey into my own designs was in the Ishikawa Welfare Annuity Hall (Kanazawa, 1977) and in the National Ethnological Museum (Osaka). The exteriors of both buildings are of Rikyu grey tiles, and all the various aluminium and stainless steel construction materials, from the rounded edges of the aluminium die-cast eaves, to the granite and Angora stone, are uniformly in hues of grey or charcoal grey. By this example, I do not wish to mislead you into thinking that the sensation of Rikyu grey is achieved only by the use of colour. Structures are built against gravity, yet in themselves express the sense of gravity. In contrast to this gravity, grey tones can create a detached, drifting sense, as do the streets of Kyoto in the twilight. It is but one technique of blotting out the materiality of the structural materials, rendering space autonomous and of double meaning, as well as dramatising that space.

What the Ishikawa Hall and the Ethnological Museum both share is the deliberate combination of mutually antagonistic, heterogeneous elements and materials, and my attempt is to create through them a sense of detachment and coexistence. In the Ishikawa building, we created an almost mystic serenity by grey aluminium panelling on the walls and ceiling.

Philosophy of *Sunyata*

In the second or third century, six to seven hundred years after the death of Buddha, the Mahayana philosopher Nagarjuna of South India wrote a treatise on the 'middle way' entitled *Mula-madhyamaka-sastra*, in which he describes the concept of *sunyata* or relativity (in Japanese, *ku*). This treatise was published in Chinese in AD409.

Nagarjuna advocated the 'middle way' in everything, saying, 'We are not nihilists. By rejecting the theories of both existence and nonexistence we will make clear the way to Nirvana', and he explains the 'Eight Negations' and the 'Middle Way of Impermanence'. Nagarjuna's 'middle way', a philosophy of great contrast to the dualism of the West, is considered the origin of the philosophy of *sunyata*. Later, in the fourth or fifth century, this theory was replaced by the 'Consciousness-Only' doctrine of the North Indian

Philosopher Vasubandhu, which produced the philosophy of the 'truly non-existent but mysteriously existent'. These teachings were brought to China by Hsüan-chuang (618-701) through his translation of the *Vimsatika-vijnaptimatratasiddhi* into Chinese in 661. Vasubandhu's teachings are explained in the *Diamond Sutra* which contains the following passage:

Treasure *sunyata*, the state which is beyond the visible world and beyond transient phenomena. The absence of form may be thought of as infinity, where there is no difference between life and death and in which one lives without fetters of any kind.

Sunyata is not a concept which opposes either substance or existence, but a nonsensual existential concept which is precisely the same as the Rikyu grey of twilight spaces.

Western architecture is the architecture of stone and sun-baked bricks, and it is thus very physical, substantial and three-dimensional. Therefore, its space is like a porous body with openings made in it. This technique is all the more certain to characterise buildings by perspective, three-dimensionality and distinct shading.

Spaces in Japanese architecture, especially as illustrated by the *shoin* and *sukiya* tradition from Katsura Detached Palace to Rikyu's tea room, are created out of wood materials which impart none of the impression of a physical body which has been carved out to form space. Rather like a stage set, each vertical side has its own viewpoint and each side seems transformed into a mental image which goes beyond substance. In the sense that Japanese architecture incorporates the *ku* and relativity, in marginal zones between substantiality and insubstantiality, it is related to the architecture of vertical two-dimensionality.

Rikyu grey, as a hue produced when mutually opposing colours are blended, also corresponds to *sunyata* (relativity) or that which shares both existence and non-existence. Japanese *emakimono* (picture scrolls) are examples which illustrate a way of drawing heterogeneous elements, measurements, aspects, distances and times simultaneously onto one plane surface, clearly a style quite different from Western painting.

In Japan, until the early modern period, architectural drawings were merely rough sketches with instructions. In the *Shomei* (*A Guide to Carpentry*) of the Hirauchi family and in the records of the Kora family there are many detailed building plans for temples. Among those in the Kora family records are plans for Daitokuin, including detailed frontal views, floor plans, cross-sectional drawings and sketches of sculpture. Whereas Western European architects often draw their plans with bird's eye perspective or isometric three-dimensional figures, Japanese master builders drew their plans only in plane or frontal views. This practice, too, illustrates the unique treatment of space in Japanese architecture as an unfolding diagram.

The technique of bringing together different worlds and different spatial dimensions can be found in various other aspects of Japanese culture. Fujiwara Teika (1162-1241), the court poet mentioned earlier, writes in his *Guhisho* (*A Private Sketchbook*) on the technique of *soku*, the poetic sequence in court poetry in which the verses are seemingly unrelated in imagery and rhetorical technique.

There is rarely virtue in *shinku* (in which the verses are closely related in theme). *Shinku* poems are much too predictable; the poem develops as would a plant, from root to branch and to leaf, and they express only the ordinary, never the unusual or exotic. Each verse of *soku* is complete, yet they always produce something strange and unique. That is why Lord Tsunenobu said that there were many superb *soku* poems.

> *Yu sareba*
> *Nobe no akikaze*
> *Mi ni shimite*
> *Uzura naku nari*
> *Fukakusa no sato.*

As evening falls,
From along the moors the autumn wind
Blows chill into the heart
And the quails raise their
                              plaintive cry
In the deep grass of Fukakusa village.[2]

In this example of *soku* technique, it is clear that there are two completely different mental images placed together. Between those two images is the same nonsensuality as represented by Rikyu grey and by the multiplicity of meaning of *sunyata*.

The same effect is achieved on the state by the *senubima* 'no-action' of the No drama, as described by Zeami in his treatise on the No, *Kakyo*:

Sometimes spectators of the No say, 'The moments of "no-action" are the most enjoyable'. This is an art which the actor keeps secret. Dancing and singing, movements and the different types of miming are all acts performed by the body. Moments of 'no-action' occur in between. When we examine why such moments without actions are enjoyable, we find that it is due to the underlying spiritual strength of the actor which unremittingly holds the attention. He does not relax the tension when the dancing or singing come to an end or at intervals between the dialogue and the different types of miming, but maintains an unwavering inner strength. This feeling of inner strength will faintly reveal itself and bring enjoyment. However, it is undesirable for the actor to permit this inner strength to become obvious to the audience. If it is obvious, it becomes an act, and is no longer 'no-action'. The actions before and after an interval of 'no-action' must be linked by entering the state of mindlessness in which one conceals even from oneself one's intent. This, then, is the faculty of moving audiences, by linking all the artistic powers with one mind.[3]

The silence and stillness in the interval between the action of the No drama must be performed with utmost care. *Senubima* represents the same quality that I have been describing in *sunyata* and in Rikyu grey. The *senuhima*, the moment when the expression of one mind communicates another, is a transitional, complex, silent space replete with meaning. The concepts of *sunyata*, Rikyu grey and *senuhima* each represent distinct areas of meaning. Naturally, I am well aware that it is problematic to discuss all these on the same level, but in order to pursue my point about the nature of intermediaries, I have indulged my penchant for fossicking in every cultural corner for contexts that will illustrate my theory of space.

In the Metabolism theory (1960), I hypothesised that there is a marginal realm or zone which unifies different spatial realms. That intermediary was the start of an approach to *sunyata*, but the marginal realm I had in mind then was too substantial.

I began to realise that the marginal zone was space without substance sometime after I became concerned with the street as a special feature of Japan's urban space; the semipublic ambiguity of such areas held great significance when compared to the spatial role of the square in Western cities.

The street has no clearly defined spatial function, but within the twenty-four hours of the day, it is at times used for private and at times for public activities. In that sense it is space without substance, space with many overlapping complex meanings. In the same way that *sunyata* is completely invisible yet possesses profound and dense meaning, so too is this 'street space' replete with meaning. In the Fukuoka Bank building the open space under the eaves is considered neutral; it is my attempt to create a relative space – a marginal zone where public and private meanings interpenetrate and where interior and exterior overlap.

If verandahs and long eaves can create spaces where nature and buildings attain continuity the intermediaries of the Fukuoka Bank are designed to produce spaces of dual meaning – that is, to be private and public simultaneously. Postwar city planning in Japan has been too firmly based on the theory of functionalism and has too severely separated private and public space. The superficial uncritical adoption of Western rationalism has resulted in the division of urban spaces into cramped, uncomfortable spaces for private use and vast expansive public spaces, including roads. Street space, which once had many functions in daily life, has now been taken over by the automobile – no longer is it a scene of dense human activity, but a channel of danger. The feeling that man is being shunted aside for the sake of the road is further alienating modern man. Rather than join the hysterical voices calling for abolition of all cars, can we not discover a way to bring back and recreate the intermediary zones which have been sacrificed in the cause of growth?

The marginal zones of the Fukuoka Bank were planned with that endeavour in mind, in order to restore semipublic space in the city which would at least create continuity with the buildings around it.

I called the Nishijin Labor Center (1962) 'street architecture' because its purpose was to recreate for people the streets where cars had totally taken over. To produce a marginal zone in architectural space requires techniques which simultaneously relate the qualities of internal and external space. The intermediary zone of the Fukuoka Bank interlocks with the building area and while it is an area in the eaves of the building, elements such as trees and ponds give a sense of drifting movement and provide an experience in the dramatic nature of space. In this sense, such intermediary spaces have gravity – the free qualities of El Greco's paintings and the ambivalence and double facetedness of the woman's expression in 'Ecstasy of St Theresa' by Bernini.

The lobby of the Japan Red Cross Main Office building was designed to create an intermediary zone linking inner and outer space through mutual interpenetration and reflection. In this case, the lobby is clearly an internal area, but there is an opening in the vaulted glass ceiling. A dry pond of polished granite was laid in the floor which reflects through the opening to the outside. In short, this lobby demonstrates very deliberate devices for reversing interior and exterior spaces. In terms of my theory of marginal zones, the Daido Life Insurance Tokyo Office building lies between the Nishijin Labor Center and the Fukuoka Bank. The building site extends from the street in front to the street at the back, and so it seemed only natural to plan a new road space passing from front to back. The thoroughfare constructed within the building is provided with exterior elements such as shops, a running stream, street lamps, street furniture and trees. Through openings in the roof light, rain can pour into the artificial stream within.

This was an effort to create a marginal zone where exterior and interior space confront one another yet coexist. In their concept of *sunyata*, Nagarjuna and Vasubandhu are not the only ones to describe the Buddhist aesthetic as the spiritual condition which incorporates both opposition and coexistence and reaction and affirmation. Daisetz Suzuki, in his logic of 'identity and difference' has clarified for us the basic philosophical principle for grasping the coexistence of relations between the parts and the whole and between mutually contradictory elements. The following description is found in the Diamond Sutra:

> *Ya eva subhute, Prajnaparamita*
> *Tathagatena, bhasita sa eva aparmita*
> *Tathagatena bhasita*
> *Tena ucyate Prajnaparamita iti.*

If the modifiers in these sentences are omitted they become: *A eva a-A. Tena ucyate A iti.* In English this is: 'A is non-A, therefore, it is called A'. This is the essence of the logic of 'identity and difference'.

The individual in the East Asian tradition is not the same as an individual of the West. He possesses no basis of self-existence within himself, but he has existence in the supra-individual which exists in the state of *sunyata*. Individuality and supra-individuality maintain their identity despite their mutual contradiction. The logic of identity and difference produces a state of suspended ambiguity with dual meaning through the simultaneous rejection and affirmation of concepts. Again, on the conceptual level, this logic is the same as the logic of Rikyu grey.

The period between 1900 and 1930 was one of great technological transformation and intellectual upheaval in Western societies. It was the advent of Planck's quantum theory, Heisenberg's uncertainty principle, Bergson's creative evolution, and Einstein's theory of relativity. Then in the thirties came a period when people pursued escapism in many forms: B Clemen's *Uncertainty and Reconstruction*, Ortega's *The Revolt of the Masses*, Freud's *Anxiety of Culture* soon followed. Individualism and the establishment of the ego had matured in European societies before the turn of the century and community was built on the schema of the individual versus the whole, and the individual versus society. For this reason European societies have swung back and forth like a pendulum. The rise of totalitarianism, for example, was countered by strong individualism tending towards social disorganisation. When social disorganisation went too far, a movement calling for social reconstruction occurred. In the world of 'Oriental individum', the parts and the whole are of equal value, individual and supra-individual (the totality) coexist without losing their identities and there is no hierarchical pyramid which unifies the whole and the parts.

Rikyu Grey is Baroque

In the West, Baroque and 'Camp' show similarities with the sensations of Rikyu grey. In his book on the Baroque, Eugenio Dorus states that when conflicting intentions are bound together in one motion, the style which results is by definition Baroque. In plain and simple terms, Baroque means not knowing what one wants to do. It is the simultaneous wish for affirmation and rejection; the attempt to fly while being pulled downward by the force of gravity. From this contradictory impulse the round column was born, for its structure is what could be described as a paradox of inspiration. The spirit of the Baroque, according to Dorus, can be represented by raising the arm while simultaneously trying to lower it.

He goes on to say that the actions of the Lord Jesus Christ in the picture on the theme *Noli me tangere* (Touch-Me-Not) in the Prado is the virtual formula for the Baroque. The picture by Correggio, the father of many instinctively Baroque masters, shows Mary Magdalene at the feet of Christ, who is rejecting her while at the same time drawing her to him. He is telling her not to touch him even as he stretches his hand out to her. Dorus says that as Christ teaches this woman the way to heaven, he leaves her in tears and desperation on earth. And Mary Magdalene, too, is pure Baroque since, while repenting her sins, she succumbs to profane love. She remains earth-bound while attempting to follow Christ. Dorus argues that this is the eternal reality of the eternally feminine and it represents a style as well: the Baroque.

I have singled out Baroque from the patterns of Western culture not through wanting to discuss the morphological types, but because Rikyu grey can be seen in Dorus' conceptual analysis of the Baroque as multipolar and continuous and as that which is eternally feminine and simultaneously desires affirmation and rejection. Though the Baroque age was scientifically and technologically more advanced than the Renaissance, probably at no other time have such efforts been made to express human spirituality and sentiment. It seems to me that this was the one time in Western history that rationality and irrationality coexisted and a nondualistic spiritual world was actually produced.

Of course, even in the Baroque there is not a great deal that fulfils the aesthetic qualities I seek to demonstrate. Mannerism, a word whose original meaning is 'affected' or 'superficial imitation', was the pejorative name given by seventeenth-century critics to the late sixteenth-century artists. The term Baroque likewise derives from the criticism of an aesthetic which strayed from the strict rules of the Greco-Roman tradition.

As an example of the view that rationalism and irrationalism coexisted in Baroque, we have della Porta's Jesuit Chapel (c1575) which was completed in the transition between the Mannerist and the Baroque periods. This church is designed in the form of a cross and combines both medieval and Renaissance styles. Its composition is very free yet achieves a restrained sense of balance.

Further examples are in the ambiguous balance of the Palazzo Massimi (c1536) by Baldassare Peruzzi (1481-1536) the Mannerist architect. A painter corresponding in style was Claude Poussin. Dorus called him an artist of rational passion, and indeed his reaction to the Baroque was an equilibrium brimming with tension between intellect and emotion. Poussin's *A Poet's Inspiration*, is an even better example of motion in stillness. Bernini's *Ecstasy of St Teresa*, El Greco's *Adoration of the Shepherds*, Domenico Tintoretto's *Goddess of Good Fortune Banishing Vices* and Gaudi's *Sagrada Familia* all demonstrate the serene equilibrium between the rational and the irrational spirit and between the impulse to fly and the force of gravity and all contain the qualities of nonsensuality and ambiguity which is unique to Baroque. However, when the Baroque comes to the decorative extreme of the interior of the Saint Agnese church by Borromini in Piazza Navona, it is too fantastic and has nothing to do with Rikyu grey.

It was Herbert Read who said that ambiguity in English prose is achieved through metaphors. William Empson, in his book, *Seven Types of Ambiguity*, 1930, takes examples from Shakespeare, Chaucer and Milton to explain the complex and alternate meanings of poetic language. He shows how single words or grammatical structures can simultaneously create different impressions on the reader's mind. This is an important key to evoking ambiguity.

Empson's seven types of ambiguity are as follows: 1) when a detail is effective in several ways at once; 2) when two or more alternative meanings are fully resolved into one; 3) when two apparently unconnected meanings are given simultaneously; 4) when alternative meanings combine to make clear a complicated state of mind in the author; 5) when the author is discovering his idea in the act of writing . . . or not holding it all in mind at once; 6) when what is said is contradictory or irrelevant and the reader is forced to invent interpretations; 7) when (there is) full contradiction, marking a division in the author's mind.[4]

However, as Masao Yamaguchi has pointed out in his work *Double Meaning in Culture*, sensitivity is produced in the marginal areas which are indicators of double meaning in art and culture. Because those marginal areas are so diverse, various kinds of sensitivity can thrive: images which are not ordinarily defined in everyday life, contradictory elements and images or symbols which have not yet been given words can ceaselessly appear and proliferate and achieve a new integration. However, such sensitivity cannot be nurtured in a world of logical consistency.

In the intellectual climate of Western rationalism, one element of which is this logical consistency, it was from the start difficult for art and culture of dual meaning or of ambiguity to grow. The Baroque era included, the phenomenon of such arts was peculiar in the history of Western culture. By contrast, as in the logic of 'identity and difference', at the base of Japanese culture is an aesthetic consciousness or sensibility which goes beyond logical consistency.

According to Masao Yamaguchi, the basic motif of Yanagita Kunio's folklore approach was the dual meaning contained in marginal zones of Japanese culture. Yanagita discusses many such phenomena, for example: the guardian gods of travellers at the roadsides; the outcastes who lived on the edges of settlements at the boundary between the wilderness and cultivated land; Hashihime, the extension of a schizophrenic border goddess who could kill men cold blood if angry but when pleased, bestow rare and precious treasures.

In the West, ambivalence and ambiguity is permitted only when discussing some special spirit of an age or the quality of some new art. The Baroque spirit and Empson's analysis of Shakespeare and Chaucer are examples of this rare phenomenon.

Masao Yamaguchi explains the marginal qualities of a culture by saying that they emerge when, on the fringes of the concentric circles that make up the pattern of a culture, attempts are made to adopt heterogeneous elements into the culture. From the point of view of Western logical conformism, which believed that cultural forms were something homogeneous and stable, anything that is on the fringes of that culture is potentially threatening, it represents vandalism and heresy. In this sense it coincides with Dorus' belief that the Baroque represents a movement to incorporate heterogeneous elements at the fringes.

The theories of architectural functionalism, developed between 1928 and 1950 in the International Style movement, in which CIAM played a leading role, were founded on the Western system of rationalism and logical consistency. The one hundred years of modernisation in Japan were also years of Westernisation. A classic example is the fact that modern architecture in the Meiji and Taisho periods as well as the teachings of Joseph Conder at the College of Engineering at Tokyo Imperial University closely followed the Western European architectural pattern. The trend in this field has not changed substantially since the end of the war, and the copiers of elements of design from modern architecture in Western Europe and America are still very influential.

However, the heyday of the uniform standard for evaluating cultures which put European culture at the top of the world hierarchy is rapidly coming to an end. International conditions are undergoing rapid and drastic change. The economic strength and political power of the US is declining. A new economic sphere is emerging in the Middle East along with a resurgence of the Islamic world. The political weight of

Third World countries, led by African nations in particular, is growing. In Asia, China is moving rapidly towards political and cultural leadership while Japan continues substantial economic growth. However, even as these violent changes occur there is a quiet movement going on which places equal value on all cultures. This may well stimulate movements in search of cultural identity in particular localities, but we must firmly reject any assertions of chauvinism and traditionalism. Each individual culture is equivalent in value to world culture in the same sense as the concept of 'identity and difference' in which equilibrium is achieved through related diversity. We must, for example, work to discover elements of Japanese tradition which can go beyond Japan and establish continuity with world culture.

This is my reason for employing the term Rikyu grey in pursuit of the Baroque aesthetic. Other architects of interest in this regard are Aldo van Eyck, Louis Kahn and James Stirling. The Dutch architect Aldo van Eyck has postulated a theory of dual phenomena. Against the traditional Western European belief that houses and cities are on completely different dimensions of a hierarchy, Van Eyck built a new order, Twin Phenomenon, based on the idea that a city is a large residence and a residence is a small city. A representative work of Van Eyck is the Amsterdam Orphanage in which fundamental units of space are combined to build the whole, while producing dramatic spaces which make one unaware of the basic units. In some places the level of the floor varies, in others building units connect in larger spaces, and in the lighting provided, the units seem to melt into the whole. This building is a concrete example of his theory of dual phenomena.

The influence of Van Eyck's theory on world architecture was very great, but of greatest interest to me is in the philosophy of Martin Buber as explained in *Ich und Du*. In *Über das Dialogische Prinzip I*, Buber explains the relation between *I* and *things* (*ich* and *es*) and the *I* and *you* (*ich* and *du*). He says that, for human beings, the world is double in that it conforms to dual human attitudes. He says that the *I* in the basic I-you relation is different from the *I* in I-it. I encounter you, because you turn towards me and approach. But the direct relation between you and me is created by my action. In this way, such a relationship entails both being chosen and choosing; it is simultaneously active and passive. I myself have not succeeded in concentrating and dissolving myself into a total entity, but it could not have happened without me. I become I in relation to you and by becoming I, am able to describe you. Buber further says that the realm of it (*es*) exists in a complex of time and space. The realm of you is not in a complex of time and space. When the relational phenomena have passed, the individual you must become one it, but individual its, by moving into relation with phenomena, can become a single you.

Buber's logic of the I and you has plainly transcended Western logical consistency and approaches Buddhist philosophy. But this is only natural, for he quotes copiously from the Buddhist sutras.

The idea proposed by Aldo van Eyck was a Buddhist, non-Western theory of ambiguity of meaning that had not up to that time been part of the philosophy of modern architecture. Yet, as Charles Jencks points out in his book *Modern Movements in Architecture*, the questions of ambivalent or multiple meaning are the most important points of departure in contemporary art, architecture and culture.

The Leicester University College of Engineering building (1964), by the British architect James Stirling, is a bold structure of glass and brick masonry. It is built of traditional English materials, brick and glass, but the treatment of glass projecting from the facade, the glass roof tilted at an angle of forty-five degrees and the cubic conclusion give the building its dramatic effect. The two quite different building materials are treated with an ordinary technique, yet the effect is one of intense tension and coexistence. Again this building seems to intend an integration of two entirely contradictory ways of thinking, the articulation yet encasing of space. Stirling later clarified this approach in the Faculty of History building at Cambridge University (1968). The glass casing on the faculty office sections slants at a forty-five degree angle, attaining not only an ambiguous spatial quality of intensified exterior space but also a sense of tension and of resistance to the articulation of the building.

Moreover, this building incorporates a whole range of architectural images – from traditional English factory styles to details of spaceships, yet they come across as very strongly controlled. It might be said to represent a similar emotion as the intellectuality of Poussin's *A Poet's Inspiration*.

The buildings of the American architect Louis Kahn are among the few examples of intelligent and dramatic space created by applying articulation and non-articulation at the same time. His Sauk Biological Research Institute allows articulation of structural beams and cores but creates an extremely controlled effect of coexistence which counters the turbulence of the articulation. This building is clearly from the lineage of the University of Pennsylvania Richards Medical Research building, the project which earned Kahn world renown as an architect.

The masonry structure and the use of arches have given the India University of Economics building a quiet but dramatic sense of coexistence which surpasses conflict between tradition and modernism, technique and art. In his Kimball Art Gallery building, space has been articulated into a world of sophistication and diversity. The entirely different materials of concrete, travertine and zinc roofing sheets create a sense of antagonism and yet extreme tranquillity – of motion in stillness.

The mind of Louis Kahn is a cross between a gaslight and a laser beam.

It is a mind full of connections, respecting the past, perceiving the future emerging from it.

It is a mind full of compassion, having known poverty, having known the frustrations born of talents isolated from opportunities.

It is a mind full of grace. Of grace under pressure.

It is mind ever searching for tranquillity amidst turbulence, and for continuity amidst contradiction.

A mind reaching out to pull tight the final ring. To amass harmony in the service of man.

(*The Architectural Forum*, July-August, 1972)

The quality of multiple meaning in space appeared early in the history of modern architecture. In a sketch of a residence for an art connoisseur drawn by CR Mackintosh, there is a feeling of 'unstable stability' – a feeling created by the subtle use of curved and straight lines. Again, Otto Wagner's Vienna Post Office, though he declares that 'art is controlled only by necessity', successfully represents space with a wonderfully ambiguous sense of space evoked by curved and straight lines. These are all typical examples of the architecture of ambiguity and in that sense they possess a sense of space which had been lacking in modern architecture.

'Camp'

'Camp' is a contemporary aesthetic which turns its back on ordinary aesthetic judgement based on evaluations of good or bad architecture and offers an entirely new standard for the appreciation of art.

Susan Sontag, in her 'Notes on Camp', 1964, says that the history of Camp can be traced back to such Mannerist artists as Pontormo, Rousseau and Caravaggio, or to the severely put-on paintings of Georges de La Tour. In the field of literature the movement has its roots in Lilly and the euphuists, in music with Belgorage and Mozart and in the Baroquists as well as Ruskin, Tennyson and Art Nouveau. The tradition also includes a whole range of works from the weird but beautiful *Sagrada Familia* by Gaudi down to Stanburg's movie, starring Marlene Dietrich, *Devil is a Woman*. The aesthetic of

Camp warns of the commonplace in modern architecture which has degenerated because of a too serious and steadfast adherence to convention.

Many Mannerist painters attempted to heighten the sensual effects through the subjective and unstable form of shot colours. One of the founders of Mannerism, Pontormo, in his portrait 'Dugolino Martelli' communicates a tension which barely arrests its unstable movement. This expresses the same sensation as his Mary and child portrait in the St Michael Bisdomini Church in Florence.

The Mannerist painters, although they employed Michelangelo's technique of contrapposto, tried to break through the artistic rules of the Renaissance and introduce intellectual foresight by creating new forms in which sensation and intelligence could coexist. The chiaroscuro shading technique is one of the best known of this school as exemplified in Caravaggio's *Palmist*. The technique creates an overall dramatic effect but maintains a subtle balance of instability.

Camp exhorts one with the complexity of human nature and of space. It is expressed by the urban pastorale, discussed by Empson in his book, *Seven Types of Ambiguity*, mentioned earlier, and by the disquietingly androgynous quality in the perfect beauty of Greta Garbo. Especially for Camp, Marilyn Monroe and Jane Mansfield are too feminine to be meaningful. Similarly, it is correct to say that some architecture is too good for Camp.

Greta Garbo was always herself, and her poor acting only heightened the effect of her beauty. As Jean Genet points out in *Notre Dame des Fleurs*, 1944, to extract polysemy from a culture, good taste must not be merely good taste but must have a sense of taste about what is bad taste. In other words, the sense of Camp is sensitivity to double meaning when a two way interpretation is possible.

The aesthetic which gives distinction to contradiction, distinguishes between different functions and pursues logical consistency is clearly a modern one. Therefore, functional architecture brought forth international forms and, together with the progress of industrialisation, a new criteria for 'good design' was created.

However, perhaps we have come full circle to face a contradictory world that is confused and possesses no logical consistency. I have no desire to deny the achievements of functionalism nor to criticise the work of many fine students of so-called good design, but I feel that the time has come for us to venture into the frontier of the spirit which stretches broadly on all sides at the fringes of our established rules and standards. The core of the human spirit is not easily divisible, it is endowed with bountiful meaning and suggestion, and at the same time with tranquillity, which is the world of Rikyu grey.

AN EXPERIMENTAL CITY IN THE DESERT

Bedouins Can't Live in California-style Housing

One of the projects I was working on in 1979 was the design of a desert city in Libya. This was an interesting case of putting the philosophy of symbiosis into practice. The town, planned for the Sarir region in southwest Libya, provided a concrete example of the symbiosis of Arab and Japanese culture and of tradition and the latest technology.

Some years earlier, I had been asked to design an international conference centre in Abu Dhabi. Although the project never materialised due to local political problems, my planning work in Abu Dhabi served as a beginning for my involvement with the Middle East. One day the leader of one of the emirates invited me to look at some housing that had recently been built. He explained that to encourage the establishment of towns in the desert they had commissioned an American architect to design housing, but it wasn't working out very well.

The population of the United Arab Emirates at that time was only about 1.3 million and its per capita income was the highest in the world. The country was trying to encourage its Bedouin population to settle down in towns and villages by providing free housing. The Bedouin were a migratory people who lived by hunting and pasturing livestock. Though they built shelters of sun-dried bricks, they frequently moved from place to place and usually lived in tents. This large migrant population made it difficult for the country to achieve the modernisation its leaders desired – providing a basic education to Bedouin children, for example, was clearly a problem – and the government wished to encourage the Bedouin to settle in towns and villages.

I went with the government leader to inspect the housing built by the American architect. When we arrived at the site, a strange scene greeted my eyes. The housing was two-storey concrete American-style residences of the kind one might encounter in California. Each unit was completely air-conditioned and had an attached garage. And there they stood in a row, in the middle of the Arabian desert.

As we approached, however, I saw that the Bedouin had set up their tents next to the houses and they had put their sheep, together with livestock feed, inside the units. I proceeded to investigate the reasons for this. The first problem, it turned out, was with the air conditioning. In the desert, the temperature rises as high as forty degrees centigrade. Air conditioning has little effect in such temperatures, and of course it breaks down; but you can't call a local appliance repairman to come out and fix it that day – repairs take at least a month. All that time the concrete boxes are ovens. Not only that, but the heat that builds up in the walls throughout the day is released at night. Though it is already cool outside, the concrete is a powerful heater, roasting anyone inside the walls. Of course no-one could live in this environment. That is why the owners had set up their tents outside and put their animals inside the California-style housing instead.

When I looked at their tents, however, I was struck by how very well suited they were for life in the desert. While the surface temperature in the desert rises and falls dramatically, there is almost no temperature variance from a point three metres below ground level. When the air temperature rises to forty degrees centigrade during the day, it is only twenty degrees at three metres underground. And when the air grows cold at night, it is still twenty degrees three meters below ground. In desert climates, the air temperature drops to as low as five degrees at night; twenty degrees is very warm in comparison.

During the day, when the Bedouin sit in the shade of their

tents, a cool breeze rises from the ground. At night, they sleep on skins and rugs spread on the ground and the rising warmth from underground protects them from the cold night air. The Bedouin exploit their centuries of experience in the desert to achieve the most pleasant and comfortable life they can in their environment. To these masters of the desert, the American architect brought California-style suburban housing.

The Value of Regional Culture

When I met the American architect, I asked him why he had designed buildings that no-one could live in. He replied that he didn't expect the Bedouin to be able to live in the houses from the start, but that eventually the peoples of the developing nations, such as these Bedouin, would have to exchange their camels for cars and their tents for homes and enter modern life. Since that was the case, it was important to teach them to do so as quickly as possible, and training them to live in that kind of housing was one step towards that goal.

Here we see a typical case of the dogma of Modernism, based on the values of the West. According to this way of thinking, the functionalism and technology produced by the industrial society of Europe has raised the quality of human life and is bound, sooner or later, to spread over the entire earth. All cultures are obliged to advance under the banner of Western civilisation; their present states are merely early stages along their delayed path of development. But this way of thinking was already repudiated by Claude Lévi-Strauss, who rejected the idea of stages in cultural evolution and insisted that each culture has its own autonomous value; and that all cultures share a structure. His study of myths and family structures in cultural anthropology placed Western culture alongside others in a larger structure, as one relative member of a whole

Of course, at certain times in history, one culture may be especially strong and can influence other cultures. At one time Egypt had such power; later, China had an equal influence. Both Rome and the British Empire had their days. The power of the United States after the Second World War was enormous; and in the years to come it is possible that Japan may exercise a similar degree of cultural influence: but no one culture can dominate the planet. We must recognise that human life is much richer if each region has its own identity and culture, suited to its people, its climate, geography and history.

Different countries and peoples must recognise their differences, and then look for ways to co-operate with each other. The important question is how different cultures can sustain creative relationships in symbiosis. From that perspective, we cannot but conclude that the thinking of the American architect who built California-style housing for the Bedouin had been poisoned by Modernism.

I recognise that it is easy to criticise others; and I am not just a theoretician, but an architect and urban planner who designs environments. From the time of that encounter in the United Arab Emirates, I continued to think about how I would meet the challenge of building a community in the desert.

Symbiosis of New Technology and Desert Culture

Several years later the opportunity to put those ideas into practice came to me by chance.

The Sarir region is several hundred kilometres to the south of Libya's third largest city, Benghazi. Great quantities of underground water were discovered there. These underground channels moved as much water as a river, and a plan was devised to use them to farm the desert. There were also oil fields near Sarir, which employed many workers. The government of Libya decided on a plan for a new city in the desert, to house the workers and engineers of the oil-fields, the farmers and their families, and the Bedouin of the region.

I was asked to design the project. The first thing I did was to develop a sand brick. It was my idea to use sand – an infinite resource in the desert – as a building material. The Bedouin had been making sun-dried mud bricks from antiquity, but these were extremely perishable and not suitable for housing of any permanency.

After three years of co-operative work with a British scientific research centre, we developed a process for making strong sand bricks that would last for several decades. Our idea was that the houses we designed could be built on a 'do-it-yourself' basis by the owners, using sand bricks.

The most difficult things for amateur carpenters would be the roof, the electrical wiring, and the plumbing. In particular, an arch-shaped roof of bricks would be very hard to build. So we decided to make roofs of a thin, pre-fabricated material that could simply be set and anchored on top of the house. We developed a comparatively simple method of roof production, too: a hollow dug in the sand served as a mould, into which a mixture of concrete and glass-fibre could be poured.

As far as plumbing was concerned, we decided to build a wall of service ducts – all plumbing and wiring were placed inside this double-walled unit. This also simplified maintenance. The builders only had to place the kitchen and bathroom next to this wall; otherwise, they were free to build whatever sort of house they liked. Unlike a public housing project, each home in this community could have the design and layout its owners wanted and could be different from all its neighbours.

To find out if amateur carpenters could actually put together our design, we conducted an experiment. Some members of my staff who had never done anything but desk-work stayed at the site for three weeks, and with the help of an English assistant, tried to assemble a house. The experiment was a success. Three weeks wasn't enough time to complete the construction, but aside from the final finishing, the houses could be built entirely by amateurs.

The houses I designed had one remarkable feature, a wind tower. This was a tower like a chimney, some fifteen metres in height with open slots at the top. When the wind blew through the top of the tower, the warm air inside the house was sucked up and cool air radiating from the floor was drawn upwards to cool the interior. This design exploited the natural air movement patterns of the desert, which the Bedouins put to such excellent use in their tents.

The community in Sarir represented the encounter between the latest in technological advances from an industrial nation and the culture of the desert, the Arab culture. In it, the scientific know-how and advanced technology which allowed us to make hard bricks out of sand combined in symbiosis with the ancient wisdom of the desert.

A New Community Development

When I made the master plan for this desert community, I gave greater importance to streets than to open squares. These streets were not laid out in straight lines. I believe strongly in the superiority of streets to squares as public urban spaces. In the Japanese tradition, the street is the front. Here, the streets, gently unfolding from one house to another, are the source of the city's enjoyment. I wanted to allow that Japanese-style street as facade to exist in symbiosis with the community in Sarir. After all, the concept of the street or marketplace (in Japanese, *tsuji*) as a public space was already firmly established in Islamic cultures as the souk, or bazaar – the shopping district in Islamic cities. In old French films you often see a criminal dashing into the streets of the bazaar and disappearing in the crowd – that crowded, seemingly confused maze of streets and shops is what I am talking about. There I found a conception of public space identical to Japan's *tsuji*.

Maze-like streets in a town set in the midst of the desert have the advantage of blocking sandstorms and winds, and they also create much-needed shade. At the peak of summer's heat, you can walk comfortably through the well-ventilated, shaded streets.

In Sarir, my philosophy of symbiosis could be realised on a

wide range of levels, from the conceptual to the most practical. The scale of the project was quite large: we were talking about building an entire city from scratch in the middle of the desert. It is still not finished. But this was no castle built on sand. Eventually, slowly, this sand-coloured city will rise from the desert, and then, just as inevitably, it will return to the sands whence it came.

Symbiosis of History and the Future

Shonan Life Town in the north of the city of Fujisawa in Kanagawa Prefecture is one of the town-planning projects that I have designed – this particular project some twenty years ago. It was designed for a population of 45,000. Some 35,000 are already living there, and gradually it is acquiring the lived-in feeling of a town. Before construction began, about five-hundred farming families lived in the area, mostly cultivating paddies. The farm houses have been preserved, together with fifty per cent of each paddy area. One of the aims of the project was to allow the symbiosis of urban dwellers and the farming community, the present and the past. This meant organising the parcels of land that became available at widely separated locations according to district, and exchanging farm plots for housing lots throughout the development.

In a farming community there is always a wooded area or a sacred mountain. To preserve the natural environment and this traditional topography, we decided against levelling all the lots and building a grid of straight roads. That would have destroyed the history and the environment of the area. Carefully choosing paths of equal elevation, we built winding, meandering roads, leaving as much greenery as possible and preserving the historical appearance of the farming village. As a result, Shonan Life Town is a great success as a symbiosis of farm and town, with roads as twisting as you could find anywhere.

At one stage, the Ministry of Construction, which was the

government agency overseeing the project, objected to the meandering roads and, because it was supplying the funds for the preparation of the site, issued an order to revise our plan. But we stubbornly held to the original plan and were finally able to carry it out. Twenty years later, this project is recognised as a model for the development of new communities in the future.

Publicly we emphasised that the preservation of the farming economy was important in the design of Shonan Life Town, but in fact this presupposed the preservation of the historical community – the human relationships – of the area. Brasilia and Canberra are both regarded as poor examples of new communities; in Japan, the Tsukuba Academic City is another rather unfortunate planned community. What is wrong with these new cities?

Many complaints are voiced that they are one-dimensional, dominated by the automobile, separated from other cities and isolated. They are cold, their populations lack variety, there is no community. To sum it all up, these cities all lack symbiosis. Put another way, they have no history. In fifty or hundred years, they will accumulate their own histories. But is that any reason why they must be unpleasant to live in for a century? Is there no way to allow these new towns a symbiosis with history from the start?

There is. As in Shonan New Life Town, new communities must be built as much as possible in symbiosis with the existing historical community or town, and the entire city should not be planned in advance. One part of it must be set aside and allowed to develop in a natural way. Such development always results in a maze. New communities that possess their own mazes, that live in symbiosis with history, will be places that are attractive and enjoyable to live in.

INTERMEDIARY SPACE

Engawa as Symbiosis of Interior and Exterior Space

One could say that the difference between Western and Japanese space is that Western space is discrete and space in Japan is continuous. Western architecture is created to conquer nature and the significance of the wall, dividing exterior from interior, is very great for this reason. Japanese space, by contrast, seeks to harmonise architecture and nature, to make them one, by enveloping nature in architecture and making architecture and nature equal partners.

The wall as a divider between outside and inside did not evolve in Japan, as mentioned earlier, partly because of a difference in the basic materials of the two cultural spheres: Japan is a culture of wood, and the West is a culture of stone or brick. But in addition, in Japan there has always been a conscious effort to integrate inside and outside.

The sense of space in traditional Japanese architecture is one in which inside and outside interpenetrate. In the country house where I spent the war years for example, we always opened the sliding exterior doors from the first light of morning, no matter how cold it was. The garden would be filled with snow; or in another season, the buds of spring would be opening and the air filled with the fragrance of flowers.

In Japanese homes of the *shoin* and *sukiya* styles, there was always this kind of unobstructed interpenetration of interior and exterior; a symbiosis with the world of nature, where house and garden are one. In the West we have the picture window; the window as a frame, with nature as the painting it frames. Nature is seen as something 'out there'. An important feature of the Japanese house is the *engawa* verandah. The *engawa* runs around the house as a projecting platform under the eaves and unlike the terrace in Western architecture, serves as an exterior corridor, intermediating between inside and outside. While it protects the interior from wind, rain, and, in the summer, the strong rays of the sun, it is also a place to entertain guests and an entrance from the garden into the house. The *engawa* takes on a wide variety of functions not provided for in the conventional plan of a series of rooms linked by interior hallways.

The *engawa* is interior space, in that it is beneath the eaves; but, at the same time, it is also part of the exterior space of the garden. In our old country house, formal guests would be received in the guest room, but local merchants and neighbourhood friends would come calling to the *engawa*, to sit down and have a cup of tea and chat. Thus the way of receiving guests was distinguished spatially according to the meaning and the role of the guest.

My concepts of intermediating space or elements are linked to the idea of reintroducing a space that permits this kind of communication among people, unobstructed by any dualistic division between inside and outside, a space free from the divisions of walls. I have identified a variety of architectural details – the space beneath the eaves, or *engawa*, corridors, and lattice doors among them – as intermediating elements, and I have also studied the ambivalence and multivalence that boundaries and peripheral spaces possess.

In discussing the theories of space in Metabolism in 1960, I emphasised the importance of intermediating elements and spaces. Just as emptiness in Buddhist philosophy is a very real, if intangible entity, intermediating elements and spaces do not always necessarily take physical form. Studying the concept of the street in traditional Japanese urban space, I began to realise that an intermediary element or zone need not always be physical. And I found in the half-public, vague zone of the Japanese urban street a kind of space that was profoundly meaningful in a way which far transcended the space of the Western square.

Open Squares versus Streets

When the Japanese first travel to a Western city, what surprises them most is undoubtedly the open squares – the Piazza San Marco in Venice, the Campidoglio in Rome, any plaza in a European city is its face. We cannot conceive of a Venice without San Marco.

Public buildings such as the church and the city hall, as well as the marketplace, are grouped together around the central square. The Western city often developed with the square or plaza as its centre, from which streets projected in a radiating pattern. As the city's population expanded, other squares sprang up, and the cityscape was given a more sculptural and spatial treatment. But behind the square, away from its lively view were the backstreets – dark, dangerous, and utterly without charm. In a city structured around central authority, these backstreets were its unseen, dark face.

In the ancient Greek city of Miletus the streets were narrow pathways lined on both sides with stone-walled houses. The only openings were tiny windows, showing that the street was not considered a part of daily living space. People met and interacted on their patios and in the marketplaces, the agora. The streets were laid out, in fact, with a secondary function in mind: they served as sewage canals to flush away waste when it rained.

In contrast, Japanese streets were not merely transportation routes. They were part of the fabric of daily life and took the role of a space for communication. As many Japanese words testify – 'crossroad sermons', 'crossroad shrines', and 'crossroad fortune-telling' among them – the crossroads (*tsuji*), or street, was an exciting space that made a variety of encounters possible. In my 1965 book *Toshi Dezain*, I pointed to this fact and wrote that, in effect, the Eastern city has no plaza, while the Western city has no street. By now this thesis has come to be fairly widely accepted, but at the time a reference to my claim in the magazine *Ekistics* was picked up in scholarly journals the world over and set quite a debate raging.[1] To rephrase my statement in a more precise if less dramatic fashion, a special feature of Eastern cities is that though they lack plazas, their streets perform the functions of the plaza. Not only do the streets of Eastern cities perform the function of the square in the Western city, that of binding the life of the private citizen to the life of his city; but the Eastern street also possesses, at the same time, an ambiguous meaning arising from its double nature: it is simultaneously public and private space, city space and residential space.

In addition, the street has no definite starting or ending point; it has a multivalence that responds to a wide variety of places and times. While the Western square has a clearly assigned function and spatial definition, the street has no single assigned spatial function. Functioning now as a space for private life and at other times as a space for public life, the Eastern city street has various complex, overlapping and profoundly multivalent roles.

Streets of the Sun and Wind

In the Vedic texts of ancient India we find the statement, 'Streets are the core of the city. Those streets are the streets of the sun and the streets of the wind.'

The Vedas offer four ideal shapes for cities: *dandaka*, *nandyavarta*, *padmaka*, and swastika. All of them are basically lattice or grid patterns of intersecting streets. In size, they range from 1,200 metres on a side to 7,500 metres on a side, with two-thirds of the total area reserved for farming plots. Houses in these cities ranged from 7.3 by 4.8 metres to 12 by 9.6 metres and each had a central court for domestic animals.

The cities' streets were laid out by first using a sundial to determine two axes. The *rajapata*, or king's way, ran east and west, and perpendicular to this, running north and south, was the *mahakara*, or broad avenue; together these streets formed the backbone of the city.

There were no squares in these ideal Vedic city plans. Public facilities and temples were set along the two main thoroughfares, and a bodhi tree was planted at their intersection. The bodhi tree was believed to have given birth to the sun, moon and stars. Though the tree was a spiritually powerful cosmic symbol, it was not the city's core. That social function was performed by the bright *rajapata*, on which the sun shone from morning to night, and the *mahakara*, cooled by the breezes constantly blowing down it.

The sunny *rajapata* must have been a lively place when the long rainy season finally ended, while the *mahakara* was a cool sanctuary into which people suffering during the sweltering summer nights could carry their beds and sleep under the stars. City festivals took place on these two avenues, while religious processions were held on another road, the *magaravici*, or road of blessings, that circled the city. In ancient India, the street was a multivalent space that functioned in many ways.

The Symbiosis of Activities in Street Space

This tendency can be seen in the urban space of Japan as well, based as it is on the open structure of our wooden houses. In the ancient capital of Heian (Kyoto), for example, there were no squares. Temples, shrines, and public facilities were set along the roads. Without a central plaza or core, it was a multi-coloured checkerboard of streets divided into broad avenues and narrower lanes. Citizens of relatively high social status lived along the avenues. These were the thoroughfares along which the ox-carts of the nobility were drawn, and down which the many festivals and processions paraded. The avenues were the framework that linked the citizens to their city both ceremonially and in terms of secular authority. In contrast, the small streets, like those that can still be seen weaving in and out among the houses of the townsmen in Kyoto's Nishijin District today, formed the actual arena of city life. The avenues divided the city into large areas and districts; the streets crisscrossed those districts.

The areas on both sides of one street would be known by a single name – for example, the smiths' district, or the armourers' district – and make up one interrelated unit. On both sides of the narrow streets, less than three metres in width, houses exploited the open construction of wooden frame design and through the device of the lattice, created a shared space with the street. On hot summer nights the streets would fill with people seeking the evening cool; through the lattice doors, people could be seen chatting and laughing. Sometimes the room facing the street was used as a shop. If the avenues were places of ceremonies, festivals, and displays of authority, the streets were an extension of residences; a place for the activities of ordinary citizens.

According to Kazuhiko Yamori, author of *Toshizu no Rekishi* (*History of City Plans*), this type of Japanese urban space developed from the latter half of the ninth century through to the tenth century. Before that time, the street was like a river, separating or encircling communities – in other words, an obstacle. In Heian in the ninth century, the square residential blocks surrounded by streets were called *machi*. These were later divided into four equal parts by drawing diagonal lines connecting the corners, and each of these parts was called a *cho*. Finally, the *cho* on opposite sides of the intersecting street were united into one unit. It was Toyotomi Hideyoshi who completed this urban structure based on the street. Hideyoshi made the streets of each *cho* the communal property of the residents of the district and exempted the street space from taxation.

This inconspicuous urban structure possesses great significance. What had previously been the basic unit of urban activity, an area bounded by streets, was transformed into a unit that incorporated streets, with its own commercial identity. Hideyoshi's policy was conceived against the historical backdrop of the disbanding of the medieval guilds (*za*), the establishment of free markets and the flourishing of a new urban culture with the rise of industry and commerce. This led to the development of the Kyoto-style urban residence (*machiya*) with the street as the core of the community – which was thus in turn a further encouragement to commerce. The *machiya* facing each other across the intersecting street evolved architectural features to exploit the common central space. In addition to lattice doors and windows, attached benches and horseguards (*kurumayose*) emphasised the continuity of the street with the open-structured wooden houses facing it.

The lattices of the *machiya*, for example, allowed an appropriate amount of openness while simultaneously guarding the privacy of residents. The people in the street outside and those inside the house could sense the others' presence as they went about their activities. The street space was neither totally public nor private but an intermediary zone, performing the same function as the *engawa* between house and garden.

Thus the street has traditionally played an important, if intangible, role in Japanese society. Since the enactment of a new system of urban districts in 1962, however, Japanese cities are divided according to a system of districts and wards. In imitation of the West, areas surrounded by streets are the new units of urban space. These have been renamed for the convenience of computerised record-keeping, and the old *cho* and their names are disappearing. Wonderful old historical names such as Kajimachi (Smithies' District), Teppocho (Armourers' District), Bakurocho and Temmacho (Post-horse District) have been replaced by inoffensive, abstract, bland names such as Heiwa (Peace), Midori (Greenery), Kibo (Hope), and Hibari (Lark). I am working, as vice-president of the Zenkoku Chimei Hozon Remmei (All-Japan Place-names Preservation Society), to revise that 1962 law, for I am convinced the new system of districts will doom our communities built around the streets to destruction.

An Inviting Architecture of the Street

The function of the street in the contemporary city continues to be of vital importance, and the revival of the street as it existed in Eastern cities is more appropriate than ever in city planning today. I do not of course oppose streets that are restricted to automobile traffic. Looking at the present state of our streets in which passenger cars, lorries and bicycles are crowded dangerously together, I have come to the conclusion that alternative systems of commercial intra-city transport must be developed (for example, underground tunnels) and that the urban motorway system, both intra-city motorways and bypass loops and belts, must be improved. At the same time, however, it is important to build city streets that also function as living space.

All over Japan today there is an interest in making the city a scenic place, and the preservation movement is also making gradual headway. But even in cities like Kyoto and Nanazawa, where so many historic buildings remain and we can stroll through history, there are not enough streets along which we can enjoy a pleasant and safe walk. Increasing pedestrian walkways is one answer. To allow automobiles and pedestrians to exist in symbiosis we need not restrict ourselves to a system of streets exclusively for either cars or people; experiments that allow them to share the same streets are now under way.

In mixed residential and commercial districts, for example, road humps can be installed to slow traffic and trees planted in islands in the road, and architecturally interesting, arcade-like streets can be built. All of these are methods which can be put into practice in order to restore the originally ambivalent, multivalent nature of street space.

When all urban space is divided into public and private, as it is today, restoring to the streets their nature as an extension of communal living space is a way to make our cities more habitable and interesting. I called my design for the Nishijin Labour Centre in Kyoto (1962) 'Architecture of the Street'; that project aimed to create a new street space to make up for the streets already usurped by automobile traffic. To create a building that presents intermediary space as architectural space, on the other hand, we may employ the technique of the symbiosis of interior and exterior space. The lobby of the headquarters of the Japan Red Cross Society (1977) is an example of the interpenetration of interior and exterior space, creating an overlapping, multivalent intermediary zone. In this work, the lobby is clearly an interior space, but the ceiling is a glass arch, through which an opening to the sky is visible. The floor is water-polished red granite in the shape of a waterless pond that reflects the whole. The lobby presents a dramatic series of reversals from interior to exterior and back again.

In the design for the Main Office of the Fukuoka Bank in downtown Fukuoka City, I allowed for a large, thirty-metre *engawa*-like space beneath the eaves. There are trees, sculpture, benches: it is a place to relax. Though the land is the property of the bank, people are free to use this space at any time of day or night. They can read or meet to chat; in the summer cicadas fly in and thrum from the trees: it is a simulation of nature.

The Daito Seimei Tokyo Building was designed for the space between the Nishijin Labour Centre and the Main Office of the Fukuoka Bank. Because the lot was bounded by two streets, front and back, I planned to create a new street space that permitted people to pass through the site. This space cut through the building and was a re-creation of the traditional *machi*, on both sides of the street: it had shops, trees, flowing water, streetlight-like illumination, and street furniture. Light – as well as rain to fill the man-made river – entered through an opening that divided the building in two. This space was designed to represent an opposition and symbiosis of interior and exterior.

Hasn't our urban planning since the war, based on the logic of functionalism, too strictly separated private from public space? Taking their cue from the Western doctrine of reason, our cities have been divided into cramped individual, private spaces and broad public spaces including our roads. Now that our streets, which once had many uses, are overflowing with vehicles, they have lost their image as scenes of dense urban life to become perilous rivers that separate us. This separateness can only increase the alienation of urban dwellers. Without going so far as to entirely outlaw cars from cities, there is certainly a need to restore the importance that the intermediary space of the street once played in our lives.

One of the important tasks of the philosophy of symbiosis is to offer an architecture that incorporates intermediary space, full of charm and mystery as an alternative to the rationalism and dualism of Modernism.

Creating Relations Between Opposites

The concepts of intermediary space and ambiguity are important keys to understanding the philosophy of symbiosis. In the West, dualisms are transcended through the dialectical method of resolving opposites on a higher level. The two opposites are either unified into a single entity, or one of the two is negated and rejected. Symbiosis instead creates a dynamic relationship between the two elements while allowing them to remain in opposition. A relationship between two opposing elements can be achieved by placing spatial distance (a neutral zone) or temporal distance (a cooling-off period) between them.

In Western society, neutral zones and cooling-off periods have historically been regarded as negative and undesirable. In the contractual society of the West, all decisions are spelled out in legal agreements; ambiguity and intermediary zones are avoided. Contemporary America is a typical contractual society; perhaps mutual trust is only possible among Americans within the rules of a contract, since the nation is a conglomeration of so many different ethnic and cultural groups. It is impossible to carry on business in America without lawyers, and situations that most Japanese would regard as easily soluble with a little discussion soon evolve into legal proceedings to be argued before a court. In contrast, many projects in Japan are undertaken on the basis of verbal promises. Except in the most extreme circumstances, acquaintances or companies in a supplier-customer relationship do not carry any grievance to the courts.

Trust, in Japan, means trust without contracts. When a problem arises it is settled by making mutual adjustments. For such a procedure to work there must be room – in other words, ambiguity and intermediary space – for adjustment. The more two parties are determined to draw up a contract that provides for every future risk and contingency, the more inflexible their positions will become. Perhaps in the process their mutual peace of mind will be assured to a certain extent, but genuine understanding and the desire to deepen the relationship with the partner in the future will be much less likely.

The limits of attempting to control all human transactions by the Western contractual system are increasingly apparent, particularly in this international age, when many different nations, enterprises and individuals are living in peace although standing in opposing relationships of benefit and harm, profit and loss.

Creating a Discontinuous Continuum

Traditionally, Japanese ambiguous means of communication, such as the verbal promise and the non-verbal communication (called *haragei*), may not be completely effective as they are; but there is a crucial need to create a new system of human transactions in which some allowance for adjustments is overlaid on the present contractual system. Allowance for adjustments would derive from those keys to the philosophy of symbiosis, intermediary space and ambiguity.

In Japan, we say that we *undertake* (literally, accept and carry) an architectural project or other contractual obligation.

The term implies more than the obligations specified in the contract. Whereas non-Japanese construction companies regard their relationship with the client firm as finished when the work specified in the contract has been completed, in Japan we feel a moral responsibility to look after a building we have created throughout its life. After a typhoon, for example, the contractor will get in touch – even though the building may have been standing for decades – to enquire whether it has been damaged and to enquire about any necessary repair work. This way of thinking applies not only to the construction industry but to all human relationships, and reflects a relationship of trust.

The concept of *ma* or interval is strongly rooted in Japanese life, the arts and in traditional architecture. One who hasn't grasped the concept of *ma* and is difficult to get along with, a fool, is called 'a person lacking *ma*' (*ma no nuketa hito*, or *manuke*). *Ma* is both spatial distance (a neutral zone) and temporal distance (a cooling-off period). Those who properly space (*ma*) their words are effective speakers who create a deep impression. When two sides are in fierce opposition to each other, it is often surprisingly easy to adjust their conflicting claims by inserting a *ma* – that is, a cooling-off period of waiting.

In the writing of Chinese ideographs, the space between the lines is more important than the lines themselves. This space is not nothingness; it means or speaks as much as the lines. *Ma* is also important in folk songs and Noh chants. The *engawa* is a space, a *ma*, inserted between nature and building, exterior and interior. This type of intermediate zone functions as a *ma* permitting two opposing elements to exist in symbiosis. Intermediate space makes a discontinuous continuum possible, so that a plurality of opposing elements can coexist in an ever-changing, dynamic relationship. The nature of intermediate space is its ambiguity and multivalence. It does not force opposing elements into compromise or harmony, but provides the key to their living symbiosis.

THE PHILOSOPHY OF CONSCIOUSNESS ONLY AND SYMBIOSIS

The *Alaya* Consciousness – neither Matter nor Spirit

I named my tea room, my place for retreat and quiet thought, Yuishikian, or the Hut of Consciousness Only, in honour of the Buddhist philosophy of Consciousness Only. For me this is the key to a philosophy of symbiosis which can help us transcend the dualism of Modernism. The philosophy of Consciousness Only is one of the major supports of Mahayana Buddhism which is deeply rooted in Japan and occupies perhaps the most important place within Buddhist religion.

The appearance of the Buddha wrought a great change on the world of Indian thought and religion. Prior to the Buddha, the concept of *samsara*, or transmigration, had been one of the central concepts of the Indian tradition: it was believed that all phenomena were bound to repeat themselves infinitely over the cyclical span of cosmic time. Another important feature of pre-Buddhist thought was the concept of the absolute self, *atman*, its identity with the ultimate truth of the cosmos, or Brahman.[1] The *atman* was destined to pass through life after life, its fate decided by the good and evil deeds of the self.

The Buddha, however, denied the existence of the absolute self. He taught that no self-existing, integral, unchanging, and imperishable subject existed. Instead, a series of selves was born and extinguished from moment to moment. This was the revolutionary Buddhist teaching of non-self (*anatman*), which denied the existence of *samsara* as a substantial entity.

It was the philosophy of Consciousness Only which eventually reconciled the opposing notions of *samsara* and non-self. According to the teachings of Consciousness Only, the subject that migrated was not a self but a consciousness –

or, specifically, the *alaya* consciousness. The *alaya* consciousness was part of the human subconscious, a source of inexhaustible possibilities and potentialities.[2] The *alaya* consciousness contains the sources or seeds, known as *bija*, of all existence and every event.

As the seeds ripen and come into contact with causes and conditions, they appear as actual phenomena. At the same time, those phenomena produce instant feedback in the *alaya* consciousness. The *alaya* consciousness is the source both of all matter and spirit. In sharp contrast to the Cartesian declaration of existence being divided into matter and spirit, the philosophy of Consciousness Only insists that matter and spirit are both manifestations of a certain primal existence. I see the *alaya* consciousness, neither matter nor spirit, as akin to DNA – a life code, a life energy – and find it fascinating that the intuitions of religious philosophers of ancient India have reached across the boundaries of time to harmonise with the discoveries of modern science.

Good, Evil and the Intermediate, Neutral Zone

The earliest teaching of Consciousness Only can be traced back to Nagarjuna.[3] Before Nagarjuna, Buddhist thinkers centred around the numerous *Prajnaparamita*, or Perfection of Wisdom, *sutras*. They are now sometimes called the *Madhyamikas*, or Those of the Middle View and their philosophy was based on the concept of emptiness (*sunyata*) in which all phenomena were no more than conventional names. The material world was a phantasmal thing, a parade of names and concepts without true existence. Nagarjuna revised and systematised this school of thought, rescuing the concept of emptiness from falling into nihilism. In his *Mulamadhyamika Sastra*, he states, 'I am not a nihilist. By rejecting both being and non-being, I illuminate the path to nirvana.' Nagarjuna articulated his 'unobstructed middle way' in the famous Eight Negations of the Middle Way, and from his interpretation of the concept of emptiness originated a philosophy that transcended Western dualism.

Some time after his death, in about AD300, Nagarjuna's thought took shape as the *Sandhinirmocana Sutra*, which is also regarded as the first scripture of the Consciousness Only school. In the centuries that followed, three great Buddhist thinkers appeared who fully developed and firmly established the Consciousness Only philosophy: Maitreya, Asanga and Vasubhandu.[4] The central concept of the Consciousness Only philosophy, the *alaya*, is described in the *Sandhinirmocana Sutra* as 'the undefiled and ethically indeterminate consciousness that contains all seeds.' Unlike Christianity, with its sharp distinction between good and evil, the Consciousness Only philosophy recognises three categories: good, evil and the ethically indeterminate, an intermediate zone between good and evil.

A Creative, Indeterminate State

Many creative possibilities with potential for today are concealed in the vague state of the 'ethically indeterminate'. From now on, people will constantly be forced to choose new systems of values. We will often find ourselves in an ambiguous situation where we cannot make clear choices. At least from the present perspective, action based on a simple yes-no dichotomy is no longer an adequate response to society's demands. I believe that a trichotomy, with a third, neither-yes-nor-no element, will become necessary. The state of neither yes nor no is a mode of thinking, when a conclusion may or may not be reached; compared to either yes or no, when thinking stops and becomes action, this is an extremely creative state.

The principle of majority rule, the *modus operandi* of democracy, does not value vagueness. Because of this, it encourages the suppression of thought. It forces us to choose either yes or no, and the simple majority wins, even if the final vote is, for example, fifty-one in favour and forty-nine opposed. But if an indeterminate category was allowed, people could show that they wished to think the issue over further; and the results of their deliberations might well be the opposite of a premature yes-or-no vote. We can even conceive of cases in which the best answer to a question being voted on is, in fact, neither yes nor no. This inherent weakness in our majority rule system will become increasingly important. How we meet the risk of ignoring the category of neither yes nor no and handle it in our social policies will be a major issue from now on.

The Buddhism that has been nurtured in Japan over the centuries is mainly Mahayana Buddhism. As the core of Mahayana Buddhism, the philosophy of Consciousness Only has also made a deep impact on Japanese thought and culture. Its teachings are the key to transcending dualism.

The Symbiosis of Life and Death

I was deeply impressed by the account of Susumu Niwa, a well-known Japanese film director, of his experience of living in the African savannah and the mixture of life and death he observed there.

In a television interview the director explained that the animal realm is one of eating and being eaten. It was completely natural to see a lion, for example, kill a giraffe and eat it. The giraffe cries out when it is killed, but only for a moment. Once the lion has finished with his meal and his hunger is satisfied, quiet returns to the veldt and other giraffes nearby go on peacefully grazing.

In contrast to the intimacy of life and death in the animal world, human beings are convinced that a single human life is the most important thing on earth, a thing of the greatest value. That belief reflects a rigorously dualistic view of life and death. The human fear of death is nearly hysterical when compared to other animals. Could it be Modernism that has inflated that fear to the highest degree?

I saw in the director's remarks a parallel with the Buddhist teaching of migration in which human beings, animals, plants and even Buddhas are given life by a great spirit that transcends phenomenal life and death. The Buddhist teaching of impermanence means not only that all is vanity; it suggests that because this is so, we must live in symbiosis in the cycle of that great life. It may well be that the time is coming when we human beings must arrive at a reconciliation: a philosophy of symbiosis of life and death. The Modernism of the West has taught us that death is fearful and Hell is frightening, so we have denied death and pursued life with all our might. Death is seen as nothingness, non-being, or something even more terrifying. Perhaps it is time to take stock of our situation and look at life and death, this greatest dualism of human existence, in the face.

THE SYMBIOSIS OF MAN AND NATURE

'Temporary Shelters' Blending into Nature

Buddhism teaches the impermanence of all things. People, animals, plants, the rest of nature and the Buddhas themselves are always changing, ever migrating within one great chain of life. As human beings existing within that ever-changing process of migration, we must awaken to the ephemeral nature of life. In that context our ideal should be not to conquer nature, nor to hunt our fellow animals, but to live as a part of nature, in accordance with its rules.

From ancient times the Japanese have built their homes as if they were temporary shelters, and they have adopted a lifestyle of symbiosis with nature based on the teaching of impermanence. Yoshida Kenko, the author of *Essays in Idleness* (*Tsurezuregusa*), says:[1]

A house, I know, is but a temporary abode, but how delightful it is to find one that has harmonious proportions and a pleasant atmosphere. One feels somehow that even moonlight, when it shines into the quiet domicile of a person of taste, is more affecting than elsewhere. A house, though it may not be in the current fashion or elaborately decorated, will appeal to us by its unassuming beauty; a grove of trees with an indefinably ancient look; a garden where plants, growing of their own accord, have a special charm; a verandah and an open-work wooden fence of interesting construction; and a few personal effects left carelessly lying about, giving the place an air of having been lived in. A house which multitudes of workmen have polished with every care, where strange and rare Chinese and Japanese furnishings are displayed, and even the grass and trees of the garden have been trained unnaturally, is ugly to look at and most depressing. How could anyone live for long in such a place? The most casual glance will suggest how likely such a house is to turn in a moment to smoke.

Since the home is no more than a temporary shelter, one should not take too many pains in decorating it; even when it has grown old and worn, it is better to leave it as it is and harmonise with it. In the *Nampo Roku*, Sen no Rikyu is quoted as advocating a simple, natural life: 'Lodgings that keep the rain out and enough food to keep us from starving – this is sufficiency.'

Japanese culture is a culture of wood. We have always regularly replaced wooden structural elements in our homes and buildings as they age or decay. In addition, many Japanese buildings have been destroyed by nature's violence, in typhoons, earthquakes, and floods, and we have been forced to rebuild after each natural or man-made disaster. Perhaps the perception of all buildings as no more than temporary lodgings is due to these circumstances as well.

Before modern times, water in Japan was not controlled as at present, by reinforcing all the banks and dykes in each drainage system with stones and concrete. In fact, the approach was just the opposite. A weak place was always built into a dyke or bank where an overflow or flood would do the least damage. This is a natural principle akin to that of the collarbone which acts as a defence of the neck and back bones, by breaking in their place.

We recently dismantled the house that my grandfather and father had lived in for many years, in the countryside of Aichi Prefecture. It was a rush-thatched house thought to date from the mid-Edo period. It had survived the Nobi earthquake in 1891, but had suffered damage on several occasions, and each time it was repaired it was added to and partly refurbished. Even so, our investigation showed that some of the timbers were from the Edo period and had been planed with the characteristic Edo-period tool, the *chona*, instead of an ordinary plane. The reed roof thatching, too, had been changed on alternating sides, once every two to four years.

All of this shows how much work is involved in the upkeep of a wooden house. But the visual appeal of such natural materials as wood, tatami mats and Japanese paper, and even their pleasant smells, are valued by the Japanese who are accustomed to living in an environment intimately linked to nature. Japanese houses exhibit a stronger tendency to merge with nature than to stand in opposition to it. Perhaps we can accept the eventual degeneration and collapse of buildings and dykes more easily because we see this as a part of the rhythm of nature.

Insect Sounds – Midway Between Noise and Music

Another important feature of the Japanese house is its openness. The characteristic post-and-beam construction produces a building with no need for walls. If the sliding paper doors and outer rain doors are opened, the house has a complete openness, with the *engawa* providing an intermediate space between interior and garden. Japanese architecture even incorporates surrounding scenery and nearby mountains into its gardens, through the technique known as 'borrowed landscapes', or *shakkei*. Living hedges, for example, are often used to encircle a home. Unlike a solid wall, a hedge or *ikegaki* doesn't completely block out the outside. While it protects the residents' privacy, it is also continuous with the surrounding natural environment, offering a Japanese type of semi-seclusion.

The word *ne* (roughly translated as sound, but slightly different in meaning, as we shall see below) is another key to explaining the continuity that the Japanese feel with nature. *Ne*, however, describes aural rather than visual continuity.

The word for music in Japanese, *ongaku*, means to enjoy sound (*on* is another way to pronounce *ne*, and *gaku* means to enjoy). *Neiro*, or sound colour, means the nature or quality of sound. When things don't work out well and we are reduced to desperate straits, we 'raise a cry' (*ne o ageru*).

In Japanese homes and restaurants, we have maintained

the custom of keeping insects in cages so that guests can listen to their sounds and be reminded of the season. To the Japanese, insect sounds are not mere noise; they are the *ne* of the insects, a natural music. The single word *ne* comprises the music created by human beings and the music of nature, insect sounds, an intermediate zone between simple sound and music – further evidence that the Japanese prefer to live in friendship with nature, linked intimately to it.

The West, Conqueror and Domesticator of Nature

In contrast to Japanese architecture in which there exists a merging with nature, European architecture stands in opposition to it and emphasises its own independence and separateness.

European cities separated themselves from nature by building fortified walls. The stone walls of houses separate the inside from the outside, with their solidity often emphasised by small windows and doors. At the heart of this thorough-going division of space into interior and exterior is the European philosophy of the opposition between humanity and nature. In the European view, human beings conquer, tame and utilise nature. Renaissance and Baroque gardens, for example, are extremely artificial and geometric, mostly comprised of lawns like huge green carpets. We can perceive them as highly idealised versions of nature; to walk through them is an expression of man's victory over nature, his domestication of nature.

What a contrast this presents to the traditional Japanese garden, which attempts to create a *simulacre* of nature as an abstraction. The main pleasure to be had comes not from walking around in the garden but from entering an imaginary world while quietly gazing at it. Of course, many famous Japanese gardens also allow one to stroll through them but the path is usually limited to a sharply circumscribed area; even those built specifically for strolling through, are designed with various stops along the walk for viewing the garden.

From Selling Forests to Sharing Forests

In their relationship with their forests, Japanese and Europeans also show striking differences. Many European forests are crisscrossed by public paths and have man-made clearings and facilities for rambles, in other words, they are a tamed version of nature. They are largely a mixture of broadleaf deciduous and evergreen trees, undergrowth is not a barrier to access and they are quite bright. Woodlands may even be incorporated into city life as a man-made green space. Many European children's tales, such as the stories of William Tell and Robin Hood, reflect life in the forest as a friendly place.

In Japan, on the other hand, forests consist mostly of evergreen conifers. The ground is very damp; thickly covered with brush and there are many snakes, centipedes, and other insects. Most Japanese forests are in the mountains and therefore inaccessible. As a result, from ancient times there has been a strong tendency in Japan to worship the mountains themselves, in an animist sense. They were regarded as sacred places, the dwelling place of the spirits; or a gravesite, the dens of great serpents. The only human being who would live there was a hermit or a defeated warrior in hiding. Forests were not a part of life's daily activities; but for looking at from afar: this was nature as a spiritual support. This Japanese relationship with nature has remained fundamentally unchanged to the present day. The mountains ringing Japanese cities are not incorporated into urban living space; they exist in symbiosis with the city as 'borrowed landscape'. Japanese do not enter the forest of their own volition as Europeans do. In fact, this is a major problem where the preservation of nature in Japan is concerned. Since the Japanese have no direct relationship with nature in their daily lives, they have no awareness of the need to protect the natural environment. The traditional Japanese attitude of symbiosis with nature stands in direct contradiction to our current relationship with our natural environment; the truth is that the natural environment in Japan is very much under threat.

In the international market, Japanese timber forests are no longer successful commercial ventures. This has resulted in a severe shortage of forestry products in Japan, and pushed Japanese forests to the brink of financial disaster. At the same time, many cities are undergoing the same sudden expansion that Tokyo has experienced. Large residential suburbs are growing up around these cities, created by a wide-scale conversion of farm and forest land into housing developments.

We no longer see such phenomena in Europe, because Europeans are accustomed to the appropriate use of the natural environment. Since Europeans know nature more directly, they feel more strongly about defending it. In the future, the Japanese will have to move beyond their abstract spiritual feeling for wilderness and link their forests with urban space, so that they can be properly utilised. To do that, the Japanese will have to change their thinking about re-forestation and the timber industry. Up to now, woods that grow quickly and sell at a high price – ie, evergreens such as cedar, cypress and pine – have been given the highest priority in Japan's forestry industry. Now we must designate zones for planting deciduous trees and create sunnier forests that can also serve as leisure areas. We must restore the symbiosis of humanity and nature in daily life by changing our strategy from one of forests for sale to forests for sharing on a national scale.

The parks of Frankfurt and Düsseldorf are filled with birds, squirrels and all kinds of insects. The symbiosis of the people of these cities with nature – all within a stone's throw of underground stations and motorways – is an impressive sight. Places such as these must be built in Japan.

The Urban Pastorale, a Garden City of Helicopter Commuters

The symbiosis of man and nature involves not only trees, birds, small animals and insects: the things manufactured by human beings also become, as time passes, part of nature. We must recognise not only man-made lakes, canals and forests, but even our cities and our technology as a part of nature. The binomial dualism that insists what God made is nature, and what human beings have made is artificial and therefore opposed to nature, no longer holds.

In the last generation, the majority of Japanese city dwellers were people who had been born in the country and migrated to the city. Their memories of the countryside were still strong and dear to them; it was only natural that they viewed the city as something in opposition to nature. But today some eighty per cent of all Japanese are born in cities. Just as naturally, today most children born and raised in the city, have neither memories nor experience of nature. Ask some children where dragonflies and beetles and other insects come from and they're likely to answer 'the pet shop in the department store'. It is hardly surprising that we have raised a generation which experiences the city as a part of nature and concrete as a kind of earth. The time may come when the city and its technology are indeed a part of nature.

I have a feeling that the twenty-first century will see a dynamic symbiosis of the city and nature such as that hinted at by Sontag in her 'urban pastorale' or by Frank Lloyd Wright's futuristic vision of a 'garden city' crisscrossed by commuters' helicopters. In both we see a move away from city or nature, to city and nature in coexistence. Edo, for example, was in fact a completely artificial city. Noboru Kawazoe, in his book *Tokyo no Genfukei* (*Original Tokyo*),[2] relates that though Edo was a city without public greenery, it was dotted with plant markets; its citizens cultivated their own bonsai trees; and the streets and alleys were filled with the blooms of morning glories and flowering gourds. The citizens of Edo were able to nurture a rich imaginative conception of nature through their artificially grown bonsai and potted plants.

The city of the future where people will live in symbiosis with technology, animals, birds and insects, together with potted plants, bonsai and man-made forests, is not far away.

The Communal Space for the Creation of Nature

Environmental protection must go beyond the preservation of Japan's existing forests to include the creation of new forests in great cities like Tokyo. As in the environmental protection and cultural preservation movements of Europe and the United States, action should begin with the contributions of individuals dedicated to protecting our natural and cultural environments. Whether it be to preserve certain cityscapes, cultural treasures or historic buildings, any such movement must start with committed people's contributions, however small, and from there develop into a national cause.

In Japan, however, such action tends to start from the top down, with a group of 'experts' calling for the preservation of nature or cultural monuments and making a loud protest against 'development'. But those same experts either make no effort to raise the funds needed for preservation or they demand the protection of the farm and forest land surrounding the cities. But farms are places for growing rice and vegetables; and forests are the sources of timber and wood products. At a time when these very industries are in trouble and losing money, it is irresponsible to insist that farms and forests be preserved without some form of economic assistance to make them commercially viable for their owners.

We cannot simply rely on the natural environment left to us by our ancestors. In exchange for developing valuable existing sites, we must also work to create new, man-made nature to leave to our descendants. In Tokyo, the huge tract of forest land attached to Meiji Shrine is a good example. This apparently primeval forest was created only seventy-five years ago. Here we have a vision of the forest not as a holy site or a dwelling place of the spirits, but as nature and as a part of the living space of the city.

In the plan for the development of Tokyo that I will describe in detail in Chapter XIII, I have proposed the creation of three forests, each of ten thousand hectares. These are reminiscent of the Musashino forest, which once existed in the Kanto region. They would be mixed woodlands of deciduous trees that would combine in function and feeling two traditional types of wood in Japan: the sacred grove, which surrounded the Shinto shrine of each village in old Japan, and the village wood, planted around the homes in farm communities to protect them from the ravages of typhoons.

This way of thinking is also relevant to the symbiosis of private and communal space in the urban environment. The city today is divided between private property, owned by individuals or commercial enterprises, and public property such as roads and parks, built and maintained with public funds. But there was originally in Japan also an intermediate zone between public and private – communal space. In agricultural communities, water rights and common rights were a sort of communal property shared equally by all villagers. And as we have seen, in Kyoto the street was a kind of communal property, administered by the *chogumi*, or district organisation. In an Edo urban district, houses were packed together with narrow frontages on the streets of a four-sided block. This district layout left an open space behind the houses, in the centre, which was called the *kaisho*, or meeting place, and this, too, was a type of communal property.

The city of Nagoya was given a unique layout during the Edo period. Each district was, like the city of Edo, divided into long narrow lots facing the main streets. In the narrow, empty space behind the houses a temple or a graveyard was built, with a single narrow path leading from it out to the street. This path was called the *kansho*, or idle place, and was also a communal space.

Nowadays, when we take one step off our own property, we are on land administered by the city or prefecture: so we have no incentive to maintain it. If it is dirty we might call the local authority and complain; but we're not likely to clean it up ourselves. In the days of communal space, however, everyone co-operated to keep the shared area tidy, and it was also a place where children could play without parents worrying about their safety. This communal space was an intermediate zone between private and public property.

The activities of the National Trust of Great Britain in preserving the environment and purchasing cultural treasures can also be interpreted as defending communal property. In Japan, too, recent interest has been shown in a Japanese version of The National Trust, and a grassroots movement to preserve the primeval forest at Shiretoko in Hokkaido is also encouraging.

In the renovation and redevelopment of our cities in the twenty-first century, we will have to revive communal property; intermediate between private and public, in many different forms. This will be linked to the creation of natural environments within the city which might be little pockets of nature, or even spaces under the eaves of a building. Or, as I created in the Head Offices of the Fukuoka Bank, they might be private property that is open to the public: we must employ a variety of means to assure this.

In Japan, in the past, borrowing landscapes was a way of achieving symbiosis with nature. The Shugakuin Detached Palace is a famous example of this technique of incorporating surrounding nature and natural views into one's own life. This was effective when the population density was low and a rich natural landscape had survived near urban areas. But today, we cannot all borrow nature. In resort areas, many people enjoy nature's beauty but forget what an ugly sight their own vacation home is. The true technique of borrowing landscapes keeps in mind the fact that we are part of the landscape and that someone is looking at us. We must be as concerned with the landscape we lend as the one we borrow.

THE PHILOSOPHY OF THE KARAKURI

A Tea Room in the Space Shuttle

In the Western world, technology and humanity have come to be thought of as in opposition to each other. We find the view of human beings as alienated and estranged from nature by technology in Jean Jacques Rousseau's criticism of civilisation and his call for a 'return to nature'. But no one who objectively considers the contribution of technological progress to our daily lives would reject modern scientific technology.

Ours is not a binomial, dualistic choice between technology and humanity. The challenge that faces us today is how to develop a philosophy that humanises technology. In Tokyo, as I mentioned previously, my study with its IBM computer opens into my tea room, Yuishikian. Here I have created a space in which the latest technology exists in symbiosis with the traditional, natural art of the tea room without the least dissonance. 'A Tea Room in the Space Shuttle' is the slogan I have invented to express the symbiosis of humanity and technology. The space shuttle flying through the heavens does not by itself represent mature technology. Only when a space shuttle is launched that includes a human space such as is represented by the tea room will this technology contribute a new enjoyment and pleasure to human life.

For the Japanese, technology is seen as an extension of humanity. The concept of the symbiosis of mankind and technology goes back to Edo, in the form of a fascination with automata, or *karakuri*. Hosokawa Yorinao's *Illustrated Miscellany of Automata (Karakuri zui)* was published in 1798, followed in 1815 by Tagaya Kanchuzen's *Instructional Illustrated Catalogue of Automata (Karakuri kummo kagamigusa)*. In the same period, Takeda Ominoshojo's automated-puppet plays became popular in Osaka, and the master carpenter Hasegawa Kambei invented various mechanical stage devices for the Kabuki theatre and introduced a new level of spectacle and excitement to the popular stage.

Hosokawa's *Automata* includes a diagram of a prototype of today's robot: the tea-carrying doll (*chahakobi ningyo*). This works in the following way. When the host, seated opposite his guest, places a cup of tea in the doll's hands, it carries the cup of tea to the guest. The guest takes the cup from the doll, and it stops. After drinking the tea, the guest sets the cup back in the doll's hands. It turns around and returns to the host with the empty cup. The mechanism of the tea-carrying doll consists of a spring made from baleen and a complicated system of interlocking gears. The doll is modelled on the form of an adorable child, rather than a machine-like robot. In the Edo period, the technology of a device was not displayed on its exterior but incorporated invisibly inside it, giving people a sense of wonder and mystery. Machines did not express their own independent identities but mirrored human beings.

Examples of *karakuri* architecture include the suspended central pillar of several pagodas and the helix structures of 'snail-shell' towers, or *sazaedo*. The five-storeyed pagodas at the Yanaka Kannoji, built in 1627, and Nikko, built in 1818, both have suspended central pillars that hang from above without actually touching the ground, supporting nothing. The purpose of these central pillars is to lower the centre of gravity of the entire structure, thus stabilising it. Such 'Snail-shell' towers can be found in the Sansodo at Rakanji, built in 1779, and the Sazaedo at Seishuji in Aizu Wakamatsu, built in 1796. The outer walls of these halls rise and fall in a helix structure, suggesting the Buddhist idea of migration through one birth after another, making a continuous journey up and down the tower possible.

Technology in Japan has thus been made infinitely attractive through humanisation, in contrast to the unadorned, exposed mechanisms of the West.

Biomation: What are the Limits of Medical Technology?

Dr Kazuhiko Atsumi, who attracted attention worldwide by transplanting a mechanical heart into a goat and keeping the animal alive for 344 days, has coined the word 'biomation' to mean the application of technology to biology. Dr Atsumi has this to say about biomation in the twenty-first century:

> The development of technology has led to the replacement of human labour by that of the machine, in other words, automation. The labour accomplished by machines has gradually evolved from physical labour – as in the steam engine, the automobile, the conveyor belt, the telegraph, telephone, typewriter and copy machine – to mental labour, accomplished by computers and the other apparatus of 'artificial intelligence'. The end result has been the widespread dissemination of information technology, which has in turn contributed to the evolution of an information society. At the same time, however, this information society has resulted in problems such as standardisation, homogenisation and alienation. To solve these problems, we must learn a lesson from the subtle behaviour of living organisms and from software. In other words, the mating of the automation of man-made technology and the *bio* of living things will give birth to the technology of a new human society. I call this hybrid product *biomation*. The age of biomation will be an age of humanity, of freedom, of multiplicity, of individuality, of art, of leisure and of health and medicine.[1]

Since Johann von Neumann's work on automata, thinking machines have greatly increased in speed until they have approached the processes of human thought. In the post-machine age, human beings and machines will grow even closer, and in certain areas, the borders between the two will be crossed, creating a symbiosis between man and machine.

For example, even today some people live with a pacemaker implanted in their heart. Artificial limbs have advanced so greatly that they approach human limbs in complexity.

Implants of machines to supplement or replace human biological functions are bound to increase.

The reverse possibility also exists: that human beings could make up one part of a machine. A recent film, for example, portrayed a plasma production plant in which thousands of bodies of human beings in permanent comas were used to produce blood that was then trucked away for use by living human beings. This could be described as a blood factory that incorporated human beings as one part of its production machinery.

Of course most of us feel a strong revulsion at the idea of using coma patients to produce blood. But this will be technologically feasible in the near future. If it should happen, or even before it happens, a tremendous debate could arise: should we permit this? And if we do, are we to think of these coma patients as human beings or as machines?

With the progress of medicine and bio-technology, new and complicated issues of bio-ethics will present themselves. Dr Atsumi has said: 'new medical technology such as heart transplants, in vitro fertilisation, genetic medicine and the synthesis of living tissue is bound to change society's ways of thinking in fundamental ways, and agreement on the values of a new ethics will be required.' One approach to this problem is to distinguish between parts of the body that may be replaced and those that may not. Human hair, for example, is used in thermometers. Hair is undeniably a part of the human body, but since it grows back its use is regarded as acceptable. Blood too is replaceable and there will be no influence on a person's individuality or character even if all of his blood is replaced in transfusion. To a certain extent, skin and organs are also renewable, and in fact they are already being transplanted from one person to another.

If we pursue this line of reasoning, we finally come to the brain, which controls the mental and spiritual activity that is at the core of human personality. As long as the brain is healthy, an individual is himself; all other parts of the body are expendable. The brain does not function in terminal coma patients; on the other hand, they have no will, no thoughts, no feelings. We can regard their state as the extreme in which only the portions of the body that are replaceable continue to live. Of course we should respect the dignity of death, but if there is no chance that brain functions can be restored and the person has previously expressed his agreement, it might well be acceptable to allow that person's body to produce blood for others. It becomes, in the end, a matter of choice for each individual.

The Boundaries Between Life and Death, Man and Machine

I once visited a German hospital where about twenty children suffering from hydrocephalus were being cared for. Hydrocephalus can enlarge the skull to nearly a meter in circumference. These children were all suspended from the ceiling, head down. They could not survive in any other position; if they tried to stand, the weight of their heads would break their necks, and lying down their head might be shaken by some vibration, again causing death. But the patients can survive for some time if they are hung upside down. The hospital was making every effort to keep them alive, in the hope that a miraculous treatment would soon be discovered that could cure them. The children smiled at me on my visit. Though their skulls were enormously enlarged, their features were normal in size and seemed to be pulled together in the middle of their faces. But in spite of their smiles I asked myself if these children who, even hanging upside down, would only survive a few years, could be called full human beings, and whether they were happy. Yet clearly the humanist position is to recognise that every person, no matter how weak, has a right to live and must have our assistance. The opposite belief, that the weak and malformed should be killed, is nothing other than Hitler's elitism, the Nazi philosophy of the Master Race.

In practice, most people find themselves somewhere

between these two extremes. For example, millions die of starvation in Africa every year. If every Japanese were to donate ten per cent of his annual income to relieving starvation in Africa, all of those victims could be saved. But no one goes that far. Saving the lives of others is a fine thing, as long as it doesn't inconvenience you. AIDS provides another example. Some people insist on AIDS patients' human rights and say we mustn't discriminate against them, while others say they should be quarantined and not allowed to come into contact with the healthy. By defending the rights of the AIDS patient we incur the risk that his fatal disease will be spread to others, as the price of the belief that human life has no meaning unless it is guaranteed to all. As a result, we must reconcile ourselves to the fact that AIDS will spread to a certain extent. Compassion is an extremely expensive proposition, and in a sense it is very inefficient. Nevertheless, we cannot adopt the Nazi philosophy that the weak and 'inferior' should die. Whatever the cost, humanity as a whole must create a structure in which the weak can live with the strong, the sick with the healthy. If the consensus of humanity is that the human race as a whole should be 'improved' and its survival take priority over individual lives, then elitism is of course one way to achieve that goal; but no doubt we will choose instead the way of living in symbiosis with the weak and ill, even if it is inefficient and curtails the survival of the human race.

The advances of science and technology have blurred the previously clear-cut boundaries between life and death, man and machine, and humanity awaits a new ethical agenda. The issue of a symbiosis of mankind and technology, including the complex problems discussed here, becomes ever more pressing as we approach the twenty-first century.

An End to Hierarchy and Anthropocentrism
Another issue the next century must face is the development of a new way of thinking about life and death, and a

corresponding way of living. Society governed by Modernism – that is, industrial society – has placed a higher value on life than ever before in human history. This excessive evaluation of human life is greatly mistaken on two counts.

First, it assigns special value to human life at the expense of all other life. Just as God was once absolute existence, now humankind is, on earth, the absolute form of existence. This anthropocentric hierarchy places human life at the centre and all other life on the periphery. As such, it is natural that this attitude should come under attack from the science of ecology.

But we cannot return the earth to the time when life first appeared on the planet. In the ecology of nature, natural selection operates, and the weak are eaten by the strong. The population explosion of one species drives another to extinction. If our criticism of anthropocentrism is nothing more than an excessive faith in ecology, we fall into the trap of a typical binomial opposition or dualism.

Humankind cannot live without eating other living things. My teacher Shiio Benkyo, in his Buddhist teachings of symbiosis, has described the human condition, the fact that we must eat other organisms to live, as a relationship of mutual living things and life. The Buddha, human beings, animals, plants and the stone by the side of the road all exist symbiotically in an enormous life cycle, living and giving each other life in symbiosis. Human beings consume other life forms as vegetables and meat, fish and rice; and when humans die they return to earth and in turn become food for plants and animals.

The minerals and inorganic materials of the stone by the roadside are necessary to preserve human life. We should neither regard human life as more important than any other form, nor suggest a return to an ecology of a 'pre-human' age. Life and death should only be viewed from the standpoint of a recognition of other life forms. A lifestyle based on an awareness that we are kept alive by other forms of life is the philosophy of symbiosis, not simply to regard other life forms as sources of food and raw materials.

Human Existence in the Intermediate Zone

The second error is to regard man as a single organism separate from all other organisms. Careful thought shows that human beings are not made up of two opposing elements, matter and spirit. Our bodies are populated by a variety of organisms, including different viruses and bacteria and all sorts of inorganic substances, some of which are necessary for life. Most of us also harbour disease organisms and disease-causing viruses. A human being is actually a symbiotic complex made up of a plurality of living things in dynamic relationship with each other.

In contrast, the modernist view of humanity is that we are an unadulterated organism composed of matter and spirit. This abstract model of a human being has come to be accepted, along with a concept of health as progress, or the unending approach to a purer human state. The invasion of any other form of life is called disease and that form is repelled as an enemy or an attacker by classic Western medicine. To kill this invader, a typical Western treatment is surgery – the cutting away of the disease producer and even the 'invaded' tissue with it.

Recently, other methods of treatment are gaining attention, including holistic medicine, which seeks to encourage the body's natural defences and to enlist mental and spiritual energies to assist the body. The techniques of traditional Chinese medicine are also being studied, but the belief that a healthy organism is one from which all foreign bodies and other life forms have been eliminated is a strong one.

An excessive affirmation of life may reflect an absolute terror of death. In the present age there is greater fear of sickness and death than of war. As Susan Sontag has said, sickness, especially such incurable sicknesses as cancer and AIDS, has become an unnecessarily prevalent metaphor for death, for fear, and has thrown society into anxiety.

In their fear of death, people try to avoid the thought of it. To enjoy life, they banish death from their awareness, denying its reality. But from birth we are half-healthy, half-sick. There is no absolutely perfect human, who from birth is completely pure, without any other form of life, who never experiences physical breakdowns. All human beings have some physical imperfection, large or small, and live in symbiosis with other organisms.

Sickness is none other than the collapse of that symbiotic balance, a change leading to death. All humans live in the intermediate zone between total life and total death. The future science of medicine will no doubt learn to preserve that intermediate state of symbiotic balance with disease organisms. The philosophy of symbiosis offers us the prospect of enjoying a coexistence of life and death.

FROM POST-MODERNISM TO SYMBIOSIS

Single-coded Modernism

As I have shown in Chapter III and elsewhere, the use of Modernism in our daily lives has reached its end. Modernism is based on the pursuit of desires fostered by a material civilisation, and the technology that has made such advances to fulfil those desires has begun to turn against humanity. Environmental pollution, for example, shows us the un-friendly face of technology and we see that even should the human race find a way to survive the practical results of the Modernist creed, it would not be a very desirable survival.

This has led to a reconsideration of the modern period, industrial society, material civilisation and Modernism as a whole, and a search for a new philosophy to replace it in harmony with the present Post-Modern issues. The search for a new culture, art, society and a new state of knowledge has become more and more active. The French philosopher Jean-François Lyotard, in *The Post-Modern Condition: A Report on Knowledge (La condition postmoderne)*, 1979, explains the term Post-Modernism:

> We call the present state of knowledge of our highly advanced society 'Post-Modern'. This term is widely used by American sociologists and critics at present . . . for the state of a culture that has undergone a transformation brought about by the sweeping revision of the rules of the game, beginning in the late nineteenth century, in the fields of science, literature and art.[1]

For the world of architecture, Charles Jencks suggested six defining principles of Post-Modernism in *The Language of Post-Modern Architecture* (1977). The first is an architecture that speaks to people on at least two levels simultaneously. A sign on the motorway, for example, 'Exit 5km', has only one reading; it would no longer function if it could be read in different ways. Unless legal codes and government documents have only one clear reading, they cannot serve their respective purposes. They are designed to have, as far as possible, only one reading, clear to all.

Documents of that sort, not surprisingly, do not make for interesting reading. This is the nature of what is called a single code. Novels, however, can be read in many different ways, though they are written with words from the same language as single-code documents. The reader uses his imagination to find meanings beyond the literal, enriching the story with his own experience – that is one of the pleasures of fiction. The more room there is for the reader to participate imaginatively, the richer is the literary quality of the work. In semantics, language that can be read in two or more ways is called a double code. Or, to borrow Charles Jencks' term, we could call such forms of expression 'multivalent'.

To give another example, an artist who paints with great realism but whose work does not move its viewers is called an uninspired sign painter. However, even among realists and super realists, there are those, such as Andrew Wyeth, who are respected as artists – and those who are not. This is the difference between one who can, and another who cannot, successfully incorporate a capacity for a multivalent reading of his work.

Inarticulate Architecture Transcended

Modern society was above all a single-code society, and Modern architecture was an unreadable architecture, an architecture of steel, glass and concrete that valued convenience and functionality only, from which no narrative could be read. The most representative work of this school is the Lake Shore Drive apartments by Ludwig Mies van der Rohe, completed in 1951. Widely regarded as a masterpiece of Modern architecture, these high-rise luxury apartment towers are extremely abstract in design, a silent architecture that has abjured all historical symbols and narrative quality. The only way in which it can be read is as an icon of Modern architecture.

When the Modern Movement was founded by Le Corbusier, Mies van der Rohe and their contemporaries, it was important as a rebellion against the status quo. The French *Académie des Beaux-Arts*, for example, concentrated entirely on the teaching of historical styles and completely dominated the world of architecture. No architect who dared to stray from its historicism, much less challenge it, could hope to find employment. The founders of the movement declared their secession from the *Académie* and their opposition to it, as to all historical styles and decoration.

But the avant-garde role of Modern architecture has now come to an end. The *Académie* long ago lost its authority to the orthodoxy of Modern architecture. At Sydney University in the summer of 1984, I was warned that Post-Modernism was a taboo subject in the department of Architecture – the faculty regarded it as a blight. That is when I realised how Modern architecture had begun to exercise the same unbending, rigid authority as that of the old *Académie*.

I do not totally reject the Modern by any means. My own work always makes use of what I regard as the positive aspects of Modern architecture. But when I see how rigid it has become, how it has lost all flexibility, I am forced to ally myself with those who attack the weaknesses of the Modernist doctrine both of architecture and society.

Modern architecture appeared at a time when abstract art was believed to be more advanced and avant-garde than representative art. Modern architecture was appreciated for its abstraction just as were the painting and sculpture of the age. There is something to be said for the superiority of abstract art over concrete representation. After all, while other animals can only respond to direct, concrete stimuli, humanity can respond to abstractions through intellectual processes. But the abstraction of Modernism is a by-product obtained as a result of industrialisation; it is only accidental. That is why it has ended up as a single-coded – or a completely silent – architecture, lacking, as Louis Althusser put it, an epistemology.

When we walk through the streets of an Italian Renaissance city – Florence, for example – the experience of just strolling along is highly enjoyable. Each building speaks to us, each sculpture engages us in conversation. We can read the streets, just as we read a novel. The city as a whole is a work of literature, and we can browse through it as we walk.

Unfortunately, cities built since the advent of Modernism are quite the opposite: they disturb and exhaust us. No tourists flock to Brasilia or Canberra, and young couples don't stroll hand in hand through the bleak banking and business area around the Kasumigaseki Building in central Tokyo. It is in this sense that Jencks has offered his first definition of the Post-Modern as architecture that speaks to us on at least two levels.

His second definition of Post-Modernism is hybrid architecture, mixing and hybridising opposing elements such as historical styles with contemporary life, and high art with popular culture. One example of this process is the use of elements of the popular cultures of Las Vegas or Hollywood which have fascinated the masses to enliven contemporary architecture. To discover the essence of charm and interest even in such paradigms of 'bad taste' is one of the strategies of Post-Modern architecture.

Modern architecture scorned Las Vegas as vulgar and, like modern literature and abstract art, made no attempt to hide its elite consciousness. Post-Modern architecture, however, has set itself the task of destroying the boundary separating high art from popular art.

Jencks also sees Post-Modern architecture as being intentionally schizophrenic. The term schizophrenia, of course, describes the mental illness in which a person is possessed of two conflicting mental states at the same time, but

Post-Modernism uses it to refer to a healthy person who intentionally behaves that way. Here we see an impulse similar to that of the second definition, the hybrid nature of Post-Modern architecture.

The fourth definition of the Post-Modern is an architecture with a language. In other words, to be read in a multivalent fashion, it must have an architectural language, while the fifth definition proposes that it is also an architecture 'rich in metaphor, new and embracing rather than exclusive'.

Finally, Post-Modern architecture is 'an architecture that responds to the multiplicity of the city'. It must be created based on a reading of the plurality of the city's values and its complex context.

The Value-added Nature of the Information Society

I would like to continue by taking these definitions and re-working them into my own argument, point by point, in the context of contemporary culture.

1) The economies of the developed countries have already moved from heavy industry to research and development, education, publishing and broadcasting – the industries of an information society – together with the service industries and the banking and financial sector. This is a major transformation of society from an industrial to a non-industrial base.

In industrial society, the production of things is paramount; quantity is preferable to quality, and the important thing is to produce goods of standard quality in great quantity at the lowest price possible. But in an information society, the added value attached to goods plays a major role. We see a shift from the goal to produce inexpensive goods, to producing goods that are also well designed. Even the old 'star' products – automobiles and electrical appliances – must take note of the value-added factor of design, which now accounts for a fair proportion of the cost of the finished product.

Japan was once an important silk-producing centre, specialising in the spinning of silk thread and exporting large quantities of raw silk. Yet it is inconceivable that Japan should be a silk exporter now. Japanese wages have risen to the highest in the world and it is impossible to make a profit by producing raw materials. Now Korea, China and Taiwan are the raw-silk producers, while Japan designs silk fabrics and sells them to foreign markets. The products of designers such as Issey Miyake and Rei Kawakubo, with the value of their designs added, are sent out into the world. This is how roles have evolved in the international division of labour.

The cost of the raw materials of a garment designed by Issey Miyake makes up less than ten per cent of its retail price. With Miyake's value-added design, however, it becomes a high-priced product. The fields of education, publishing and broadcasting are based, too, not on hard costs but on 'soft' costs. The hotel industry is another example: four-star and five-star ratings are determined by such value-added features as the quality of the service, the restaurants and the decor of the rooms.

In this evolution of an information society, we look to city planning and architecture for more than mere convenience, function and pleasantness. It is not enough to regard Post-Modernism as a movement of art and literature that has influenced architecture and urban planning. The production base of our society itself is changing profoundly, and as we evolve from an industrial to an information society, the defining traits of Post-Modernism are converging as an accompaniment to this great transformation of the values of society as a whole.

City Space Becomes Novelistic and Private

2) In the age of Modernism, much was made of 'humanism'; we could even call this the slogan of industrial society. Humanism was the dispensation that permitted the un-checked development of technology. But in the post-modern age, this concept of an idealised, abstracted humanity must be cast away.

What, for example, does it mean to design with such a notion of humanism in mind? There are no abstract human beings but men and women, old people, middle-aged people, young people, children – individuals of both sexes and different ages. There are Japanese, Americans, British – individuals of different countries; and if we pursue this line of reasoning to its end, there is person A and there is person B.

You can search the world in vain for the abstracted, average human being, the 'humanity' that has served so long as the slogan of Modernism, for it is no more than an icon labelled as human. In this age however, we must build cities and design buildings and homes for the actual, real person A; for a man, for a woman, for an elderly person – for individuals, with their own identities and personalities. This is the task of bringing human beings down from their pedestal of ideal abstraction and returning them to the milieu of private life.

Let us enter a Gothic cathedral: this cathedral is a work of architecture inspired by devotion to God. When we lift our eyes, light pouring through the stained-glass windows falls on our heads. The music of the organ also cascades down on us from above. In that imposing space we fall to the earth in submission, we repent, and we pray that we may come nearer to God. This is the Medieval cathedral.

Following the Renaissance, the achievement of Modern architecture has been to create a humanist architecture that replaces God with man, and is offered to a mighty, faceless, ideal image of humanity. Since that architecture is offered to an abstraction of humanity, and to human society, the individual person not only finds no peace or comfort in its superhuman scale but also feels a crushing alienation.

As the role of government has grown with the rise of a modern industrial society, public spaces in cities have been enlarged in the name of the public welfare. The lobbies and halls of public buildings are enormous spaces with no place for a person to make himself comfortable. To return to a normal living environment, where they can laugh and cry, people have to rush back to their own homes. In other words, the city denies the possibility of private life. But in the post-modern age, architecture and the city will restore private life to its rightful place, in many different forms. For example: narrow streets that one can walk along alone; pocket parks just the right size for a couple to squeeze into, hand in hand; a bench set under a single tree; space with the excitement of a maze; special places, restaurants, shops that suggest you are the only one who knows where they are; places that are so frightening that you never dare to return; places that come alive at night; a little hidden corner where you can lose yourself in your own thoughts. By incorporating such core images of private life into the city and into its public spaces, we will make our cities more complex and interesting.

The reason that the old Shitamachi area around Asakusa is so interesting; and the crowded, twisted, up-and-down, ever-changing back streets of Harajuku and Akasaka are so much fun, is that they have achieved a good combination of public and private living space. In the cities and buildings before Modernism, we find a mixing of the frightening, the fascinating and the reassuring. In old Edo, there were 'haunted houses' (*obakeyashiki*) where you could go for a good scare, there were frightening old streets that people used for tests of courage; and the night was different from the day: a dark, mysterious time when spirits reigned. But modern city planning tears down haunted houses, destroys the mazes, and banishes a city of night that might satisfy our curiosity. Now night is inferior to day, little more than a diluted version of it. We need to recapture the symbiosis of the cities of day and night.

Making space novel and private again is just this: restoring interest, surprise and stimulation to our curiosity in our monotonous cities, so that the people who pass through them can weave their own stories from the environment. Much is made of the present as the age of private enterprise. But 'private enterprise' has a greater purpose than simply to reduce the role of government by placing a greater part of the financial burden on the private sector. Private enterprise can do much to re-create the city of night, the city of private, novelistic space in contrast to the public centres of the daylight city.

Ruled by an Invisible Icon

3) The pre-modern age was the age of the central authority. The king or ruler – or, in his place, a vast government – was always in the centre from which all rules, all lines of sight, radiated out.

In the urban planning and architecture of the pre-modern age, and that of the Renaissance in particular, a square or plaza occupied the centre and the streets radiated out from it. Standing in a square in Rome or Paris and looking down one of those streets, we see buildings of equal height neatly lining both sides and extending off into the distance in a dramatic demonstration of the law of perspective. Our lines of sight extend into infinity from the central square, symbol of authority.

If the pre-modern age was an age of a transcendent code, then the modern is an age that has liberated itself from codes. Michel Foucault has offered Jeremy Bentham's Panopticon as a model for the pre-modern age.[2] The Panopticon was a prison design with radiating wings made up of blocks of cells. Between every two wings was a tower from which the prisoners could be observed. The design ensures that the prisoners feel the eyes of their guards on them at all times, even if there are actually no guards in the towers.

Similarly, in the pre-modern age the 'king' of the lectern, the teacher, stood at the front of the class, and all his pupils faced him. In the modern age, the authority figure of the teacher no longer exists, but the pupils still feel his gaze on their backs. The modern reality is that though the authority figure is gone, we are each ruled by his icon inside ourselves. For example, when we drive a car we observe the rules of the road. We may say that we do so because the rules exist; but this can also be an example of rule by an invisible authority.

The rule of the icon manifests itself in a variety of fields – education, industry and all other aspects of life – as self-control and self-discipline. The International Style of Modern architecture is an icon of this sort; although an architect who refuses to design according to its laws will not be punished by society, architects have been possessed by an internal fear of liberating themselves from the Modern; an obsession that they must design in the International Style.

In the post-modern age the spell of the teacher's gaze on our backs will be broken: I call this the age of the third classroom. In the first classroom, the teacher stands in front. In the second classroom, we feel the teacher looking at us from behind. In the third classroom, there is no teacher, either real or perceived, in the front or at the back of the classroom.

At first glance it may seem a confused age, and there will be those who will seek to restore hierarchy and order. But a new age cannot be forced to bloom through political or moral coercion. In the end, no one will want to return to an order of the past.

Introducing Diachronicity and Synchronicity

We can compare the absence of the king, or central authority, to the movements of a school of fish. When a school of minnows changes direction, the action is not initiated by any established leader. An individual within the group volunteers to lead by making the first move, and the rest of the fish follow as if they shared a single mind. The school has no king or authority. Each individual member can act as leader at any moment, yet the group as a whole does not lose its dynamism.

The concepts of diachronicity and synchronicity will become important. In time, Modern architecture cuts itself off from the past and places the future far ahead; in space, it regards the West as the leader and all other places as inferior and less advanced. But my philosophy of architecture is to introduce diachronicity and synchronicity into urban space, thus relativising space and time.

How are we to consider the past, the present and the future with regard to architecture? In Giambattista Piranesi's *Imaginary Prisons* (*Carceri d'Invenzione*, c1743), there is neither present nor future; in the *New City* (*Città Nuova*, 1914) drawings by Italian Futurist Antonio Sant'Elia there is no past or present.[3] Modern society is a society of the present, with no interest in past or future. That is why Modern architecture rejected the history and tradition of the past, along with its symbols and decorative language. At the same time, it rejected the future as unfathomable: Modernism could only conceive of the future as an extension of present trends.

All that was required of Modern architecture was that it rationally serve its present functions and meet the demands of present-day people and society. Le Corbusier's Unité d'Habitation apartment complex outside Marseilles (1945-52) and Mies van der Rohe's Lake Shore Drive apartments are both examples of contemporary architecture as offerings to the frozen icon of an ideal image of society.[4] Modern architecture conceives of time as a pyramid of three layers: the past is a base on which the present stratum rests, and on top of the present sits the future stratum. In this model, past and future are only articulated in terms of the present, which forms the central layer of the pyramid. For me, on the contrary, architecture is an evolution from the past to the present and on into the future, a maturing and metabolising process.

Time is not a linear series, nor does it have the hierarchical structure of a pyramid or a tree. It is an interwoven network, a rhizome. The term 'rhizome' as used by Deleuze and Guattari, represents a model in which there is no clear hierarchy, unlike the pyramid, or the tree with its trunk and branches. It is like a spider's web, with neither core nor periphery; neither beginning nor end. A rhizome never ossifies – it is a series of relationships that are always dynamically re-forming and regrouping.

If the past, present and future are conceived of after the model of a rhizome, we can consider ourselves at an equal distance from all times and freely engage in relationships with any. No longer do we feel close only to the present, while past and future are distant. This relativity of time is what is meant by diachronicity.

Synchronicity, on the other hand, is the relativity of space. Lévi-Strauss linked all cultures on earth and thereby relativised Western culture, which had been accorded absolute superiority until then. Structuralism gave the cultures of Western Europe, America, Africa, the Islamic countries and Asia all equal status, with each placed at an equal distance from the others.

In the age of the 'third classroom', time and space are made relative in this way. As a result, we are able to weave different times and histories – past, present and future – and different cultural values – those of Western Europe, Japan and Islam – into a single work of architecture where they can exist in symbiosis.

Sacred, Profane and Pleasure in the City

4) A major feature of the post-modern era is the elimination of dualism and binomial opposition. The boundaries between such apparent opposites as flesh and spirit, religion and science, artifice and nature, technology and humanity, pure literature and popular literature, seriousness and irony, work and play, and life and death will gradually become hazy, and from the intermediary space between these pairs of opposing poles many creative possibilities will well up. The post-modern sensitivity will be one in which we straddle the spiritual and the material, the sacred and the profane. Things that seem contradictory at first glance will turn out to be compatible, even all of a piece, like the Klein bottle. And from this situation a new set of values will arise.

Roger Caillois, in *Man and the Sacred* (*L'Homme et le sacré*),[5] proposes adding a third element to the traditional dualism of sacred and profane: pleasure. The sacred corresponds to the 'first classroom' where the king, or authority, claiming to be sacred, looks down over the people. The profane corresponds to the 'second classroom' and Modernism, the age of the masses, of mass production, of an Esperanto-like universality, of Heidegger's *das Mann* – man as an ordinary person. To be ordinary is the value that Modernism has lauded; it rejects variety and difference; its paradigm is ordinary domesticity.

Pleasure is the 'third classroom', the post-modern age, which rejects the division of sacred from profane. In architecture, for example, the neighbourhood police boxes of Japan are designed in a multiplicity of shapes and styles: in brick, with onion domes, or other curious shapes; and the thought of the familiar policemen glaring out of them is a delightful image. This will transform the city into a blend of the sacred and the profane.

In the world of thought, the New Academism discusses difficult concepts with the flippancy of the comic strip in a blending of sacred and profane. Deleuze and Guattari write: 'Be the Pink Panther and your loves will be like the wasp and the orchid, the cat and the baboon.'[6] In the past, philosophy restricted itself to a rigorous, self-enclosed language of its own, but here we see a mix of philosophical investigation and everyday words and images that will appeal directly to the mass sensibility, while the authors place themselves at an equal distance from both languages. This, too, is an example of the rhizome.

The age when philosophy is restricted to philosophical terms has come to an end; the rule of dualism and binomial opposition is already starting to crumble.

From Association to Bisociation
5) The post-modern age will have conviviality which is another way of expressing Zeami's *hana*, or pleasure, novelty and enjoyment.

Modernism allied itself with a type of purism, and made the functional the highest good while rejecting play, ease, interest and pleasure as extraneous elements. In the Baroque, Renaissance and earlier architecture, decoration was regarded as an important element. The rejection of decoration began with Modernism, and this is one reason why the Modern is an architecture that cannot be read.

6) Post-Modernism recognises the value of the world's variety and the worth of hybrid styles, acknowledging that Western values are not the only legitimate ones and that a near infinite variety of cultures exists around the globe.

As Western culture, hitherto regarded as totally superior to all others, is recognised as just another local culture, English and French, for example, will be seen as no more than local languages, and the world will be enormously transformed. In the post-modern age, we will be forced to recognise the divergence among cultures world-wide and allow different cultural identities to live in symbiosis.

In architecture, this will lead to the reappraisal of combinations of elements from different cultures and a new hybrid style. This will no longer be criticised as the product of compromise, 'neither bird nor beast', but seen as a positive expression of a multivalent energy. My high regard for the architecture of the late Edo and early Meiji periods – the Tsukiji Hotel, the Mitsuigumi House – is because they are fine examples of this creative hybrid style.

7) The concept of the whole will crumble and part and whole will exist in symbiosis in the post-modern age. The modern age was an age of Hegel, an industrial age, in which the concept of the whole – the nation, massive industrial and scientific complexes – was formulated. The post-modern age instead will be a utopia after the fashion of Charles Fourier's phalanxes, or co-operative communities.[7] It will be a world in which small groups take the initiative to form co-operative federations. Arthur Koestler calls this a change from 'association', with the nuance of free and friendly co-operative

relations among groups that recognise their mutual differences, to 'bisociation', a more delicately balanced relationship that even includes a certain degree of mutual opposition.

Koestler remarks: 'The essence of creativity is to be found in the integration on a new plane of two previously unrelated structures of consciousness.' Association is a relation between two parties with some connection to each other, but bisociation is the collision of two completely unconnected parties. Naturally, a tremendous tension, resistance, and stimulus results, in which Koestler finds the essence of creativity. Koestler described the Janus-like relationship between part and whole with the acronym SOHO, meaning 'self-regulating open hierarchic order'. The atomism of the nineteenth century was akin to Koestler's thought in its concern with the part. But the 'self-regulating' part is quite distinct from that earlier line of thought. The shared observation and management of the 'third classroom' can be identified in this self-regulation which has led me to call my own concept of a society based on shared management a SOHO society.

In short, the post-modern world will be one where equal value is accorded to the whole and to the individual; industry and the individual; and society and the individual. It will be a society of a type rejected by Modernism, to some extent inefficient. According to the logic of Modernism, to maximise its efficiency society must be unified and highly organised. Whatever ideals may be professed in our age, and however much capitalist societies claim to value the individual, in reality the trend has been to cede priority to the whole. The great challenge of Post-Modernism will be whether it can achieve a society of symbiosis in which the part, or the individual, is valued as much as the whole.

My own holistic approach to the actual work of architecture, outlined earlier, is to design details such as door handles at the same time as I am making sketches for the whole building. I thus design from both the part and the whole simultaneously. Most architects first settle on the overall shape of the work and then proceed to think about the shape of the rooms inside it while the door handles are the considered last.

In urban planning, too, it is the roads, the parks, the large spaces and facilities that are decided on first, and last of all the houses that will line the roads are considered. That, however, is wrong. We cannot create new cities unless we consider the city and its houses at the same time and give them equal value. True creativity emerges from the process of conceiving the part and the whole together.

A complete deconstruction of the social status quo took place between about 1900 and 1930, three decades which perhaps best represent the special character of the twentieth century. Planck's theory of quantum mechanics, Heisenberg's Uncertainty Principle, Bergson's creative evolution and Einstein's theory of relativity were all articulated at that time. Then, as we entered the 1930s, a transcendence of that deconstruction was explored on various fronts. These years saw the appearance of Ortega y Gasett's *The Rebellion of the Masses*, Benjamin Crémieux's *Inquiétude et la réconstruction*, and Freud's *Civilisation and its Discontents*. The Western concepts of individualism and the self had reached maturity before the twentieth century began, and now a community based on those concepts was created on the basic model of part and whole, individual and society. In reaction to emphasis on the whole, the individual is given more importance, or theories for the deconstruction of society become popular. When deconstruction proceeds too far, the reconstruction of society is called for. This pendulum swing has repeated itself again and again in Western society.

The Arts and Crafts Movement in England was a reaction against industrialisation that called for a renewed recognition of the value of the craftsman's hand labour. In Europe, ages that emphasise the whole have alternated with ages that emphasise the part, the individual. Periods when technology is encouraged alternate with movements to preserve nature in oscillation – a reflection of the dualism of Western civilisation. In the post-modern age we must transcend dualism, and the part and the whole come to live in symbiosis.

From the Economy to an Exchange of Symbols

8) The materialism of the modern age has valued things in terms of their function and utility; parts of things that have no apparent function are rejected as frivolous. But in the post-modern age, spiritual elements will become important.

I do not reject the principle of functionalism *per se*, nor will it be rejected in the post-modern era, because functionalism is not really a product of Modernism. It can be traced back to ancient Greece and Rome. Edward Robert de Zurko, in his book *Origins of Functionalist Theory*, traces functionalism back to Aristotle and the Roman architect and engineer Vitruvius, on through Saint Augustine in the fourth century, Saint Thomas Aquinas in the medieval period, and the Renaissance architects Leone Battista Alberti, Leonardo da Vinci and Andrea Palladio.[8] Functionalism has been advocated by such eighteenth-century figures as Claude-Nicolas Ledoux, Lessing, Goethe and Schinkel, and, in the nineteenth century, Horatio Greenough and Louis Sullivan. From there the baton was picked up by Modern architecture, and it will just as surely be passed to the post-modern era.[9]

The essence of the problem is not functionalism but the one-sided over-dependence on the intellect and rationalism that is the basis of Western culture. Intellect is more highly valued than emotion; rationality is seen as the essence and true form of humanity, the ultimate and unadulterated good. Industrial society developed from scientific thought and experimental and analytic methods that are based on such a thorough-going rationalism.

Rationalism has played an important role in industrial society, but it has also led us to disdain and devalue philosophies emphasising the role of consciousness, spiritual phenomena and emotions. In the post-modern age, the material and the mental, the functional and the emotional, the beautiful and the terrifying, analytic and synthetic thought will have to exist in symbiosis.

We might say: 'The ability to look at a thing and discover its function is due to our analytical capacities, but the ability to discover its aura is due to our perceptive capacities.' The non-functional aspects of things – their design, their aura, intangible context, their spiritual nature – will become increasingly important in an information society. The ability, the sensitivity, the perception to see what is not visible to the eye will be much sought after. Jean Baudrillard has used the bold term: 'the death of the economy' to describe the new age, which will be one of the exchange of symbols.[10] In the age of a mass consumer society great quantities of goods and currency are exchanged: manufactured products are bought and discarded again and again, in a repeating cycle. But in an information society it is not goods but symbols, information and signs which are consumed. The frequent redecoration of shops and restaurants that has become popular can be regarded as a sign of the tendency to discard things. When cafe bars are popular, suddenly there are scores of them, all with the same white walls, revolving overhead fans, and generic high-tech atmosphere. But this style is soon finished and shops made from renovated warehouses are the next rage. Fads and fashions change at an amazing pace, and premises are constantly being redone to keep up with those changes.

They redecorate not because the shop no longer functions well, or because the heating no longer works, but because the symbols and signs their store presents have grown old. What is being so avidly consumed here is not goods but symbols, information, the value-added part of the store. Baudrillard, in his *L'échange symbolique et la mort*, offers a radical criticism of the ideology of production. In modern society, production and economics have, through long association, merged together. He suggests that we are moving away from an age of the accumulation of value and meaning to an age of *la poétique*, in which all excess value and meaning is pared away in what he calls the 'exchange of symbols'. Poetry can be thought of as the creation of atmosphere, but the contemporary age is one in which an aura, the likeness of a thing, is created from signs that possess no particular meaning. A piano that has never been used, a clock that does not tell the time, a chair that can't be sat on, weapons that cannot be fired – our lives are filled with evidence of an age of the exchange of symbols, which Baudrillard calls *simulacres*.

The *Simulacre* as Symbiosis of Sanity and Madness

This age of the exchange of symbols will effect great changes in human relationships. Even among friends, information that you don't have but your friend does, which may not be available through the mass media, will be extremely valuable. The value of information will link people in relationships.

In search of new information, people will come together and separate, or join special groups. A person who told you a wonderful story yesterday will be dismissed out of hand if he tries it on you again today: his information has already been consumed and no longer has any value.

This represents a great change from modern society. The age has come when we find our purpose and interest, and our difference from others, in the information we have that is different from what others have. Compared to the lukewarm relationships in the modern age, the pleasures, stimulation, and joys of life will be intense. But on the other hand, each of us will need his own gyroscope to seek an independent lifestyle, different from that of others. In that sense, it will also be an extremely challenging time. Because each of us will have to select information for ourselves, we will need heightened sensitivity and mental powers.

The times are changing from an easy-going, hedonistic mass society to one society that will make great demands on our intelligence. On television, news shows, debates, and other 'hard' programming will be popular. The appearance of the New Academism in philosophy is a sign of the same trend, which will only increase in intensity from now on.

The key word in the age of the exchange of symbols will be *simulacre*. Baudrillard says, 'A *simulacre* is the structure of atmosphere, or a system constructed of the extraordinary.' The film director Yoshimitsu Morita has made a film titled *Something Like It (No Yo na Mono)* – which is precisely the definition of a *simulacre*.[11]

In Morita's film *Kazoku Geemu (The Family Game)*, an automobile acts as a *simulacre*. Whenever a problem arises, the hero, with a wink, calls his wife or the son's tutor out to the car in its parking place to have a talk. His car is not something to drive; he uses it as a private room – a reflection of Japan's housing situation. The hero also uses it as a space that he controls, a metaphor for a space where he can regain intimacy and take the initiative in his life. Here the car has already been transformed from a vehicle into 'something like a car'.

Consider the sale at a tremendously high price of the Rolls Royce that once belonged to the Beatles. It was precisely because it carried the cultural cachet of having been their possession, not because of its functional value, that it sold for an enormous figure.

In the future we will live in a world surrounded by *simulacres*: 'things like' other things. The Japanese have a long tradition of appreciating objects for their background and context as well as their function. This is their sensitivity to *ki*, or aura, energy. The element *ki* (also pronounced *ke*) appears in words such as *kehai* (presence or seeming), *fun'iki* (aura), and *kibun* (feeling or mood). It has the sense of a symbol or spirituality, a cultural value attached to, arising from or surrounding an object. *Ki* is also used to point to the irrational, the religious, the transcendent. Through the concept of *ki*, a corridor is opened linking the symbiosis of function and aura, material and spiritual elements with the symbiosis of sanity and madness, science and religion.

La Poétique: Deconstruction Beyond Meaning

The theory of the exchange of symbols is linked with the linguist Ferdinand de Saussure's theory of *la poétique*,[12] the symbolic function of language which he uncovered using anagrams to decipher poetry.

According to Baudrillard, '*la poétique* is an exchange of symbols from which, ultimately, nothing remains, a reverberating interplay of structural elements.' Language reverberates within the bounds of the poem and then perishes of its own accord. Whereas the role of literature and philosophy is to point to a subject, such as a transcendent God, and make 'meaningful' statements about it, in poetry, that meaning is completely extinguished.

Let us apply this concept to architecture. The creation of meaning is the task of a certain type of architecture, one with a strong, clear narrative quality. Examples of this are frequently encountered in socialist countries in the one-dimensional, aggressive attempts to create a city district devoted to a mythologised Lenin, with symbolic statues of Lenin and streets named after him. But this monumentality is a thing of the past.

Though I have said that our living environments, our cities and our architecture should be novelistic, with many different readings, I also believe that this 'novel', when finally deconstructed, should be akin to a poem that expresses, finally, nothing. As Baudrillard has written, '*La poétique* as the exchange of symbols brings into play a strictly limited and determined group of words. Its purpose is to totally exhaust those words.'

The Science of Ambiguity or Fuzzy Logic

9) In the modern age, vagueness and the 'irrational', were rejected or forced into a dualistic mould. We were faced with a choice between exterior and interior, public and private, eternity and the moment, good and evil. But at last the truly ambiguous nature of human existence is being rediscovered.

We have learned that the human brain, especially the frontal lobe, is more creative than analytical, and has a high tolerance of ambiguity. The more we learn about ourselves the more we discover that human beings are an ambiguous form of existence that, in many respects, confound analysis.

Modernism makes a great mistake in assuming that this ambiguity remains simply because science has not yet advanced far enough to solve all these mysteries. Human beings are not made up exclusively of parts that can be clearly distinguished and analysed. Ambiguity is also essential in the human make-up. Shuhei Aida, a professor at Denki Tsushin College, comments from the perspective of engineering in his book *Aimai kara no Hasso* (*Thinking from Ambiguity*):

> The dictum 'I think, therefore I am' is famous as a philosophical expression of the essence of humanity. The wellspring of the 'ambiguity' of human beings is thought, which depends upon the activity of the brain. The brain is a miracle of nature, made up of a tremendous number of groups of cells that form a mass of matter which can perform an infinite variety of functions.

The brain processes not only physical stimuli such as sound, light and heat but human feelings as well. It exercises a subtle control over our emotions and each part of the body, and to preserve both our biological balance and our emotional balance, initiates many different activities. The brain's information processing and transmission of instructions are carried out by electric impulses. Thus, when 'I think', impulses within the brain flash in many different patterns, are unified according to a certain order, and take shape as thoughts and mental images.

In each person's brain there is an independent environment, a world, a language, props and a stage, and every day a grand drama unfolds there, directed by thought and intellect. The body is not only a tool or prop for implementing one's thoughts and will, but it is also the very thing that makes the self possible. Here lies the special character of the human being as a form of coexistence of brain and body. Ambiguous engineering starts here, and from this perspective reaches out to include many other phenomena. This multivalent system is based on the recognition that the coexistence of brain and body is the essential nature of the human being.

Nowhere are life and matter more intimately intertwined than in our brains. The broad, dark valley that lies between the worlds of thought and matter is where ambiguous engineering arises. By building bridges across that valley it seeks to gradually discover methods for grasping ambiguity, and eventually construct a system to bring the machine and contemporary civilisation closer to mankind.

Lotti Asker Zadeh, of the Department of Electrical Engineering at the University of California has advocated what he calls 'fuzzy logic'. If we think about it, the language, colours, forms and sounds that surround us are all ambiguous information. There is room for judging, interpreting and understanding all of these data, and in that margin of ambiguity we come to a mutual agreement. This is precisely why words can mislead and different colours and shapes convey different images to different people.

Traditionally, engineering has tried to eliminate the naturally existing margin of ambiguity. Fuzzy logic, however, attempts to put ambiguous information to use in engineering. Its advocates seek to build a fuzzy computer and software that can steer an automobile by remote control.

This ambiguity, the intermediary zone that cannot be explained by dualistic logic, is an important element in the post-modern age of symbiosis. We find a new image of humanity in the 'moratorium human being', a concept articulated by Keigo Okonogi in his *Moratortiamu Ningen no Jidai* (*The Age of the Moratorium Man*). The 'moratorium person' is one who remains uncommitted, unfinished, with no rigid self-definition or social role. This is a human being as potential, a human being in waiting – a very similar concept to the idea of mankind as an ambiguous existence.[13]

The Non-linear, the Fractal and Implicate Order

Ambiguity has become a major theme in science and philosophy as well. In his book *The New Scientific Spirit*, Gaston Bachelard describes this new age:

> If the modern age sought an all-encompassing truth, the new age will seek relative truths. If the modern age was the age of Euclid, the new age will be one that combines the Euclidian realm with a non-Euclidian realm. If the modern age was one of rejection or contradiction, the new age will be a combination of rejection and contradiction. In mathematics, the modern Euclidian realm will be pushed into a non-Euclidian realm by the new age. In physics, if the modern age is one of a Newtonian realm, the new age will be moved into a non-Newtonian realm. In science, if the modern age is that of Lavoisier, the new age will be a move into a non-Lavoisieran science. In logic, if the modern age is one of Aristotle through Kant, the new age will be non-Aristotelian and non-Kantian. And, in contrast to the age of Modernism, the age that waits for us will be one in which all of those negations of their predecessors will encompass and embrace their opposites, in other words, the ideas and beliefs that existed before.[14]

Up to now, progress and revolution in Europe have occurred through a complete rejection of the status quo, an about-face reversal; but Bachelard tells us that the new age will be one in which the status quo will be at once rejected and embraced, a time of symbiosis of old and new. This Bachelard calls the new science of negation.

From this perspective, Japan's Meiji Restoration may come in for a re-evaluation. It was pronounced ambiguous and incomplete in comparison with Western-style revolutions as it did not reject all tradition, but sought to carry tradition into a new realm. This Japanese characteristic of continual revision and reform is well adapted to Bachelard's new age.

In mathematics, Benoît Mandelbrot's fractal geometry and non-linear analytic geometry have replaced Nicolas Bourbaki's systematic, axiomatic mathematics and the Newtonian world view. Non-linear analytic geometry analyses phenomena such as wind currents and tornadoes, previously regarded as non-mathematical phenomena without structure or order. Fractal geometry, too, treats the 'nested structures' found in nature, revealing chaos within order and order within chaos. Ilya Prigogine's dispersal theory and Hermann Haken's synergetics also describe the state of chaos, where order and anti-order exist together.

Traditional science is limited to simple phenomena possessing a clear order, ignoring the disordered and chaotic. Post-modern science will study both order and disorder and pursue the relations between them. Returning to a Leibnitzian view of the world, the previously ignored realm of disorder will live in symbiosis with order in each branch of learning, and a theory of chaos will be born. Leibnitz declared that the whole exists in the part, a view that has much in common with Koestler's *holon*.

As post-modern science and the science of ambiguity develop, Christian civilisation will receive a great shock. Christianity teaches that nature and man are both the creations of God, but for post-modern science, each of us possesses within ourselves the power to create nature. This would appear to mean the irrevocable death of God. Post-modern science is approaching the Buddhist teaching, that all existence – animals, plants and minerals – is inhabited by Buddha nature.

Since his encounter with the Indian philosopher Krishnamurti, David Bohm, the logician and physicist, has begun to develop a unique new physics. For Bohm every part of the natural world contains an 'implicate order' that embraces the rest of existence. He quotes Spinoza's remark that 'Mind is incorporated in matter, and in that sense matter is all-embracing. Matter is an extension of God.' Bohm goes on to say that 'In classical physics, matter is regarded as exclusively material, a mechanical form of existence. There was no room for mind, feeling or soul in this model. But in the new physics, there can be no true separation between inhabitants of the same zone. The mind is born from matter.'

From this revolutionary new position, Bohm advocates holistic medicine. Conventional medicine has treated the body as if it were only matter, but our spiritual and physical functions are interrelated. In Japan, the word for sickness is 'afflicted energy' (*byoki*); traditional Oriental medicine has long regarded mind and body as a unit in a way very similar to holistic medicine.

We have examined several defining characteristics of Post-Modernism as a new current transcending Modernism. To sum them up, we can regard Post-Modernism as the philosophy of symbiosis.

In architecture there is a post-modernist group represented in America by Robert Venturi and Michael Graves, and in Japan Arata Isozaki is often called a post-modern architect. But in my opinion, they are post-modern only in the narrowest sense of the term. Their method is to incorporate the architectural styles of the past – predominantly the European past – into contemporary architecture. They do not subscribe to the broader Post-Modernism I speak of, which seeks to eliminate the domination of the West and transcend Modernism.

THE SYMBIOSIS OF REDEVELOPMENT
AND RESTORATION

Non-economic 'Life Factors' in Regional Planning

The towns of Vasto and San Salvo in southern Italy, along the Adriatic coast, are beautiful cities that still look as they did in Roman times. Agriculture is their main industry, and since they have not succeeded in introducing any secondary industries, per capita income is low compared to the industrialised cities and towns of northern Italy.

At a public meeting on regional planning in the provincial assembly, people from the region declared that their aim was not the high per capita income of northern Italy. They didn't want to bring all sorts of factories into the area and make it like the north, but wanted to preserve their beautiful coastline, their lovely cities, their delicious seafood and their lifestyle. They sought, accordingly, a plan for their region based on a true understanding of these wishes.

I was deeply impressed by this declaration of the people of Vasto and San Salvo. When the day arrives that we hear the same sentiments expressed by the people of various regions in Japan, we too can have regional cities that preserve the unique character of each area. As long as every city aims to match and mimic Tokyo, we are bound to see thousands of mini-Tokyos sprout across Japan; but how much more attractive is the image of regional cities, each distinct and rich in local character.

If the increase of per capita income is the guiding economic principle of regional development, distinct local character and lifestyle, in contrast, are decidedly non-economic principles. 'Character' and 'lifestyle' are instead life principles which guarantee that the local residents will be able to live a human life with pride in their surroundings and their history. We cannot afford to ignore these life principles: today we need a plan for regional development that balances the economic and non-economic factors.

From the 1960s, Japan's national planning has consistently been linked with the economic policy of achieving a standard per capita income throughout the country. The Ikeda cabinet (1960-64) was the first to make this a national goal. Its 'Plan for Doubling Per Capita Income' (1961-70) spurred the Japanese on to greater productivity, towards a goal that could be clearly grasped by anyone. That government constructed what is now known as the Pacific coast industrial belt. The region was chosen for development because of its excellent harbours, ready supply of labour, and proximity to a large consumer market. It was very well suited for the development of the secondary industries of processing raw materials, which made up Japan's leading industrial sector at the time. The intensive development of this region so rich in potential led, in the end, to a concentration of the nation's capital, industrial power, and population in the Pacific coast industrial belt. In response, there arose a cry from other regions of Japan, particularly those along the Japan Sea coast, for a fairer share of the national productivity and a rectification of the gap between per capita income on the Pacific coast and the rest of Japan.

The slogan of the succeeding Sato cabinet (1964-72) was 'Social Development'. This government sought to decentralise industry, which had become too concentrated, planning and building new industrial cities throughout Japan. These cities were supposed to stop the flow of labour, especially of young workers, from local areas to Tokyo and the Pacific belt. If that exodus could be stopped, local economies would revive, tax revenues increase, and public works projects could be undertaken and the local environment improved.

This was the rationale for the new industrial cities and the start of decentralisation. This strategy appeared to be an ideal plan for the improvement of local life throughout Japan, highly advantageous to the residents of those regions; and, in fact, within certain limits, the 'decentralisation = standardisation of per capita income' equation was effective. The gap between earnings in Tokyo and other regions shrank.

But the complete decentralisation of Japan proved to have some major disadvantages for local areas, too. First, it was extremely wasteful in terms of the investment required in public works and facilities. The old ideal of a regional city was of a self-sufficient unit that could meet all the needs of its residents, from cradle to grave. People were born, educated, married, raised families and died in their city. A very strong community spirit, almost a family feeling, is promoted in such a city.

However, isolated and static communities of this sort need all the goods and services of modern life brought to them, which thus have to be supplied to a very limited market. In its most extreme form, this policy would mean that all the facilities of contemporary life, from cinemas and department stores to universities and research centres, Kabuki theatres and opera houses, would have to be constructed and supported in each region, for a limited local population. But every city does not need its own Kabuki theatre or opera house; several cities can share one. The market or audience for these arts is then greatly increased. We must conclude that entirely self-supporting small and medium-sized regional cities are economically unfeasible.

Network Cities for the Age of *Homo Movens*

The second disadvantage of complete decentralisation is that it makes it difficult for people to move between regions. The title of my book *Homo Movens*, (meaning of course, man on the move, after the models *Homo sapiens*, man as thinker, and *Homo faber*, man as maker), expresses the importance of mobility as the special characteristic of contemporary humankind. Just as the concept of *Homo faber* is linked to principles on which industrial society is based, *Homo movens* is linked to the principle of industrial society.

The mobility that characterises modern society cannot be explained simply in terms of the development of transportation. The fact is that in our information society, mobility has begun to possess considerable value for its own sake. It is choice that makes movement possible. According to your own inclinations and values, you can now choose things that are not found in the place you were born. People today look on the availability of choices as one of the riches of life – 'a wealth of choices'. The city of the future, as we continue to evolve into an information society, should be a city that guarantees freedom of choice and makes positive provisions for movement.

The third disadvantage of decentralisation is that, economically speaking, a small city simply cannot compete with a big one. There is no way that a small city can match a large one in the amount of available capital, population, or consumer activity. Simple decentralisation only leads smaller cities to make fruitless efforts to achieve that which they never can.

All in all, a policy of total decentralisation has many disadvantages and is no better than the opposite policy of total concentration in a single region. A truly ideal plan can never be achieved as long as the dualistic choice is either decentralisation or centralisation. National planning in Japan has been grappling with this problem, and at last has produced a New National General Development Plan. A completely new policy of regional development, neither centralisation nor decentralisation but a network city is at last taking shape.

The concept of the local city as an independent and self-sufficient unit will be abandoned in an age of *Homo movens*, with people always on the move from city to city. Cities will be connected by transportation and information networks that will weave a spider's web of linked cities, in a symbiosis of centralisation and decentralisation.

The network theory of cities is based on two major assumptions. One is that an information society will supersede our industrial society. The second is that each city in the network will establish its own cultural identity and pursue its own development based on that culture. If the kind of network we are talking about is formed in an industrial society, there is great danger of a 'siphon phenomenon' occurring between large and small cities: the economies of the smaller cities, which have less accumulated capital and labour, might be siphoned off by the larger cities with densely concentrated resources. This has actually happened along the bullet train lines. The leading sector of industrial society, manufacturing finished products from raw materials, depends to a great extent on concentrated capital, productivity and consumption, so the 'siphon phenomenon' is very likely to occur.

By contrast, in an information society, the leading sector of the economy is made up of such tertiary industries as broadcasting, publishing, education and the service industries. These depend mostly on accumulated culture, and so the economies of small cities do not fall victim to the 'siphon phenomenon'; they may even take an enormous lead over large cities.

Kyoto, for example, cannot be compared economically with Tokyo or Osaka, but its accumulated cultural wealth is one of the highest in the world. In the twenty-first century, the information value of cultural treasures, skills and scholarship will continue to increase. As a source of information, Kyoto is far superior to Tokyo, and this will be a powerful weapon for Kyoto, and cities like it, in the information age.

An 'Event Economy' for the Regions

In the information age, the character of each regional city, no matter how small, will be a source of economic strength. At the same time, the evolution from an industrial to an information society will be a move from an age of economic priority to one of the priority of knowledge and expertise. Already it is becoming possible to enlarge regional economies, which have been strictly limited up to now, through the power of knowledge.

The 'event economy' that I propose is an example. A calendar of local events can generate enormous income by attracting visitors from outside the region. The economic scope of tourism and resort industries is completely unrelated to the size of the local population.

Another example is the sweet-potato liquor 'Downtown Napoleon', which has expanded its market to the entire nation. The governor of Oita Prefecture, Morihiko Hiramatsu, has led a successful 'village product' campaign, in which many events have been held. When local groups hold exhibitions and fairs, promote international conferences and cinema festivals and encourage local festivals, they can sell their agricultural and other products on a nationwide scale. Regional efforts to expand local markets now achieve success through these kinds of events.

Local tax revenues have until now been determined by certain set, inflexible figures: the taxes on forestry, farming and the local population. In the future, however, local governments will start offering financial support for ideas. The conduct of regional government itself will change as it turns to supporting ideas for events that will get the region's economy moving.

In an information age, an age of ideas, networks between big and small cities will avoid a one-way siphon phenomenon, promoting the symbiosis of cities. As this continues to develop, small cities will increase their own information-generating capacity and exploit the markets of large cities. This is one reason why regional planning should adopt the concept of the network.

Cities with High Information-generating Capacities
The Japanese Fourth National Development Plan (1983-2000) focuses mainly on the Tokyo metropolitan zone, and many have criticised the plan as another attempt to centralise Japan

around the capital. Let us look at a portion of the plan's intermediary report that has stirred considerable controversy, under the heading 'Tokyo as an International Centre':

Tokyo is not only the capital of our country but, in such respects as international finance, for example, an international centre. It also provides information of international scope to other cities of Japan, and with its highly developed capacities contributes to the development of the economies of Japan and the world. To ensure that the entire Tokyo area can function as an international centre, we recommend the general development of the Tokyo Bay area, for which high-use demand continues to increase, and the adjacent coastal areas, while encouraging at the same time the selective decentralisation of various functions to other business centres and the reform of regional structures. We also recommend the development of access by regional cities to Tokyo, so that Tokyo's highly developed capacities may eventually be carried out across the nation. We especially recommend the creation of a data base of high-priority government and business information, now concentrated in Tokyo, together with a lowering of communication costs, so that other regions will have easy access to this information.

This section of the report caused a great stir among regional governments, as these newspaper headlines show: 'The Flames of Discontent Spread: Fourth National Plan Favours Tokyo'; 'Many Problems Remain with the Fourth National Plan'; 'The Regional Argument Against the Fourth National Plan: Mere Terminals of the Main Computer?'; and 'An Outdated National Plan – Concentration on Tokyo, an End to Regional Development and Support'.[1]

Of course, we cannot fail to recognise various problems with the present implementation of the plan. My own suggestion for the plan is that, since it has spotlighted Tokyo as an international centre, it must also offer the other regions methods for resisting Tokyo's dominance. Concretely speaking, it is time to rethink the traditional system of allocating public works projects uniformly across the country. Instead, the national government should make more investment in regional cities that have already achieved a certain degree of concentration and accumulation of resources, capital and population: Osaka, Nagoya, and Kyoto, as well as Sapporo, Sendai, Kanazawa, Hiroshima, Takamatsu, Oita and Kumamoto. These cities must be allowed to develop an appeal as living and working environments that can rival Tokyo.

An attractive city, in other words a city with a strong information-generating capacity, contributes enormously to establishing a regional identity and is linked also to the economic development of the region. One of the reasons regional cities are not as attractive as Tokyo is their relative poverty of choices: they simply offer far too little to choose from. People are drawn to a city that has more than one department store, or more than one university.

The relocation of the universities from Tokyo is a good idea. It would be confusing for various reasons to move universities with place names, such as Tokyo and Kyoto, positive steps should therefore be taken to get around this, such as renaming the universities with numbers, as was the practice in the previous century: First University, Second University, etc. When these major regional cities attain the functions of information centres they will lead the development of the entire region in an information society.

My second suggestion to the Fourth National Plan is to look for large-scale projects to undertake in other regions.

A Tunnel Connecting Shikoku and Kyushu

In 1988, the bridge connecting Honshu and Shikoku was completed, and right now the New Osaka International Airport project is under way. We need to continue to look for this type of project as we approach the twenty-first century.

Those projects, in addition, must be linked to the creation of a network of regional cities. Unless they link regional cities into a federation that can rival Tokyo or contribute to the further development of major regional cities which will then provide leverage to the surrounding towns, the investment will be of little meaning. One of the first projects that comes to mind is the expansion of the bullet train lines, indispensable for the creation of a network linking regional cities. Another project that I have been promoting for years is a tunnel linking Kyushu and Shikoku. This would play a major part in forming the network of regional cities.

Today all of Japan, with the exception of Okinawa, is linked. Hokkaido and Honshu are joined by the undersea tunnel from Aomori to Hakodate. The Seikan undersea tunnel connects Honshu to Kyushu, and three bridges span the sea between Honshu and Shikoku. Yet there are no plans to join Kyushu and Shikoku. If those islands were linked by a tunnel, a network comprising Kyushu, Shikoku, and the Chubu region of Japan would be created. This would be an enormous economic zone and an important urban federation.

The privatised Shikoku Railway Company is not doing well because at present Shikoku is a dead end. Yet one of the bridges joining it to Honshu is constructed so that a bullet train line can travel over it. If that bullet train line passed through Shikoku to Kyushu, the fortunes of the railway company would be revived in a single stroke. If the highway under construction in Shikoku now – also said to be very uneconomical – was linked to a Honshu-Shikoku bridge on one end and to Kyushu on the other, it would become a major national artery, and an economically justifiable one at that.

These projects would not only increase Shikoku's economic performance but would have a major economic impact on the Chugoku region of Honshu, on Kyushu, and even on the Kinki area of Honshu, contributing to the formation of a regional urban federation.

Encouraging more investment in the major regional cities and undertaking projects outside Tokyo will establish and enrich the regional network needed in an information society, and these are highly effective strategies for fostering the ability of other regions to rival Tokyo in activity and drawing power. Only when regional cities have acquired this power can there be a symbiosis of centralisation and decentralisation.

The Symbiosis of Three Networks

A third network is formed by international capitals of finance, which has now arrived on the Japanese archipelago.

With the deregulation of finance, Japan's short-term money market is growing at a rapid pace. When the total from trade in foreign currencies and interbank transactions, excluding reciprocal trading, is added to that of the open market, Japan's short-term money market reaches 627 billion dollars. This is the figure for 1989, converted to dollars at the 1989 rate. The Japanese market has already surpassed that of West Germany and Great Britain and is second only to the United States.

The Japanese money market will continue to grow. As the financial sector is completely deregulated, companies that have been investing overseas because they were unhappy with Japan's regulations are likely to return to domestic bonds. Japan's low interest rates make Japan's money market extremely attractive to international investors. The low interest rates are a result of Japan's huge economic surplus. The surplus for 1989 was seventy-seven billion dollars. This enormous amount of money sits in the Japanese financial market, and of course, interest rates are low.

With its excess of money, Japan is investing in bonds and real estate in other countries, and buying up companies as well. Today, Japan's purely foreign investment capital totals more than 266 billion dollars, and it is predicted that within a few years it will reach 500 billion dollars. This is the enormous amount of capital that Japan is investing overseas. The more extensive this relationship with other countries becomes, the more important Japan's money market becomes. Whether we like it or not, we are a part of the network of the international financial markets.

The major American commercial bank, Banker's Trust, moved the general manager of capital markets division from New York to Tokyo in 1985. When IBM transferred the headquarters of its Pacific Group from New York to Tokyo, it made quite a splash in the weekly news magazines. Dupont Japan and Japan Texas Instruments have established research facilities in Japan. All of these are further demonstrations of Tokyo's importance in the eyes of the international financial market.

Another reason that Tokyo finds itself in the centre of the international financial network is geographical. The world of finance is in the age of twenty-four-hour dealing. Making use of the time differences among different markets across the globe, twenty-four-hour trading has become possible by moving on to Tokyo after New York closes, and then to London after Tokyo. Lights may remain on all night in the offices of major trading companies and banks. To keep up with twenty-four-hour dealing, they have to watch the yen and the dollar and the international markets around the clock, in shifts.

The international money market needed an opening in time somewhere between New York and London – somewhere in Asia. Hong Kong and Singapore have been regarded as promising, but Tokyo, with its far superior investment capability, has taken the lead. Tokyo now exists in symbiosis with three networks – a federation of Japanese regional cities; the three major urban centres: Nagoya, Osaka and Tokyo; and an international money market network of an entirely different dimension.

This multilayered network has resulted in the following conditions in the city. According to the estimates of the Fourth Plan, by 2025 the number of non-Japanese residing in Japan will have reached 2.3 million. This is a conservative estimate, and I believe that 2.5 million is closer to the mark. This is equivalent to a city the size of Osaka and it will have a great influence on the country. The 'internationalisation' that had been little more than a vague slogan will take concrete form before our eyes.

The majority of those non-Japanese residents will be living in the international financial capital, Tokyo. Just as today New York has become a thoroughly international, global city, Tokyo will support its end of the international network. As a city, it will no longer belong completely to Japan.

While some will insist that the other regions of Japan should also internationalise to counterbalance the concentration of human and economic resources in Tokyo, Tokyo's development is linked with the development of the regions just as the development of another prefecture only occurs when it has a major city – an Osaka, a Nagoya or a Hiroshima – with its own concentration of people and information. We need simultaneous decentralisation and centralisation; we need, in other words, more urban centres.

France, for example, is now following a decentralisation policy, in a way which offers an interesting contrast with the Japanese. A communications and liaison committee of all government departments for the 'grands projets' under President Mitterrand has been at work on the redevelopment of Paris. The new Bastille opera house has been completed; the largest museum of science in the world and a unique music centre have been constructed in Parc de La Villette; the Musée d'Orsay has opened in the restored Orsay station; the Institute of the Arab World has been built on the Seine; an international competition (of which I was one of the judges) was held for the design of an international communications centre (La Tête Défense) to be built in the newly developed Défense area. Major additions are being made to the Louvre, after the move of the Ministry of the Treasury, which had occupied part of the Louvre's space. These new cultural facilities commemorate the second centennial of the French Revolution, just as the Eiffel Tower commemorated the first anniversary in 1889.

What is interesting is that there has been no resistance from other parts of the country to the further concentration of cultural facilities in Paris, already so richly blessed with them. As long as Paris continues as one of the leaders in the international network of global cities, the rest of France will have access to the same level of information through its domestic networks. Other regions of France are confident that they will prosper, their unique local cultures intact, by remaining linked with Paris.

In the 1920s, Berlin created a unique cultural environment, often labelled 'cabaret culture', as a world capital of cinema, theatre and architecture. In 1987, the 750th anniversary of the founding of the city was marked by an international architectural exhibition: the IBA. Some fifty architects from around the world were invited to participate in this ambitious project, including myself representing Japan. Each was given a site and asked to design a plan for its redevelopment, which should be left as architectural exhibits for the twenty-first century. The exhibition aimed to restore the divided city, long out of the international limelight, to a new glory equal to that of the 1920s, when it led all of Germany.

My idea that centralisation and decentralisation must exist in symbiosis is essentially the same as the idea behind the Berlin project. Tokyo must be developed and, through its participation in the network of international cities, all of Japan will be linked to the rest of the world.

A Man-made Island in Tokyo Bay

A major redevelopment of Tokyo is required to enable it to function as an opening to the network of international cities. This redevelopment is no more than the preparation of the access route through which one of the networks of a world on an entirely different, much higher level, will enter a network that will create a new age in every region of Japan.[2]

Millions of non-Japanese will pour into the city, and even now Tokyo does not have sufficient housing. The coastal areas are being recommended for new developments, but it is not ecologically sound to continue to increase landfill along the shore; this method also drives up land prices in adjacent areas and makes public works more expensive.

I believe it is much wiser to preserve the shoreline more or less as it is and build a man-made island off Tokyo, like Portopia in Kobe. Let us assume we are building an island of 30,000 hectares in Tokyo Bay. At its deepest, the bay is twenty metres, and it is estimated that the sludge on the bay bottom is another seven metres deep, so for an island five metres above sea level, you would need landfill to a depth of thirty-two metres. The amount of landfill to create an island of 30,000 hectares – approximately two-thirds the size of the present twenty-three wards of Tokyo – would be nine billion cubic yards. This is equivalent to two-thirds of Mount Fuji. Where could this amount of landfill come from?

First, from the dredging of Tokyo Bay itself: this would produce 4.5 billion cubic metres of soil. The other half of the total needed would be provided by excavating a Boso Canal – a canal five hundred metres across, connecting Tokyo Bay with the Pacific Ocean through the Boso Peninsula. If the Boso Canal were built, the difference in the tides would mean that three or four metres of water would come rushing in and out of Tokyo Bay daily. This would cleanse the bay and increase its marine life, in a symbiosis with development.

At present, several hundreds of thousands of boats ply the waters of Tokyo Bay annually. The creation of a man-made island would disrupt their traffic, so the port of Tokyo would have to be moved to the tip of the island. At the same time, an outer Tokyo Port would be constructed at the Pacific mouth of the Boso Canal. Products that did not have to be unloaded in Tokyo Bay could be shipped from there by pipeline.

The cost of constructing this 30,000-hectare man-made island would be about eighty trillion yen. Computing the net land cost from this, 3.3 square metres would cost about two million yen. If we suppose a land-use ratio of four-hundred per cent, that is reduced to five-hundred-thousand yen, a cost that would permit the average white-collar worker to buy a condominium. In that projected cost of two million yen per 3.3 square metres, all construction and support facility costs are included: undergrounds, bridges, roads, parks, water, and energy plants. A pleasant, liveable apartment from which one could commute by underground, by car or even by boat need not be an impossible dream.

The intent of this project does not contradict the larger policy of decentralising population and technological capacity across the archipelago. It is merely a plan to improve the appalling living circumstances of Tokyo's working class, to meet the needs of the rising foreign population and to improve the business efficiency of Tokyo as an international financial centre.

The projected population for this man-made island is five million. Of that total, 1.5 million will be non-Japanese. The projected population increase for the native Tokyo population by 2025 is another 1.5 million. The remaining two million will be previous residents of 'mainland' Tokyo, lessening its population density. The completion of the man-made island will not intensify the concentration of population in Tokyo.

As far as the eight-trillion-yen construction cost is concerned, we can see that, with the enormous amount of Japanese money invested overseas, this is a far from impossible figure. Furthermore, there is a clear and certain demand for this new island. Land sells for about 12.7 million yen per 3.3 square metres today, so the profit to be had from this project is approximately two-hundred-trillion yen. If the project were carried out by private enterprise, the capital that is now floating around in the domestic stock market and foreign bonds could be attracted by this potential profit. The tax revenues from this two-hundred-trillion yen could be used for further redevelopment of Tokyo and the major regional cities. In other parts of Japan, the same pattern could be followed: encouraging projects based on private enterprise, and using the profits to initiate yet other projects. This would be a way to bring funds that float like disembodied spirits through the stock market and foreign investments down to earth, in Japan.

For the Japanese government, facing the challenges of institutional reform and the restoration of government finances, large-scale regional projects and the redevelopment of Tokyo are burdens too heavy to bear. It is in the country's best interests to push surplus funds from profitable enterprises into increased circulation and pursue regional development on the private level. In the future, this new strategy will attract considerable attention.

Preserving the Jumble of Tokyo's Rhizome

The new island in Tokyo Bay will provide the elbow room necessary for the redevelopment and resuscitation of Tokyo. The recent jump in land costs has made redevelopment of the present city increasingly difficult. The new land of the man-made island will be useful here, providing land of the same value in exchange for land in mainland Tokyo.

The aims of Tokyo's redevelopment will be to make the city safer in the case of a natural disaster on the scale of the Great Kanto earthquake; to increase the space per person in Tokyo's housing, currently far below the national average; and to add to the city's green spaces. If two or three million people can be drawn away from Tokyo to the new island, two loop-shaped canals can be excavated in the land that they vacate. A belt of high-rise buildings can then be constructed along both sides of these canals. These loop cities will be effective firebreaks in case of a natural disaster.

Aside from the canals' construction and their high-rise loop cities, Tokyo can be left as it is. The maze-like chaos of Tokyo is a natural rhizome that possesses the potential for becoming a city of night, a post-modern city of symbiosis. Tokyo today seems chaotic, without order. If order means the Avenue des Champs-Elysées in Paris, where the buildings on both sides of the avenue are standard in height and consistent in design, then indeed Tokyo is chaotic. While there's nothing wrong with broad boulevards and high-rise buildings, we also want cluttered maze-like districts to explore. Tokyo's attraction is in its complexity, its variety and its wide range of choices. Its constant transformation is also enjoyable. It is a city that doesn't distinguish between the wealthy, the middle class, and poor students; a city that is fun and interesting to walk through (unlike Los Angeles, for example); it also has buses, an underground and taxis, and this wide range of choice is what makes Tokyo human.

Modern Tokyo is a city in which old things and places are preserved, even if they lack historical value, but at the same time a city that is being rebuilt with the most advanced technology, the most pioneering designs and avant-garde architecture. We must not lose this source of Tokyo's attraction through redevelopment. If we supplement Tokyo with the elements it lacks and proceed pragmatically with the required changes, it may well become the most attractive and interesting city in the world by the twenty-first century. Aside from doubling the amount of park land and greenery and increasing the size of living space, the city should be left alone. Leaving it as it is, we can proceed slowly, taking our time with Tokyo's revitalisation.

The development of the loop cities along the canals and the preservation of the present city are a package. We could call this the symbiosis of development and preservation. There is also a need to invest in the suburban areas outside the present belt motorway number eight to foster the development of an urban network there. And we should also restore the Musashino Forest, creating a ten-thousand-hectare deciduous grounds that is a combination of castle grounds and sacred forest.

Contemporary Tokyo has three important overlapping meanings for the Japanese people: it is their greatest metropolis, the capital and the home of the Emperor who symbolises the nation. This degree of concentration is unnatural. The nation's capital should be transferred to the new island in the bay, which will then become a special administrative district. Kyoto is celebrating its twelfth centennial in 1994. Why not mark the occasion by building a new imperial palace in Kyoto? It could become the first imperial palace, and the present palace in Tokyo could be a second palace. Couldn't we have the Emperor spending half the year in Kyoto?

A linear motorway that would connect Tokyo with Osaka in only an hour should be built, and the functions of the nation's capital split among Tokyo, Osaka and Nagoya. Even now several ministries – the Imperial Palace Agency, the Ministry of Education, the Agency for Cultural Affairs and the Science and Technology Agency – have relocated one or another of their divisions, and the belt from Tokyo to Osaka can already be regarded as a 'capital corridor'. One way of invigorating Hokkaido and the Tohoku region would be to run the bullet train through the Seikan tunnel, build a 'super port' in Hakadate and relocate the Supreme Court in Sapporo.

It is widely held that Japan's current huge budget surplus can only last another three decades. Now is our chance to build a new Japan for future generations. Nor do I think that Japan will end its age in the sun as just an economic giant. In the new age that is dawning across the world Japan will for the first time make its own creative contributions to world thought and culture.

TOWARDS THE EVOCATION OF MEANING

The Name of the Rose

The title of Umberto Eco's powerful novel is taken from a hexameter composed in Latin by a twelfth-century Benedictine scholar-monk, quoted at the end of the book: *'Stat rosa pristina nomine / Nomina nuda terminus'* ('The name of the rose is given by God; our roses are roses without names'). This is Eco's contemporary, semiological challenge to the great philosophical controversy of the Middle Ages, the debate concerning the existence of universal natures.

The novel is set in a northern Italian monastery in the fourteenth century. A Franciscan monk, William of Baskerville, arrives at the monastery with his pupil, Adso, to investigate a strange series of murders that has occurred there. As they make their inquiries, they learn that hidden in the monastery library there is a labyrinth, where the second, lost half of Aristotle's *Poetics* is kept. Aristotle's work is said to teach that laughter is the remedy that prevents us from becoming the slaves of truth (universal being). This is a powerful rebuttal of the doctrine that universal natures actually exist, of Plato's doctrine of ideas, and of the Scholastic philosophy that was the servant of theology in medieval Europe.

The meaning of 'catholic' is, of course, universal. The Catholic Church is not simply a congregation of believers but a universal, and therefore sovereign institution that exists prior to and beyond its members. And without this abstract notion applied to humanity, the concepts of original sin and salvation through Christ are also inconceivable.

The English scholastic philosopher William of Ockham, on the other hand, proposed that universals exist only as terms, signs that stand for and refer to individual existences. Eco's name for his leading character William of Baskerville is a pastiche of William of Ockham and the 'Baskervilles' of the famous Sherlock Holmes story. Here we can decipher the intent of Eco the semiologist, with his belief that meaning is invoked as words (or signs) to produce more words (more signs), and interpretations create interpretations. In addition, Eco sprinkles his novel with references to Thomas Aquinas, Roger Bacon, Meister Eckhart, and Sir Arthur Conan Doyle, and quotations from and references to church architecture, philosophy, politics, pharmaceutics, and many other fields of art and learning.

A look at the layout of the monastery depicted in the novel reveals that the church, which is set in the centre of the complex, is not the centre of the novel's action. The main events take place in the *aedificium*, a large castle-like structure located at the edge, the periphery of the complex. The scriptorium, where the story reaches its climax, is also located here at the monastery's periphery.

In the centre of the library that houses the second volume of Aristotle's *Poetics* is an octagonal, twelve-storey scriptorium and a stairway with sixty steps connected in labyrinthine fashion. The steps lead to a wall with a hidden door in it, disguised as a distorted, fair-ground type mirror and moved by secret springs. The number eight of the octagonal labyrinth that represents the universe is a multivalent symbol: it refers to the eighth day, when the universe had been completed; to the last day of our universe; and also to the sequential steps in the sequence of the development of Eco's novel.

I begin this chapter by introducing Eco's *The Name of the Rose* because I believe it is a masterful presentation of the most pressing contemporary issues not only in literature but also common to philosophy, architecture, art and technology. The world depicted in this novel is the new world – whether we call it Post-Modern, Next-Modern, or whatever – to come.

From Epistemology to Ontology

From Greek and Roman times to the modern period, architects have tried to answer the question 'What is architecture?' The epistemological question of what being is, and the nature of the existence of the world, has been the central issue of Western metaphysics from the time of Aristotle, through Plato, Descartes, Hegel, and the thinkers of the modern age. This presupposes a single, true notion of existence that can be described in terms of logos, or reason. The epistemology of architecture has been that there is one universal, true phenomenon 'architecture', which can be comprehended logically by people of every nationality and culture. This is the epistemology of Modern architecture, whose ideal image, the International Style, was conceived as a universal creation that transcended all differences of culture and applied the world over.

What system of values produced this universalised icon? Clearly, the answer is the values of industrial society, based on the pursuit of material comfort; or in other words, the values of Western society. Here we have a phenomenon that is similar to the creation of Esperanto. However, don't we enjoy a more richly creative world when Arthur Miller writes in English, Dostoyevsky in Russian, and Yukio Mishima in Japanese? Then, through the media of translation and interpretation, we can be moved by our readings of different cultures and participate in mutual communication.

Yet the notion of the universal persists. The Cartesian linguist Noam Chomsky postulates an infra-structure, a universal grammar, beneath the surface of the various languages of the world. Some, encouraged by such theories, go so far as to suggest a meta-level hierarchical structure common to all humanity within the heterogeneous cultures of the world, and from which a single and unified notion of existence can be extracted. But this meta-linguistic theory of existence is an issue restricted to the context of Modernism, and has been fiercely attacked by the forces of Post-Modernism.

For example, JM Benoist, in *La révolution structurale*, criticises Chomsky's universal grammar: '. . . the concept of a universal grammar is nothing but the extreme generalisation of a particular notion that is specific to Western culture. This concept can be easily challenged by the theory of the relativity of all cultures'. The Cartesian definition of substance demands a reduction of reality to an unchanging unit, which is why Chomsky, with his theory of deep structure as universal grammar, calls himself a Cartesian linguist.

The application of transcendent meta-statements to the exterior of individual works and the meta-theory of a universal image of existence (architecture with a capital A) has been the target of criticism from the Post-Modern movement. Lyotard, in his *La condition postmoderne*, has remarked:

As long as science refuses to limit itself to expressing a simple functional regularity and aims to pursue the truth, it must legitimise its own rules of operation. In other words, a statement that legitimises the status of science is required, and that statement goes by the name of philosophy. When that meta-statement is based in a clear manner on some grand scheme – the dialectic of the mind; the study of the deciphering of meaning, rational man, or the liberation of the proletariat and the creation of wealth – in order to legitimise itself, we call the science based on those schemes or stories, 'modern'. At the risk of greatly oversimplifying the matter, Post-Modernism is, first and foremost, a suspicion of these meta-schema.[1]

If we can say that Modern architecture created a universal icon based on Western culture, we can see that this was very much a meta-statement (architecture with a capital A).

Culture and tradition are not limited to the tangible. Styles of life, customs, aesthetic sensibilities and ideas are intangible, indivisible aspects of culture and tradition. Japanese culture, in particular, transmits its traditions with greater emphasis on its mental and spiritual aspects, aesthetic sensibilities and ideas, than on physical objects and forms.

While Modern architecture in Japan is extremely contemporary in its forms, it also manages to incorporate the cultural tradition. In the same fashion, the city of Tokyo seems at first to be a modern metropolis of no nationality; but actually Tokyo contains extremely Japanese characteristics and elements.

For me, architecture based on the philosophy of symbiosis is created by being deeply rooted in one's own history and culture and at the same time making positive efforts to incorporate into the work elements from other cultures. Since no single, universal ideal architectural iconography exists, architects must first express their own culture. At the same time, they must collide with other cultures, engage in dialogue with them, and, through symbiosis, create a new architecture that is both local and global.

The history of Modernism in the West reflects the control and suppression of nature by logos. The city is created by controlling nature, and modernisation has meant that cities that had grown and evolved naturally had to be efficiently reconstituted on a geometric plan. Architecture was seen as a means of controlling space and demonstrating the rational capacities of human beings. Reason was the means of controlling and subjugating nature which was exterior to human existence. Modern man is a person whose interior nature – his spontaneity and sensitivity – is controlled and subjugated by his reason. Reason, science, technology and economics take precedence over culture, art, literature and thought. To challenge Modernism and Modern architecture is to challenge Western rationalism. Contemporary Post-Modern architecture has not yet achieved the essential conquest of Western dominance and rationalism. Lévi-Strauss' structuralism, which relativised Western culture, is being further developed by the post-structuralists who deconstruct metaphysics (philosophy based on logos) and Western dominance.

The essential transformation of the Post-Modern age can be described as a change from epistemology to ontology. In his *Sein und Zeit*, Martin Heidegger writes, 'The epistemological question has been whether we can properly describe being. In contrast, ontology asks what the nature of existence is'. While the question 'What is architecture?' is an epistemological one, in seeking the right order of architectural being (its single, universal, ideal image), ontology asks the question 'What is the meaning of architecture?'. Ontology is linked to semantics; both disciplines seek not a single, true order (a notion of architecture) in the form of the universally applicable International Style, but rather the evocation of meaning in architecture.

They do not assume a single, ideal image of architecture that exists as a truth transcending time, history and the differences among cultures. Rather, it is the very differences that arise in the unfolding of time and history that produce meaning. From the epistemological standpoint of Modernism, which asked 'What is architecture?' the truth was given *a priori*, and the problem was how to attain that truth through the power of reason.

It is easy to see that Post-Modern architecture will evolve as an architecture of minor, heterogeneous cultures, an architecture of deconstruction that seeks to reintroduce 'noise', and that sets itself off-centre. In this sense, the Post-Modern is often an architecture of *mélange*, with tendencies towards hybridisation – but a hybridisation fundamentally different from a style that simply mixes together historical architectural styles. Since there is no single ideal architecture and no one correct order, architecture does not express a single system of values. It is a conglomeration of many different value systems, or an order that embraces many heterogeneous elements. As the ontological question suggests, architecture will be the stage for the evocation of a variety of meanings. The collision of different cultures and their introduction as 'noise', creates a new culture. This is the discovery of meaning by means of our sensitivity to differences. In architecture, the conscious manipulation of elements from different cultures evokes meaning through difference and disjunction, and this distinguishes it fundamentally from a simple hybridisation.

Eco's *The Name of the Rose* is rich with quotations, metaphors and signs. But who would say of this bestselling novel that it is nothing more than a hybrid pastiche, lacking in creativity? For Eco, medieval Europe served as a *prétexte* to transcend Modernism. All of the quotations, metaphors and signs of his novel are extracted from the culture, religion and philosophy of the Middle Ages. His method is similar to my own, as I have chosen Japan's Edo period (the seventeenth through to the nineteenth century) as my own *prétexte* from which I have extracted my own quotations, metaphors, and signs.

A hybrid style, produced by the aesthetic combination of different historical styles, is a clever technique that produces beautiful proportions on a surface level. In this formal manipulation we cannot expect to find the intellectual operation of creating new interpretations of historical periods and cultures and pointing to the future. The indefinite, merely aesthetic quotation of architectural styles of the past clearly results in a contemporary hybrid style of architecture, and because of that I am opposed to this sort of historicism in Post-Modern architecture.

We must ask why a particular period is chosen as a *prétexte* from which we extract quotations. For Eco, the Middle Ages in Europe served as the *prétexte* for his thought. The same phenomenon can be observed in many others: for Schinkel, the classical architecture of Greece had a special import as a *prétexte*; for Le Corbusier, the architecture of the Mediterranean had special significance; and for Picasso, the primitive art of Africa had special meaning.

My reason for focusing especially on the culture of Edo-period Japan is that Edo at that time was the largest city in the world, and it produced a unique popular culture. Another reason is that the unique character of that culture resembles my own philosophy of symbiosis. At any rate, for the artist the decision of which historical signs to extract and how to incorporate them in his work is an extremely creative process. There is a fundamental difference between imitation and hybridisation.

Modern architecture has regarded the abstract forms of steel, glass and concrete in the form of the International Style as its universal. The quotation of historical signs and the symbiosis of heterogeneous elements has been regarded as impure, and rejected. But I believe that the presence of historical signs and the symbiosis of heterogeneous elements lend a richer significance to works of architecture. Very few today would argue that a city in which historical buildings are preserved and exist alongside contemporary works of architecture in symbiosis is not preferable to the purely abstract ideal city of Le Corbusier or Oscar Niemeyer. Nor is it appropriate to dismiss this city in which history and the future exist in symbiosis as hybrid.

Of course, we cannot assume that the ten million readers of Eco's *The Name of the Rose* all grasped each of the author's quotations, references and signs. As can be seen from the many different essays of criticism and interpretation on the novel that have appeared since its publication, there are many different ways of understanding it. This multivalence and ambiguity will take the place of the universal, and they are precisely the essence of the new age, in which we will transcend the logocentrism of Modernism.

Will = Text

I have noted how Modern architecture, as a modern episte-mology, is deeply rooted in Western dominance and 'logos'. If we are to move on to Post-Modern architecture, which asks ontological and semantic questions in its attempt to create an evocation of meaning, how must we transform the design methods of Modern architecture?

The basis for Modern design methods has been an ideal image of architecture (an order) which is single and universal, known as the International Style, articulated by means of reason. The design processes of analysis, structuring, and organisation were stressed, always pursued according to principles of reason and logic. The final result of the design process was expressed as a synthesis with universal application.

Heterogeneous elements were excluded from this design process, and everywhere the operations of introduction, connection, clarification, denotation, and co-ordination were given greatest importance. Reason and logos were always called upon to control and subjugate intuition.

We have seen how dualism and binomial opposition are inherent in Western metaphysics and logos: the dualisms of reason and sensitivity, body and spirit, necessity and freedom. In the history of architecture as well, the binomial opposition of reason and sensitivity has always manifested itself in a pendulum phenomenon. The industrial revolution was followed by the Arts and Crafts Movement, which was followed by Art Nouveau and *Jugendstil*. They in turn were followed by the Rationalism of Peter Behrens and Tony Garnier; and after the expressionist and futurist movements, Modern architecture emerged, waving its banner of functionalism. This dualistic process of action and reaction has had an unfortunate effect on Modernism.

In Modern architecture, dominated by reason, the wild revolts of sensitivity by such architects as Alvar Aalto, Frank Lloyd Wright, Hans Scharoun, Paolo Soleri, and Bruce Goff have always been regarded as exceptions. These men have been declared geniuses, and have thus been excluded from the mainstream of Modern architecture; but their revolt of spontaneity and sensitivity against the rule of reason is also a product of the age of Modernism. With the advent of a new age, the advocates of sensitivity and spontaneity are not likely to play any role in the defeat of Modernism. If we have no need for one true image of architecture (order) provided *a priori*, where should we direct our search for architecture? When there is a universal order, it is sufficient for architects to be led by it, to try to approach as near to it as possible. The architect's talent is to successfully ride the current or flow of that order and express his personality in the appropriate manner within the confines of that rational order.

We live in an age of the transformation of the paradigm of Modernism. Post-Modern architecture must begin from the expression of the will towards the changes of the new age. The will or philosophy that tells us what we should transform and how, will become the driving force that motivates the creativity of architects the world over. The ontology suggested by the question 'What is the meaning of architecture?' will be established through the expressions of the wills of this wide variety of people.

The expression of my own will is, as I said earlier, the transformation of Western domination and logos. My will is linked with the expressions of will that are taking the form of battle lines unfolding on a variety of fronts – in literature, philosophy, art, and many other areas. The philosophy of symbiosis is the present expression of my will, previously articulated as Metabolism and metamorphosis, and it enables me to search in my architecture for an evocation of meaning. The philosophy of symbiosis is not another metaphysics; I believe it is more accurate to call it the text of a movement.

An architect's text or philosophy is rooted in that person's history and culture. The architects of the modern age sought an internationalism, a universalism that transcended their own personalities and regional characteristics. Post-modern architects, on the other hand, must set out from the expression of their own will, deriving from their own history and culture. A keen sensitivity to the differences in history, time, and culture will enable them to evoke the meaning of architecture.

Whereas the ultimate goal of Modern architecture was to achieve synthesis, the ultimate goal of Post-Modern architecture will manifest itself as evocation. As far as the methodology of design is concerned, symbolisation will replace analysis, deconstruction will replace structuring, relation will replace organisation, quotation will replace introduction; intermediation, synthesis; transformation, adaptation; sophistication, clarification; and connotation, denotation. These design methods will have an important and conclusive role in the evocation of meaning.

These methods will not necessarily be carried out more under the direction of intuition than of reason or logos. Rather, we can expect the simultaneous operation of reason and intuition. The processes of symbolisation, deconstruction, relation, quotation, intermediation, transformation, sophistication, and connotation, however, depend greatly on a keen sensitivity to differences among times, cultures, and among elements.

The philosophy of symbiosis is a text for the deconstruction of metaphysics, logos and Western domination. This philosophy encompasses the symbiosis of heterogeneous cultures, of human beings and technology, the interior and the exterior, the part and the whole, history and the future, reason and intuition, religion and science, human beings (their architecture) and nature.

This philosophy of symbiosis finds its sources in the Indian Buddhist philosophy of Consciousness Only and Japanese Mahayana Buddhism. In other words, this expression of my will is rooted both in my own identity and in Japanese culture. I do not regard tradition as being restricted to the transmission of tangible forms but as including such intangibles as styles of life, customs, thoughts, aesthetic sensibilities and sensitivities.

In the transmission of Japanese culture in particular these intangibles are paramount. While we can transmit Japanese culture by injecting it into contemporary architectural expression employing the latest high-tech materials, it is also possible to represent very traditional forms within the Japanese aesthetic sensitivity, including the absence of a centre, open-endedness, asymmetry, the expression of detail, and disjunction (deconstruction).

These elements of the Japanese aesthetic appear as a sense of balance, not in the form of a system but when they are disposed as separate elements. We might also say that their special character is that they possess form as aura, mood, feeling. The essence of Japanese sensitivity can be described with the philosophy of symbiosis, which is a text both for the special nature of Japanese culture and for the transformation of the modern paradigm.

Mood, feeling and atmosphere can each be described as a symbolic order without an established structure. It is through a variety of dynamic, intersecting relationships and juxtapositions – the relationship between one sign and other symbolic elements with which it stands; the way the content of the sign changes when it is quoted; the existence of a medium, an intermediating space introduced between different elements; the relation of the parts to the whole – that mood, feeling and atmosphere are created.

In architecture, the meaning produced by the individual elements placed here and there, and by their relationships and disjunctions, is multivalent and ambiguous. When this meaning creates a feeling and an atmosphere, architecture can approach poetic creation.

To regard architecture as no more than actual space, a stacking of bricks on top of each other, is to accept the models of the pyramid and the tree. But the alternative is to consider all elements of architecture as words (signs), between which new meanings and atmospheres can be created. Since all elements of the work of architecture – the pillars, ceilings, walls, stairways, windows, skylights, rooms enclosed by walls, entranceways, open spaces, furniture, lighting, door handles, the treatment of the walls – exist as quotations, transformations, sophistications, connotations, symbolisations and intermediations, the solid, substantial architecture, the stack of bricks is already deconstructed.

Another way of describing the discovery of meaning in the intermediary (vacant) space between elements is to say that we are evoking meaning by setting elements in relation to each other. Pillars and walls, which have only had meaning as structural elements in architecture up until now, can be deconstructed from the hierarchy of structure and given independent symbolic existence.

The four bamboo poles that are set up at the Shinto-style ground-breaking ceremony which is observed before commencing each construction have a fictional connotation. Their physical nature as bamboo poles disappears and they connote the symbolic aura of the place for the descent of the gods. In his work *Le Système des Objets*, Baudrillard wrote of space enclosed by elements he calls things:

> Space, too, has a fictional connotation. All forms are relativised as they pass through space. A spacious room has a natural effect. It breathes. When there is a lack of space, the atmosphere is destroyed because our breath is robbed by the things crowded into it. Perhaps we should read a reflection of the moral principles of separation and division in this distribution of space. If that is so, it is a reversal of the traditional connotation of space as a full, existing substance.

The space he refers to is the vacant space between objects, called in Japanese *ma*, or 'in-between space'. It is natural in the sense that it is outside existing, wild and breathing. Unlike a pile of bricks, it does not have the connotation of solidity, of actuality, but of emptiness, of nothingness.

Atmosphere is evoked along the ties of relation that link thing to thing. Baudrillard's theory of architecture brilliantly reverses the epistemology of Modern architecture, transforming it into an ontology.

If the pyramid and the tree are models of modernist hierarchy, the models of post-modern order are the semi-lattice structure and the rhizome of Deleuze and Guattari. The rhizome represents the principle of union and difference, a multiplicity in which relations are possible at any number of points. It is completely different from the tree, which is a model of a unilateral, frozen hierarchy. The concept of the semi-lattice resembles the rhizome's multiplicity. It, too, is an open-ended order in which different points are continually evoking meaning in their relations. Julia Kristeva describes this type of ontological relationship as a 'polylogue', the condition in which 'many different logics, many different selves, exist in different places and at different times.' It is 'an active, parallel order of things that arise in the process of the evocation of meaning.'

In any case, the evocation of meaning is not realised through some established hierarchy, but is an active state evoked in the process of relation.

Architecture for the Information Society

Just as Modern architecture and the International Style belong to the industrial society, Post-Modern architecture will be the architecture of the information society. The present collapse of Modernism and repudiation of Modern architecture can be attributed to the transformation of the paradigm of industrial society. The most advanced nations are rapidly shifting from industrial production to the production of information. And, while industrialisation has followed the stages of evolution described by the American economist Walt William Rostow, handed down from developed to developing nations, the information society transcends economic and technological evolutionary stages and differences of ideology, enabling the entire world to progress at the same time.

Specifically, the information and related industries include: broadcasting, publishing, finance, research, education, tourism, design, fashion, trade, transportation, and the food, leisure and service sectors. What all these industries have in common is that they do not depend mainly on the production or assembly of things; instead, their products are information, added value and culture itself.

In the fashion industry, the added value of design is worth many times the cost of the materials themselves. In restaurants, the skill of the chef, the quality of the service, and the décor are worth far more than the cost of the ingredients that make up the food served. Even in industrial products, there is a shift from mass production to limited production of a greater variety of goods giving added value through variety, and the added value of design is receiving increased attention.

While the industrial society aimed for universality and homogeneity, the information society will aim for multiplicity. Universal, homogenised information is of reduced value; in order to establish their own identities, people try to distinguish themselves from others. In this manner, things, people, and society will grow infinitely various, and architecture is no exception. The differentiation of architecture will be achieved in the evocation of new meanings, bringing differences and variety into new work.

It is mistaken to regard the Post-Modern as a chaotic transitional period. The appearance of a highly differentiated architecture, the eruption of the evocation of new meanings is the manifestation of the architecture of the information age. Differences are created by giving consideration to relations, or by Heidegger's 'care' (*Sorge*). The evocation of meaning through difference requires a keen sensitivity as an essential prerequisite.

The information society will create trans-global relationships in real time through travel and communication. Different languages, ways of life, and different cultures come directly into our homes via television and other media. This allows for a depth of multivalent meaning unthinkable in the age of Western dominance. The transformation of the paradigm of an industrial society to one of an information society is playing a large role in shifting the world from the dominance of the West and logos.

Roland Barthes, in his *Mythologies*, calls this the 'age of the power of meaning'. Since the age of an information society is a time when meaning will be evoked through differences, we will see a shift from the 'syndigmatic' linear, explicit thought patterns of Modernism and denotation to 'paradigmatic', non-linear, latent thought patterns and connotation.

Barthes refers to transformations or expansion of meaning achieved through connotation as a mythological function. Theodor Adorno, the German philosopher, also speaks of the importance of the mythological function (mimensis) in contemporary society. In his *Aesthetische Theorie*, he describes mimensis as the 'reason of harmony', and predicts that the unfortunate dualism and binomial opposition of reason and intuition in Western metaphysics will be harmoniously resolved through mimensis.

Modernism and modern rational thinking were given their basic nature through the objective rationalism of Galileo, Newton and Descartes. The principle of identity, in which there is an objective and universally applicable view of the world common to all, is epitomised by the perspective drawing, used in architecture and the visual arts. Perspective, which depicts the entire world from a single, visible point, is like the head of Medusa, turning all who look on it to stone. In perspective, not only is the viewer himself eliminated from the picture, but all that is beyond his line of vision is rejected.

We must abandon single-point perspective and move the point of vision so that it reveals the relationships among all things. A point of view in which the world and people are seen from the perspective of things is probably also necessary. This would imply a point of view of the infinitely varied whole. Modern man, who has depended too much on his eyes to view the world, cannot understand why a person from a 'primitive' tribe doesn't wear clothes. The 'primitive' man answers: 'My entire body is my face'.

Recently, the theory of measurement in quantum physics has revealed that even the one true measurement made through scientific processes is actually nothing more than a state which has been accidentally selected, whereas that selection itself causes the instantaneous collapse of the quantum wave function, rendering the state perceptible – that is, measurable – to us. In fact, all possible states exist at the same time, overlapping each other. This is called the Copenhagen Interpretation.

The image of architecture revealed through reason alone, a whole established solely from the point of view of the visible, the single, correct measurement made by science, is actually no more than a partial glimpse of a rhizome-like multiplicity.

Without a doubt, the architecture of the information society will shift from a paradigm of symmetry to one of asymmetry, from being self-enclosed to being open-ended, from the whole to the part, from structuring to deconstruction and from centrality to non-centrality. It will aim for the freedom and uniqueness of all human beings, for the symbiosis of different cultures, and for a spiritually rich pluralistic society.

The Realisation of Architectural Works

The Symbiosis of History and Nature

The hill of Hijiyama now stands in the centre of Hiroshima City, but it is said to have once been an island in Hiroshima Bay. Hijiyama was chosen as the site for the construction of a new symbol of contemporary Hiroshima City, as distinct from the Hiroshima Peace centre built after World War II as a symbol of 'No more Hiroshimas'. After the completion of the master plan for the layout of the facilities and the general design of the Hijiyama complex eight years ago, work proceeded in stages, as roads, the observatory, the park area, and the Aozora Library were completed.

The Hiroshima City Museum of Contemporary Art is situated on the ridge of the hill, just off the axis of the Aozora Library. With the eventual completion of a natural history museum and a museum of local history, the Hijiyama complex will become a cultural centre – a new symbol of the city of Hiroshima.

The design of the Hiroshima City Museum of Contemporary Art is based on the philosophy of symbiosis. The reappraisal of Modernism and Modern architecture means the reappraisal of the dominance of the West and the logos which are part and parcel of Modernism. The cultural references of Post-Modern architecture in Europe and the United States are also based on the West, and in that respect Post-Modern architecture does not differ from Modern architecture. The doctrine of rationalism and logos meant that humanity (and architecture) were called on to control and restrain the nature that lay outside. In addition, human reason was to control and restrain the nature that lay inside: the 'wildness' or sensitivity. The concept of the symbiosis of humanity (architecture) and nature is a transformation of that paradigm of the dominance of logos.

Modernism was also a doctrine of the present, and the quotation of historical signs and symbols was deprecated as 'hybridisation'. Instead, pure, abstract geometric figures were regarded as the triumph of reason.

This obsession with the present must also be reconsidered, yet the method of quoting historical symbols and styles directly, is especially likely to degenerate into mere hybridisation. In order to evoke a more creative and multivalent meaning, a symbiosis of history and the future, the historical signs and symbols must be subjected to transformation, articulation, sophistication and intermediation.

The Hiroshima City Museum of Contemporary Art was carefully situated on the ridge of the hill to give priority to the preservation of as much of the wooded areas on the slopes of the hill as possible. In order to keep the height of the building from exceeding that of the surrounding trees, part of the exhibition space was set underground, so that some sixty per cent of the total floor space is below ground. Many intermediary zones between the work of architecture and its natural setting have been incorporated into the building's exterior – a central approach plaza with a colonnade, a patio, a corridor, a stone garden, a stairway sculpted from stone – facilitating the symbiosis of architecture and nature, interior and exterior. The materials used on the building exterior also evolve gradually, from the natural stone foundation upward to roughly finished stone, polished stone, tile and aluminium; from earth to sky, from ground to the universe, from the past to the future – all are in symbiosis. I have been using this method for nearly a decade, for example at the Melbourne Central and the Okinawa Prefectural Government Headquarters, now under construction.

The overall shape of the museum is a linked series of gable roofs. It is segmented, a work of architecture that is a village, a group of dwellings: we might call this the symbiosis of part and whole. This has permitted the museum to achieve a scale that does not dominate its natural setting.

The gable roofs are a quotation of Edo-period earthen storehouses, but the use of the contemporary material aluminium transforms that historical sign and imbues it with ambiguity. This is the efficacy of connotation. The central approach plaza is a quotation of a Western city, yet there is no fountain or work of sculpture in its centre, indicating an empty centre, or the absence of a centre. The roof of the colonnade that rings the central plaza is cut away at the front, in the direction that faces the city centre, connoting the site of the atomic bombing, and the pillars of the colonnade rise from stones exposed by the blast. Like the *roji* entrance-way garden leading to a tea room, this approach plaza has no particular function, yet it is an important area in the evocation of the meanings of the symbiosis of history and the present, and of heterogeneous cultures.

A Henry Moore arch is set in the outdoor sculpture garden opposite the approach plaza, and from the cut-away section of the plaza, it suggests a gun sight that automatically leads the eye to the site of the atomic blast. The approach plaza also acts as an intermediary zone between the permanent exhibition space on the right and the galleries for special exhibitions on the left. The circular corridor that links these is a dynamic intermediate area. The stairway that connects the permanent exhibition space with the first floor and the underground level is a sculpture created by Inoue Bukichi, a new experiment in the symbiosis of architecture and sculpture. The Hiroshima City Museum of Contemporary Art is the first museum in Japan to include works of contemporary architecture, industrial and graphic design in its collection: in 1988 it exhibited the architectural models and plans of Le Corbusier in its possession. It continues to pursue a unique collection, including works which it has commissioned from some eighty Japanese and foreign artists on the theme of Hiroshima, and I believe it will prove itself a museum of international calibre and interest in the years to come.

THE SYMBIOSIS OF HISTORY AND THE PRESENT

The theme of the design for the Honjin Memorial Museum of Art is the symbiosis of history and the present. As in the Hiroshima City Museum of Contemporary Art, I have quoted the Edo-period storehouse as a metaphor. The pure geometric form of the circle is displaced, and a complex, fissured space has been created for the facade.

The square moat and lattice-style fence that surrounds the perimeter of the building is a modern manifestation of the ancient Chinese theory that the Heavens are round and the Earth is square. The moat surrounding the building is a sign that this lot was once the site of a moat-surrounded castle. The centre space of the interior has a simple two-storey open space, but even this is unfinished, and with its wedge-shaped skylight it expresses the absence of a centre and a rejection of the universality of pure geometry. By emphasising asymmetrical forms, the work challenges the centrality of logos and the West.

The basic theme for my prize-winning plan for the New Osaka Prefectural Headquarters Complex is the symbiosis of past and future. Since the historical monument Osaka Castle is located on the same site, its moat, its stone walls and the castle itself have been quoted as historical allusions. While other designs submitted included twin high-rise towers, one for the administrative headquarters and the other for the police headquarters, my plan has only one, for the administrative headquarters. The rest of the structure is of medium or low height, in an attempt to attain a symmetry with Osaka Castle. Administrative, police and prefectural assembly blocks, the governor's mansion, a family court, lodging for assembly representatives, a separate administrative block and a cultural hall are all planned for the ten-hectare site. Geometrical forms such as domes, vaults, four-sided pyramids, triangular roofs and patios have been employed symbolically to distinguish the different architectural forms. The high-rise administrative block is a three-tier superstructure, which, aside from its own intrinsic meaning, is an allusion to the form of Osaka Castle.

THE SYMBIOSIS OF HETEROGENEOUS ELEMENTS

Fukuoka Seaside Momochi is presently serving as an exhibition for the work of eight architects, but eventually it will be a multipurpose structure housing a branch of the Fukuoka Bank, a bookstore, and an information centre. This is an attempt to allow these various works of architecture to function individually and, while permitting each of them to express itself in the signs of it own unique form, to forge them into a fluid and yet composite whole.

The exterior walls are made from water-polished stone mixed with natural stone; the trusses are made of wood, and natural light enters from the skylights; all of these are metaphors for nature. Signs of traditional Japanese architecture are quoted in the designs of the windows and the lattices. The light tower and the curving walls are connotations of European culture. The exterior space is designed to be complex and to create an intermediary space that leads people into the interior, so that they may experience the symbiosis of interior and exterior that characterises traditional Japanese architecture.

The Shibuya Higashi T Building is a small office building in the middle of Tokyo. The narrow approach hall of this building is filled with many different signs: a metal folding screen, a polyurethane screen alluding to lacquerware, an unfinished concrete wall and a granite wall all exist in synthesis. Here is the symbiosis of past and future, the West and East. Though the work is a simple square form, several wedge-shaped aluminium exterior curtain walls serve to reject the universal, the pure, and to cast the building off-centre. The roof, suggesting a cross-section of an aircraft wing, alludes to flight, defying the building's gravity.

The methodology that all these designs have in common is that the philosophy of symbiosis – the expression of my will – is at their base, and they present a challenge to the dominance of the West, of logos, of dualism, and of the universal.

In contrast to the methodology of Modern architecture – analysis, structuring, organisation, introduction, synthesis, adaptation, clarification, denotation – the processes adopted in the plans I have introduced above are symbolisation, deconstruction, relation, quotation, intermediation, transformation, sophistication and connotation.

Following each respective method, the signs that are quoted in these designs are situated as free elements, and each person who reads them is free to adopt his own method of interpretation. There is no one accurate reading of each sign; the objective of this method is to permit the various signs to operate in free combination and to contribute to the evocation of meaning, create *la poétique* and produce an atmosphere of its own narratives in symbiosis.

EPILOGUE
LIBERATION FROM CRAVING
AND IGNORANCE

From the Philosophy of Coexistence to the Concept of Symbiosis

I first began to use the phrase 'the concept of symbiosis' in 1979. My interest in the idea began when I was chairman of the Yokohama Design Conference, on the theme 'Towards the Era of Symbiosis', but I had been discussing 'the concept of coexistence' since the 1960s. In a book I published in the early sixties, *Toshi Dezain* (*Urban design*), the section 'The Philosophy of Coexistence' commented in part:

Isn't dualism a sickness that has taken root in all areas of modern thought and methodology? To put it impetuously, we cannot conceive of European civilisation without Christianity. European civilisation is, in other words, Christian civilisation. Christianity presupposes such dualisms as that between a good and an evil deity, the god of goodness and light and the evil material world, or the creator and his creation. This is true of Western philosophy as well. The philosophical dualism in which the fundamental principle of the universe was the separation of existence into mind and matter was already established in ancient Greece. In modern times, Descartes postulated a dualism between mind as a limited entity that depended on God for its existence on the one hand, and matter on the other. Kant, who divided existence into the thing in itself and phenomena, freedom and necessity, was also a typical dualist.

European rationalism has been the spiritual backbone that has supported the industrialisation and modernisation of society. This rationalism is based on dualism. Our thought has been articulated from head to tail in dualistic forms: spirit and body, art and science, man and machine, sensitivity and rationality.

Humanity has relentlessly pursued these two extremes, terrified of the deep chasm it has discovered between them. Without a doubt, the impressive modern civilisation born of European rationalism is the product of the recognition of this deep abyss and the will to somehow or other bridge it.

The discoveries of contemporary design, too, are based on dualism, giving us such contrasting pairs of terms as beauty and utility, form and function, architecture and the city, human scale and urban (superhuman) scale. All debates about design up to now have been pendulum-like, swinging back and forth between such extremes. The father, as it were, of functionalism, the American architect Louis Sullivan, proclaimed that 'form follows function'. From the more modest position that the pursuit of function will produce its own distinct beauty to the most extreme dictum that beauty is to be found only in function is only a difference in degree. The weight of this way of thinking in modern design is considerable indeed.

But the other side of this dualism is just as extreme: that humanity, sensitivity, beauty, are independent entities opposed to function, and that functionalism compromises humanity, represents the defeat of humanity. From this is born the dogma that only the beautiful is functional. The debate is then reduced to a simple counting of heads on each extreme side of the issue, from which no creative thinking is likely to result.

When we try to resolve problems with dualistic methods, the concept of harmony comes into play. Here is an example: in urban space, there are two scales, one human and the other superhuman, and they are regarded as antithetical. To bridge the gap between them, a hierarchy of several graded scales leading from the human to the superhuman is created, and that is how these extremes are harmonised.

If these two scales are really antithetical, there will always remain an unbridgeable gap between them, no matter how many intermediary steps are constructed. Conversely, if the gap can be bridged, that means that the two scales were never actually antithetical. As long as dualism is to be a creative logic, it will always arrive at either compromise or escape.

Our task is to move from dualism to pluralism, and from there to advance to a philosophy of coexistence.

My philosophy of coexistence began here; its roots are in the Indian philosophy of absolute non-dualism that can be traced to the Vedanta philosopher Nagarjuna, and the Mahayana Buddhist concept of emptiness.

This is the source of my present concept of symbiosis which first began to take shape as early as 1959, and has been growing and developing ever since.

The City of Symbiosis, a Way to Liberation

In the early 1960s, together with Noboru Kawazoe, Masato Otaka, Fumihiko Maki, Kiyofumi Kikutake, Kiyoshi Awazu, Kenji Ekuan, Shomei Tomatsu, and others, I laid the foundations of the Metabolist movement.[1] We borrowed the term metabolism from biology: just as living organisms have metabolisms, we believed that cities and architecture grew and metabolised. The Metabolist movement touched many different fronts and although it is impossible to summarise it in a word, it is fair to say that the issue of the symbiosis of past, present, and future, of human beings and technology – in other words, the issues of diachronicity and synchronicity – were central to it.

Also at the core of Metabolism was the tradition of Eastern thought. At the time, I remember reading with great interest Hajime Nakamura's *The Ways of Thinking of Eastern Peoples*. The work traces the evolution of Buddhism as it was transmitted from India, its land of origin, to Tibet, Thailand, China, Korea and finally Japan. He investigates the way in which the Buddhist scriptures were translated from Sanskrit and Pali into other Asian languages and explores the changes that took place in Buddhism as it encountered other peoples and cultures. His book had a very great influence on me, and through it I was directed to other sources of stimulation: the Edo-period Japanese philosopher Miura Baien, for example, and the Consciousness Only current of Buddhist thought that is one of the bases of Mahayana Buddhist philosophy. The book made me aware of the rich and unique cultures of India, Tibet, Thailand, China, Korea and Japan, about which I had previously had no clear idea. It also marked the beginnings of my commitment to Buddhist philosophy, which I had encountered at school as a teenager. I attended Tokai Gakuen in Nagoya, which is affiliated with the Jodo, or Pure Land, sect of Japanese Buddhism. This school was established in the Edo period, and even today most of the teachers are monks. The Principal of the school when I attended it was Benkyo Shiio, the head of the huge Zojoji temple complex in Shiba, Tokyo. His lectures over six years had a profound influence on my way of thinking. Only recently did I learn that the term symbiosis had been coined by Shiio in 1923. He began a Foundation for Symbiosis (Zaidan Hojin Kyosei Kai), which published religious verses on symbiosis and a manual of symbiosis. In those works we find:

> We take the truth of coexistence as our guide and concentrate on the realisation of the Pure Land, for both the sharp and the dull, the strong and the weak, hand in hand. No one exists divorced from the thoughts of those around him. All comes into existence through an assembly of causes. All things are interrelated. In accordance with this principle, it is our aim to build an ideal world, step by step.

This is the true teaching of symbiosis. In Shiio's Buddhism of symbiosis, he reads the characters *kyosei* as 'living together', or coexistence. At the base of his philosophy is the conviction that all existence not only lives, but, at the same time, is being given life by the rest of existence. Inorganic substances such as minerals are crucial for human life; if even one vital mineral is lacking, we cannot survive. Human beings live and are kept alive through their coexistence with animals, plants and minerals. Shiio calls this essentially Buddhist vision of life 'true life'.

In Buddhism, human suffering is said to be caused by two things: craving and ignorance. Craving is attachment to things and the delusions that arise from that attachment. Ignorance means not to know what our universe is, what our self is. When you think that you are living entirely on your own, you begin to cling to your own life and to fear death – in other words, craving arises. The arrogant attitude that you know everything there is to know is based on ignorance. The escape from those two kinds of suffering is called liberation, and that escape is based on grasping and living the concept of symbiosis.

This Buddhism of symbiosis has exerted a strong influence on me. But I have not written this book as any sort of religious expression. I wrote it to suggest a new principle of order in general, encompassing all fields – government, science, philosophy, art and culture. I mention architecture from time to time because I happen to be an architect. But an age when we must learn to think in a way that transcends all divisions among different fields of specialisation is dawning. It is my hope that this book will be read by specialists in a wide variety of fields and people with a wide variety of beliefs and values.

NOTES

Chapter I
From the Age of Machine Principle to the Age of Life Principle

1   Sergei Mikhailovich Eisenstein, (1898-1948) was a Russian
    film director born in Riga. His 1925 film *The Battleship
    Potemkin* was a story of the revolutionary soldiers of the ship
    in the Black Sea in 1905. It was a silent movie, which shocked
    the world with its location and montage methods.

    Filippo Tommaso Marinetti, (1876-1944) was an Italian
    poet and the ideological founder of Futurism. His major
    written work was *Mafarka il futurista*.

2   Togo Murano, (1891-1984) was a Japanese architect whose
    major works included the World Peace Memorial Hall and the
    Nihon Seimei Hibiya Building. He was awarded the Order of
    Cultural Merits, Japan, and the Art Academy Award Blue
    Ribbon Medal.

    Seiichi Shirai, (1905-83) was also a Japanese architect. His
    projects of the Head Office at the Shinwa Bank and the Shoto
    Museum are viewed as his major works. His work has been
    recognised by the Kotaro Takamura Award and the Japan
    Architecture Academy Award.

    A contemporary of Shirai, Kunio Maekawa's, (1905-86)
    major works are the Nippon Sogo Bank and the Tokyo Metro-
    politan Museum. His awards include: Japan Art Academy Award;
    Mainichi Art Award; Japan Architecture Academy Award.

    Kenzo Tange's (b 1913) Olympic Yoyogi Gymnasium,
    Tokyo, and the Metropolitan Government Office established
    his architectural career in Japan. He has been awarded the
    Japan Architecture Academy Award, the Order of Cultural
    Merits and the Royal Gold Medal for Architecture, RIBA.

The Japanese architect Arata Isozaki's, (b 1931) most important projects are the Saint Jordi Sports Palace, Barcelona and the Art Tower Mito, Mito. His work has been recognised by the Architectural Institute of Japan who awarded him its prize for design. He has also been awarded the Royal Gold Medal for Architecture, RIBA.

3   Walt Whitman Rostow, (b 1916) the American economist, was special aide during the Kennedy era. He wrote *The Stages of Economic Growth*.

4   The Austrian architect, Hans Hollein (b 1934), principal works include the Jewellers Shop Schullin I & II; Austrian Travel Agencies, Vienna. His awards include the Reynolds Memorial Award and the German Architecture Award.

The American linguist and political critic, Auram Noam Chomsky's (b 1928) theory of transformational generative grammar has had a profound impact on the field of linguistics. His writings include: *Aspects of the Theory of Syntax*, Cambridge, Massachusetts, MIT Press, 1965, and *Language and Mind*, New York, Harcourt Brace, 1968.

5   Richard Rogers, (b 1933) is a prominent British architect, whose most famous projects include the Georges Pompidou Centre, Paris, and the Lloyd's Building, London. His work has been awarded the Royal Gold Medal for Architecture and the Chevalier, l'Ordre National de la Legion d'Honneur.

Renzo Piano, (b 1937) is an Italian architect whose chief works include the Kansai International Airport, Osaka and the Italian Institute of Culture, Tokyo. He has been awarded the Chevalier, l'Ordre National de la Légion d'Honneur.

The British architect Sir Norman Foster's (b 1935) works include the Century Tower, Tokyo and the Hong Kong Shanghai Bank Headquarters, Hong Kong. He has been awarded the Royal Gold Medal for Architecture, RIBA and the Japan Design Foundation Award.

6 Claude-Nicolas Ledoux, (1736-1806), a French neoclassicist architect, developed into the most adventurous and extreme exponent of neoclassicism. His most representative work is perhaps Les Barrières (custom house) in Paris.

7 The German philosopher, Edmund Husserl (1859-1938), was the founder of the philosophical school known as phenomenology, and in 1887 became a *privatdozent* at Berlin. He is without doubt one of the most significant philosophers of the twentieth century. His writings included *The Crisis of European Sciences and Transcendental Phenomenology: An Introduction to Phenomenological Philosophy*, Evanston, Illinois, Northwestern University Press, 1970 (translation of *Husserliana*, vol 17).

8 Galileo Galilei, (1664-42) was an Italian physicist and astronomer who discovered the constancy of a pendulum's period. He completed the telescope in 1609. His other great achievements were his discovery of the satellites of Jupiter, the rings of Saturn and sunspots. He pursued a series of astronomical investigations, which proved to him the correctness of the Copernican theory. His works include: *Dialogue Concerning the Two Chief World Systems*, 1632, *Discorsi Intorno a due Nuove Scienze*.

   Sir Isaac Newton, (1642-1727) the English mathematician, physicist and astronomer, was born at Woolsthorpe, Lincolnshire. His research included the rule of universal gravitation and in 1687 he published *Mathematical Principles of Natural Philosophy (Principia)*.

   Regarded as the founder of modern chemistry, Antonie Laurent Lavoisier (1743-94) established the theory of combustion. His *Traité Elémentaire de Chimie*, of 1789, was a masterpiece. He also wrote *Mémoires de Chimie et de Physique*.

   Euclid, the Greek mathematician, taught in Alexandria in around 300BC. His main work is the series of thirteen books, entitled *Elements* which sets out the principles of geometry.

Charles Robert Darwin (1809-82), the English naturalist and discoverer of natural selection, was born in Shrewsbury. He cruised the southern hemisphere, observing geology and plant and animal life. In 1939 he published *Journal of researches into the natural history and geology of the countries visited during the voyage of HMS Beagle round the world*. Then in 1959 he published his famous treatise on the theory of evolution, *Origin of the Species*.

9   Plato (428-348BC), the Athenian philosopher who formed the theory of eternal ideas was one of the great philosophical geniuses of all time. He became a disciple of Socrates but later became increasingly opposed to Sophist doctrines. His major works include *The Republic*; *Laws*; *Phaedo* and *Crito*.

René Descartes, (1596-1650) was a French rationalist philosopher and mathematician. He sort to achieve a unitary universal science using geometrical methods. Widely regarded as father of modern philosophy, he wrote such works as *Discourse on Method*, 1637 and *Meditations*, 1641.

Jürgen Habermas, (b 1929) a German philosopher, was the theorist representative of the Frankfurt school in the postwar era.

10   Democritus (460-370BC) was the greatest naturalist philosopher of ancient Greece. He developed and systematised an atomic theory of the universe.

The Roman politician, Critias (b 5BC), was a friend and disciple of Socrates. One of Plato's most famous dialogues, the *Crito*, is named after him. This represents Crito's dialogue with Socrates on the nature of citizenship and a citizen's duty to obey the law.

Epicurus (341-270BC) was a Greek philosopher who founded a school in Mytilene in around 311BC. He is respected as one who advocated relief to the soul. He taught that *ataraxia*, seeking pleasure and avoiding disturbance and pain, is the supreme good.

11 In 1675 Gottfried Wilhelm Leibniz, (1646-1716) the German philosopher and mathematician, single-handedly established calculus. His major work was *Metaphysics*.

Baruch de Spinoza, (1632-77) was a Dutch philosopher and theologian who used geometrical methods to develop, deductively, a consummate theory of monism and pantheism in which mind and matter were seen as aspects of God. His main work is *Ethica (Ethics Demonstrated in Geometrical Order)*, 1663.

The Austrian philosopher, Ludwig Wittgenstein (1889-1951), was active mainly in England. He claimed that philosophy was not theory but linguistic criticism, a 'language game' analysing the relationship of language to the world. His *Philosophical Investigations*, is an album of arguments compiled in a solitary hut on the Galway coast in Ireland in 1948.

12 The French philosopher, Gilles Deleuze's (b 1925) major works include *Differénce et Répétition, Anti-Oedipus, Capitalism* and *Schizophrenia*. See note 1, Chapter III.

13 Ilya Prigogine, (b 1917) is a Belgian physicist and scientist. Born in Moscow, he pursues a unified physics/chemistry of nonequilibrium open systems. He discovered dissipative structures, reactions in biochemistry that increase in complexity rather than decrease, thus providing a theoretical framework for the origin of life. In 1977 he received Nobel prize for chemistry.

The German physicist, Hermann Haken (b 1927), was a leader in the theory of biophysics in post-World War II West Germany. He created synergetics, arguing spontaneous creation of order in a random system. His most significant works included *Synergetics; Nonequilibrium phase transitions and self-organisation in physics, chemistry and biology*.

Theodor Wiesengrund Adorno, (1903-69), the German philosopher and sociologist, fled to America to escape Nazi persecution. He wrote *The Authoritarian Personality* and returned to Germany in 1949. Together with Max Horkheimer he established Social Research Institute.

14 Umberto Eco, (b 1932), the Italian critic and semiologist, is an important member of New Avant Garde School. He is noted for his historical novel *The Name of the Rose*, 1981.

Karlheinz Stockhausen, (b 1928) is a German composer and theorist, who creates electronic music with Cologne's electronic music studio, which he co-founded.

Pierre Boulez, (b 1925) is a French composer and conductor who in 1971 became the musical director of the New York Philharmonic and BBC Symphony Orchestra.

Chapter II
Symbiosis in Economy

1   Japan Inter-Design Forum (ed), *Kyosei no Jidai*, Kodansha Ltd, Tokyo, 1981. Kurokawa's principal lecture, 'Towards the Age of Symbiosis', is included in this volume. In addition, the reasons for selecting the theme 'Towards the Age of Symbiosis' are discussed in the afterword to the book.

2   Kisho Kurokawa, *Kyosei no Shiso (Philosophy of Symbiosis)*, Tokuma Shoten Publishing Co Ltd, Tokyo, 1987. Revised edition, 1991.

3   Kisho Kurokawa, *Hanasuki – Reflections on Traditional Architecture*, Shokoshu-sha Publishing Co Ltd, Tokyo, 1991.

4   Kisho Kurokawa (ed), *Rikyu Nezumi Ko: Ryogisei no Geijutsu (Rikyu Grey: Art of Ambiguity)*, Geijutsu Shincho, Tokyo, June 1978. Also, Kisho Kurokawa, *Guree no Bunka (Cultures of Grey)*, Soseiki Publishing Co Ltd, Tokyo, 1977; Kisho Kurokawa, *Michi no Kenchiku – Chukan Ryoiki e (Architecture of the Street: Towards intermediate Space)*, Maruzen Co Ltd, Tokyo, 1983.

5   Kisho Kurokawa, *Metabolism in Architecture*, Studio Vista, London, 1977.

6 *Newsweek*, Japanese Edition, TBS Britannica Co, Tokyo, October 1989, no 19.

7 Akio Morita, 'Crisis on Japanese Management', *Bungei Shunju*, Bungei Shunju Co Ltd, Tokyo, February 1992.

8 Tsuneo Iida *Kyosei wa Caruteru no Betsumei (Symbiosis: Another Name for Cartel)*, The Nihon Keizai Shimbun, Tokyo, August 4th, 1992.

9 Kisho Kurokawa, *Intercultural Architecture: The Philosophy of Symbiosis*, Academy Editions, London, 1990.

Chapter III
Transcending Modernism

1 Gilles Deleuze (b 1925) is professor of philosophy at the University of Paris. His philosophical method is characterised by a rejection of the theories of consciousness of traditional metaphysics and a focus on will and desire, from which he proceeds to analyse modern society. In *Anti-Oedipus*, co-authored with Felix Guattari (see below), he postulates the two principles of schizophrenia and paraphrenia in contemporary society. According to Deleuze, the 'modern intellect', which seeks to know all, ignores the fact that life itself is inherently anti-hierarchical. In modern capitalist society, the desire to see all existence as orderly has become an independent entity that intervenes between people and is reborn as a feeling of pressure and anxiety.

   Felix Guattari (b 1930) is a psychoanalyst at the Borde clinic. He has also been in the forefront of the development of a new, revolutionary psychoanalysis in the face of the largely British-American reaction against psychoanalysis in general.

2 Jacques Lacan (1901-81), under the banner 'Return to Freud' established a structuralist psychoanalysis by interpreting

patients' non-intellectual accounts on the symbolic levels of metaphor and suggestion. In Lacan's thought, the signifier – that which transmits meaning – is given precedence over the signified – the content of meaning – and the former is represented by S while the latter is represented by s. In other words, for Lacan it was not the content that was important but the symbolic expression of content, its linkings, its condensations, its displacement as an event. He placed less importance on the individual and more on the unconscious call from the S; here it was the language functioned, and it was in this dimension that the human being was created. Lacan's seminars were attended by many contemporary intellectuals, including Guattari and Louis Althusser, and his ideas had a great influence on the post-structuralist movement.

3   René Girard (b 1923) found the image of the scapegoat at the core of human culture and also developed a theory of culture as the 'imitation of desire'. According to Girard, desire cannot exist on the level of the individual. He offers the love triangle as an example. In a love triangle, the desire of B for C is linked to B's awareness that A desires C. In this triangle of desire, a reciprocal imitation of desire is carried out, and this paradigmatic relationship extends infinitely to encompass the entire world until it produces a violent confusion, exposing all groups of human beings to danger. In reaction, the natural defence mechanisms of these groups are activated and the reciprocal imitations of the groups of human beings are transferred to a relation between the group and one individual, and that individual's relations to other individuals. This individual becomes a scapegoat and the symbol of the evil which has brought chaos to the group. At the same time, he is a symbol of the group's salvation. The scapegoat possesses an ambivalent significance. Girard points to Jesus Christ as an example of the scapegoat. He also seeks to liberate contemporary society from this scapegoat phenomenon.

4   Jacques Attali (b 1943), professor of economic theory at the University of Paris, has been active in the French Socialist Party since Francois Mitterrand became president in 1981. Transcending the traditional boundaries of economics through his research into semantics, cultural anthropology and sociology, he has attempted to deconstruct orthodox economic theory into new paradigms.

5   Claude Lévi-Strauss (b 1908) held that we must observe phenomena not from an established theory but from the perspective of their own structure. The system of distinctions among phenomena is their structure; existence is the system of relationships among different things. Lévi-Strauss applied these ideas to the study of anthropology, especially kinship relationships and mythology. He is sharply critical of the modern notion of the self as a discrete entity, and refuses to accord a higher value to the entity of 'civilisation' than to the entity he calls 'the unknown'. He discovered so called 'uncivilised thinking', that is, non-rational thought, and revealed that the equation of thinking with rationality only applies within the context of European culture; he went on to criticise the principles of substance and existence, based on rationality, as an oppressive ideology.

6   Yamaguchi Masao (b 1931) has, from the 1970s, been investigating new ways of perceiving the problems of linguistics and cultural anthropology. Among his concepts is that of the core and the periphery. Yamaguchi claims that a culture develops more from the power of its periphery, which energises the culture as a whole, than from a concentration of power in its core. The core forever tries to reject the periphery, and the periphery continues to stimulate and enliven the core. The ambivalence of the relationship between core and periphery is to be found in all binomial relations: the sacred and the profane, heaven and earth, order and chaos, man and woman, regulation and freedom.

7   CIAM was founded in 1928 at Las Sarras, Switzerland. The Athens Declaration outlined the social principles of city planning.

8   Le Corbusier (1887-1965) was born in Switzerland, but was active as an architect in France. He is also famous as a painter and writer. In architecture, his work spanned many areas, from residential housing design to city planning. He was also a major theorist of Modern architecture and set forth its five principles: the *pilotis*, independent skeleton structures, unobstructed interior space, self-supporting walls and rooftop gardens.

9   Jan Mukarovsky was a Czech dialectical thinker of the 1930s. Mukarovsky held that while a structure possesses a tendency towards integrity that preserves its continuity and establishes regularity it also possesses factors that seek to destroy that integrity. A structure is forever repeating a cycle of stability, upset and restoration. The internal integrity of a structure is preserved by the opposition of the forces of harmony (affirmation) and conflict (negation), but Mukarovsky places the greater emphasis on negation. In other words, the dominant structural elements are renewed through the introduction of negation of tension into the system, and the subsequent upset of the system's balance. In this model, structure is always in the midst of reformation.

10 Maurice Merleau-Ponty (1908-61) was a French philosopher and essayist. He began as a political realist akin to Sartre and evolved into an existential idealist. His thought is characterised by an enthusiasm and a fascination with visible, tangible reality.

11 Paraphrased by the author.

12 See Chapter IX for a further discussion of the Consciousness Only school of Buddhist philosophy and the *alaya* consciousness.

13 William Morris (1834-96), the English poet, painter, craftsman and social reformer established the manufacturing and decorating firm Morris, Marshall, Faulkner & Company in 1861 and then embarked on the production of room interiors, stained glass, metalwork and wallpaper. He was opposed to industrialisation and sought to bring beauty to daily life through the handicrafts. As a poet and artist, he promoted medievalism in the midst of the Gothic revival of the nineteenth century and believed that was possible in the context of socialism.

14 Peter Behrens (1868-1940) was a German architect who was a leading influence in the emergence of Modern architecture. His style evolved from Art Nouveau to a highly modern purism. Gropius, Le Corbusier and Mies van der Rohe worked in his office in the 1920s. Tony Garnier (1869-1948) was a French architect who pioneered the use of reinforced concrete and is known in France as the father of Modern architecture. Auguste Perret (1874-1954) started out as an engineer and, together with Garnier, developed reinforced concrete into an acceptable building material. His later style had neoclassical affinities. Le Corbusier and other famous architects worked in his atelier.

15 Arthur Koestler (1905-83) was imprisoned as a spy in 1937 during the Spanish Civil War. He claimed to have experienced 'the third reality' in prison. Koestler writes in *The Holon Revolution*:

> The third reality cannot be explained on either the perceptual or conceptual levels. It is like a magical meteorite perceived by primitive man streaking across the round dome of the heavens, and it is when we have occasion to gain access to that level that we encounter occult phenomena . . . Just as we cannot feel the pull of a magnet with our skin, we cannot hope to understand this ultimate level of reality through language. It is a text written with invisible ink.

Koestler's essay, 'The Tree and the Candle', was published in

Unity Through Diversity – a collection of papers published to commemorate the seventieth anniversary of the birth of Ludwig von Bertalanffy, the originator of general systems theory.

16 David Bohm (b 1917) is an American physicist. He has suggested that both mind and matter have an 'implicate order', which links the two. Bohm uses the image of a drop of ink in a glass of water. If we stir slowly, the ink will spread out until part and whole are completely inseparable. This is the world of implicate order. If we could slowly stir the water backwards, the ink would slowly separate from the water and return to its form as a single drop, becoming a part again, a distinct phenomenon. According to Bohm, this is the process through which atomic particles are formed, as well as mental process and nerve impulses.

17 Suzuki Daisetz (1870-1966) is perhaps the best-known populariser of Zen in the West. According to Suzuki, the total self-identity of 'I am I' is the state of non-time and is equivalent to the emptiness of Buddhist philosophy. In that state, the mountain is the mountain. I see it as it is; it sees me as I am. In other words, my experience of seeing the mountain is identical to the mountain seeing me. From this, Suzuki moves to the conclusion that absolute subjectivity is identical to absolute objectivity. That which is inside me is at the same time that which stands opposed to and outside of me. Human beings and nature, God and nature, are one, and the many and the one are also one. In this way, Suzuki arrives at an absolute monism.

18 Miura Baien (1723-89) was a doctor by profession, but studied a wide range of subjects, from Confucianism to traditional astronomy to mathematics. The originality and profundity of Baien's trilogy marks him as a universal philosopher who transcends all genres and his age.

19 By Professor Hiroto Saigusa of Tokyo University, in his *Philosophy of Miura Baien*, 1953.

Chapter IV
Edo, the Pretext for the Age of Symbiosis

1 Shitamachi, the 'low city' or 'downtown', is now east central
   and northeast Tokyo. It was traditionally where townsmen
   and craftsmen lived, as opposed to the feudal lords and their
   entourages, who lived 'in the hills', the Yamanote area. The
   Shitamachi district preserves more of the old character of
   Tokyo-Edo than other parts of the city.

2 Yamagata Banto (1748-1821) was a scholar of the merchant
   class. He was adopted at thirteen by his uncle and moved to
   Osaka, where he became the manager of a rice business.
   While carrying on his trade he also studied Confucianism,
   astronomy and Western science, or Rangaku, and wrote
   Instead of Dreams. This work is divided into twelve sections,
   on astronomy, geography, mythology, history, government
   policies, economics and other subjects. The section on
   astronomy is especially well-known. Banto's achievements as
   an economist and a thinker rank him with his contemporaries
   in Europe, America and Asia.

   Shizuku Tadao (1760-1808) was a scholar of Western
   science, or Rangaku, who translated many Dutch works in
   addition to his own writings. His main work is *Reki Sho Shin
   Sho*, a translation from Dutch of an original English commen-
   tary on Newton's *Principia*. The theory of the Earth's movement appears there, and Tadao's appended theory of the
   origin of stars rivals the Kant-Laplace hypothesis.

3 Ino Tadataka (1745-1818) is famous as a cartographer,
   although until he was fifty he was the manager of a brewery. It
   was only after retirement that he began to study astronomy,
   geography and mathematics and began drawing maps. In
   sixteen years starting from 1800, he spent 3,736 days travelling around Japan and charted 43,708 terrestrial miles, taking
   hundreds of thousands of readings. His maps are accurate to
   about a thousandth of a degree. Ino's maps became the

standard maps of the country during the Meiji era.

4   Joruri is Japanese puppet theatre, also called Bunraku. In the
    Joruri theatres, serious dramas were enacted for an audience
    of adults. The large puppets were eventually operated by
    three puppeteers dressed in black and visible from the waist
    up. The drama was accompanied by a ballad narrative called
    Joruri, which gave its name to the theatrical genre.

5   The dates of Toshusai Sharaku's birth and death are unknown,
    but he was active in the late Edo period. His output of more
    than 140 prints is concentrated between May 1794 and
    January 1795; after that we know very little more of him.
    Various theories about his true identity have been suggested,
    but there is not enough evidence to confirm any of them.

6   The Rimpa school of painting started around 1600 by Sotatsu,
    also associated with his contemporary Hon'ami Koetsu. The
    paintings of this school are characterised by their decorative-
    ness, delicate shading and colouring and the abstraction of
    their layout and design. Though the Rimpa painters were keen
    observers of nature, their work is highly stylised. Sotatsu was
    active in Kyoto from 1600 to 1640. Hon'ami Koetsu (1558-
    1637) was widely admired for his calligraphy, pottery and
    lacquer designs, and encouraged Sotatsu by giving him many
    painting commissions. Ogata Korin (1658-1716) is known for
    his gorgeous screen paintings in rich colours against gold
    grounds. Ogata Kenzan (1663-1743) was a potter as well as a
    painter, and combined the rigour of the Chinese literati style
    of painting with Japanese decorativeness.

7   *Kumadori* make-up, in contrast to the make-up of Peking
    Opera, for example, is based on the muscles of the face,
    abstracted in stylisation. It is said to have been influenced by
    the iconography of Buddhist images, especially those of
    fierce guardian deities such as Fudo Myoo.

8   Suzuki Harunobu (died 1770) was the originator of the multicoloured woodblock print, or *nishiki-e*. In addition to his prints of beautiful women (*bijinga*), he designed many scenes of loving couples and sights of daily life about town. He is often regarded as having introduced the sophistication of aristocratic art into the woodblock print, but his role in commercialising the print is probably even more important.

9   Fukugawa still exists, though no longer a red-light district. As a brothel district, it had a reputation for a lower (and cheaper) class of courtesan than its rivals in Yoshiwara and Shinagawa. Many courtesans took male professional names and they developed a refined and satiric dandyism that Edoites enjoyed immensely.

10 Kobayashi Rekisai (1884-1959) was a maker of miniatures, including tiny, perfectly crafted ink boxes, incense stands, dressers, samisens and other furniture and accessories.

11 *Maki-e* is a process in which mother-of-pearl, gold dust and other decorations are embedded in lacquerware, creating beautiful painterly designs.

12 *Komon* means small crest or design. Edo *komon* is characterised by a repeated pattern of tiny motifs, produced with a paste-resist dyeing technique.

13 In the *shoin* style of residential palace architecture, several large buildings are linked by elevated, roofed corridors. The main building is open to the south, and the typical *shoin* layout forms a U, with a garden including a pond enclosed in its middle. The design details of *shoin*-style architecture are relatively formal and elaborate.

14 The Flying Cloud Pavilion is located in the southeastern corner of the Nishi Honganji temple compound. It is said to have originally been part of Toyotomi Hideyoshi's Juraku no

Tei Palace, which would mean Hiunkaku was built around 1586 or 1587, although another theory suggests it was built in the early 1600s. It has an unconventional design, containing *shoin*-style rooms, a steam bath and a famous tea room.

15 The *soan* style refers to the simplest and most austere type of tea house or tea room design, in which the structure is modelled after a hermit's hut. Simple, homely materials are used in a style that is at once rough and highly sophisticated.

16 From the tenth century in Japan a theory was current that stated that Buddhist deities truly existed and Shinto deities did not; what appeared to be a Shinto deity was only the manifestation of a Buddhist deity in Shinto form. This doctrine was an attempt to establish the pre-eminence of Buddhism over the native religion. It resulted in a duplication of deities: a multivalence of the sacred.

17 The 'Civilisation' prints showed scenes of the latest Western inventions (railroads, steamboats, curling irons), fashions, and even scenes of Westerners and Western capitals. The Yokohama prints specialised in scenes of Westerners and their activities in the port of Yokohama, where a Western settlement had been established.

Chapter V
Hanasuki, the Aesthetic of Symbiosis

1 A tea room in Japan is, of course, a unique architectural unit where the tea ceremony and related arts such as flower arrangement are practised. However, it is also a place for quiet contemplation and the appreciation of works of calligraphy, painting and ceramics. *An* means 'hut' and is often used to describe a tea room or tea house.

2 These key terms in Japanese aesthetics are notoriously

difficult to define in English. *Wabi* suggests a highly austere, severe aesthetic of a sort of sacred poverty. *Sabi* carries additional connotations of sadness and loneliness, reflection and isolation. These highly emotional 'sensibilities' – for they are not rigorously defined concepts in any sense – are more often associated with each other than accurately distinguished. They are applied to a wide range of visual, plastic and literary arts.

3   Shokado Shojo (1584-1639) took up residence in Takimotobo when he was seventeen. Later he became the head monk of Takimotobo, but he is better known for his tea room and collection of tea utensils, paintings and works of calligraphy, now preserved at Iwashimizu Hachimangu. Shokado is also credited as the inventor of the traditional Japanese lunch box, the *bento*. This is a rectangular lacquer box divided into four compartments for rice and various foods. Shokado was a noted connoisseur and man of taste of his age.

4   Kan'unken was built in the style favoured by Kobori Enshu. Though destroyed in 1773, it was reconstructed in almost identical fashion in 1922, and the tea room in Takimotobo today is that reconstruction. It is often confused with another tea house designed by Shojo, which stands on the property of the Atsuda family in Kyoto and is called the Shokado. The latter tea house was built by Shojo in his last years, after retiring from Takimotobo to take up residence in Izumibo.

5   Kobori Enshu (1579-1647) was a member of the samurai class, but best known as a master of the tea ceremony. He is the founder of one of the schools of tea, and he was also commissioned by the Tokugawa shogunate and the imperial house to design major works of architecture, such as the dungeons of Edo Castle and Nagoya Castle, the central compound of Fushimi Castle, and the Sento Gosho palace, as well as many gardens and tea rooms. He introduced his personal aesthetic preference, which he called *kirei sabi*, or

gorgeous *sabi*, into the tea ceremony. The private library of Horiguchi Sutemi, editor of the encyclopaedic *Chashitsu Okoshiezu Shu* (*Fold-out Plans of Tea Rooms*), contains a work called *Sukiyashiki* (*Sukiya Mansions*), which includes a floor plan with the legend 'The Takimotobo in Hachimangu shrine is built from the same plan as Enshu's Fushimi tea room'. *Sukiya* is a style of architecture characterised by a sophisticated taste that blends the formal and informal, the heavy and the light. It was strongly influenced by the evolving aesthetic of the tea ceremony and is the dominant style of non-official architecture in the Edo period. *Suki* means 'taste' or 'style' and is used in compounds such as *eabisuki* and the author's neologism *hanasuki*.

6 A *daime*-sized mat was slightly smaller than an ordinary tatami mat. It was usually the size of the space from the host's mat to the *daisu* tea-utensil stand.

7 A *kaiki* is a detailed record *(ki)* of a tea gathering *(kai)*. The *Matsuya Kaiki* is one of the most valuable of these records, as a rich historical source for the development of the aesthetic of the tea ceremony.

8 Designed by Oda Uraku, this tea room is a national treasure and survives in the Urakuen of Oyama castle town in Oyama City, Aichi Prefecture. It is said to be the *sukiya*-style portion of the retirement residence that Oda Uraku built in the Shoden'in at Kenninji in Kyoto. The name derives from Oda's Christian name, Joao, which he received upon his baptism in that faith. In 1908 the tea room was brought to the Mitsui residence, and in 1971 reconstructed at its present site.

9 Oda Uraku (1547-1621) was the eleventh son of the warlord Oda Nobuhide and the younger brother of Oda Nobunaga, who ruled Japan in the mid-sixteenth century. Born Oda Nagamasu, he adopted the name Uraku, by which he is usually known, after joining the Buddhist order. He survived

the reigns of his brother and the two rulers who came after him in succession, Toyotomi Hideyoshi and Tokugawa Ieyasu, and was made a feudal lord of a moderate-sized domain. His line continued on through to the Meiji period. The names of the present Tokyo districts Yuraku-cho and Sukiyabashi derive from his mansion, which was located in those areas. He is also the founder of the Uraku school of the tea ceremony.

10 Yuin is one of the tea rooms in Kyoto's Urasenke school of tea compound.

11 Nambo Sokei was a master of the tea ceremony from the port of Sakai, near modern Osaka. He was active during the rules of Oda Nobunaga and Toyotomi Hideyoshi. He describes himself as a Zen monk, the second-generation head priest of the Shuun'an at Nanshuji. He was the foremost disciple of Sen no Rikyu and regarded as his successor, but disappeared after the third annual memorial observance of Rikyu's death. He was completely devoted to the aesthetic expression through the art of tea of his Zen ethic of 'pure poverty'. The *Nampo Roku* is a secretly transmitted manual of Sen no Rikyu's school of tea, regarded as having been composed by Nambo Sokei. The earliest copy we have of the work is in the hand of Tachibana Jitsuzan, a senior minister of the Kuroda clan in Fukuoka fief. Because of the strange 'coincidence' that the work was discovered on the one-hundred-year anniversary of Rikyu's death its authenticity is suspect. Nevertheless, it offers an accurate record of the world of tea, and based on this work, Jitsuzan founded the Nambo school of tea. Though the Tachibana family line terminated eight generations later, the school has continued to be active in Kyoto and other areas as the Namboryu Meikyoan school.

Takeno Joo (1502-55) was a wealthy merchant of the port city of Sakai who made a name for himself as a leader and patron of the art of tea. He was the teacher of the great tea masters of the age, including Imai Sokyu, Tsuda Sogyu and Sen no Rikyu. With his wealth to support his innovations, he introduced the aesthetics of the linked-poetry (*renga*) gatherings which had been popular for many years, and brought Zen to the tea ceremony. He is the leading figure in the period of the evolution of the so-called *wabi*-style tea ceremony (*wabi cha*). His three followers mentioned above were also all from merchant families, and they eventually became tea masters for the samurai class and spread the art far and wide.

The major masters and schools of tea are as follows: Murata Jouou (1422-1502); Oda Uraku (1547-1621); Furuta Oribe (1544-1615); Hosokawa Sansai (1563-1645) and Kobori Enshu (1579-1647).

Fujiwara no Teika (or Sadaie; 1162-1241) was a distinguished poet and compiler of the *Shin Kokin Shu*. He is renowned for his critical writings. The full title of the anthology is the *Shin Kokin Waka Shu*, or *New Anthology of Ancient and Modern Poetry*. Compiled by Fujiwara no Teika in around 1205, it is one of the greatest of the twenty-one imperial poetry anthologies.

12 Robert H Bower and Earl Miner, *Japanese Court Poetry*, Stanford University Press, 1971, p307.

13 The *daisu* was a tea utensil stand used in the elaborate and formal tea ceremony of the aristocrat's mansion (*shoin*), which was practised before the spread of the much simpler tea ceremony of Murata Juko. By the time of the *wabi*-style tea ceremony, the *daisu* was usually no longer set in the much smaller tea room.

14 Murata Juko (1422-1502) is regarded as the founder of the tea ceremony. After becoming a monk at Shomyoji in Nara, he returned to lay status and began to practise the art of tea. He is not directly linked to Sen no Rikyu or his followers and descendants, but he is the undisputed founder of the Way of *wabi*-style tea. He was instructed in Zen by the famous monk Ikkyu Sojun, and he was also a curator of Chinese art and tea master to Ashikaga Yoshimasa, the shogun. He created a tea

for the common people based on his deep knowledge of the tea ceremony as it was practised among the elite.

15 A record of Rikyu's life, compiled by Rikyu's first disciple, *Yamanoue Soji Ki* (1544-90). Soji was also Toyotomi Hideyoshi's tea master, but he was of extremely unattractive appearance and had a sharp tongue, which eventually led to him being dismissed from Hideyoshi's service. He became the guest of the Hojo clan in Odawara (in modern Kanagawa Prefecture) and spread the way of tea there. When Hideyoshi attacked the Hojo, Soji had his ears and nose cut off.

16 Tanizaki Jun'ichior, *In Praise of Shadows*, Thomas J Harper and Edward G Seidensticker (translation), Tokyo, Charles E Tuttle Co, pp13-14.

17 Matsuo Basho (1644-94) is the most famous haiku poet. He travelled throughout Japan composing haiku and poetical prose called *haibun*, and he also contributed significantly to the aesthetics of these genres.

18 Mukai Kyorai (1651-1704) was Basho's disciple. Basho placed great faith in him and he was the editor of the collection of haiku called *Sarumino* (*Monkey's Raincoat*). Kyorai's greatest achievements, however, were in criticism and theory of the haiku. He was born in the samurai class, but gave up his status to become a yin-yang diviner, which remained his profession for the rest of his life.

19 *Kyorai Sho* is Kyorai's masterwork, in which he identifies and discusses many of the distinctive properties of the haiku and *haibun* genres, including 'unchanging flux'.

20 Zeami (1363-1443) was a Noh actor, theorist, director and composer. Together with his father Kan'ami, he created the theatrical genre of Noh. Zeami made his first real debut as a performer at the age of twelve, when he and his father

performed for the shogun Ashikaga Yoshimasu, who was much taken with Zeami. Yoshimasu showed such affection for and protection of Zeami that it was widely believed they were lovers. Zeami based his Noh on that of his father, which had a broad popular appeal, but he placed a tremendous emphasis on beauty and raised the art to great heights. After suffering persecution from Yoshimasu's successor, Zeami increased the intellectual content of Noh, formulating the art as we have it today.

Fushi Kaden is a systemisation of the theories of Noh that Zeami had inherited from his father. It is a practical work, dividing the life of an actor into seven periods and prescribing the correct practice for each one. Zeami composed *Kakyo* when persecution by the new shogun threatened to destroy his theatrical troupe; it contains the marrow of Zeami's thoughts. The 'flower' (*ka*) found in the titles of both works refers to the power to continue to be attractive on the Noh stage, and it is related to Zeami's key concept of the ideal of beauty: *yugen*, or dark mystery.

21 J Thomas Rimer and Masakazu Yamazaki, (translation), *On the Art of the Noh Drama: The Major Treatises of Zeami*, Princeton University Press, 1984, p12.

22 Sen no Rikyu (1522-91) was born into a merchant family in Sakai, the port city near Osaka. He studied tea under Takeno Joo. When Oda Nobunaga demanded payment of a huge indemnity from Sakai, Rikyu and Imai Sogyu were sent as members of a party to negotiate a settlement. After Nobunaga's death, Rikyu became the tea master of Toyotomi Hideyoshi. Rikyu is known as the great formulator of the art of tea; we owe the transmission of the art of tea down to the present not only to his aesthetic vision but also to his success in promoting tea among high-ranking samurai. His seven disciples, most of them of samurai origin, are called the Seven Sages of Rikyu, and he also taught tea to such well-known feudal lords as Date Masamune. Rikyu's increasing political influence may have

played a part in Hideyoshi's decision to sentence him to death by *seppuku*, or self-disembowelment.

23 Furuta Oribe (1544-1615) was of samurai birth, and he served under both Oda Nobunaga and Toyotomi Hideyoshi, rising to a fairly high rank in the feudal hierarchy. Oribe studied under Rikyu, but he adapted Rikyu's style of tea, which was essentially quietist, finding beauty in stillness, to a more dynamic style that would please members of his class. He is said to have purposely broken tea utensils and had them repaired with gold. His disciples included Kobori Enshu and Hon'ami Koetsu, and a type of ceramics has been named after him. He was tea master to the second Tokugawa shogun, Hidetada, but when, at the age of seventy-two, his involvement in plans for a *coup d'etat* in Osaka was discovered he was condemned to commit suicide.

24 En'an, or Swallow Hut, was designed by Furuta Oribe and survives, designated as an important cultural property. It is located in Kyoto, on the grounds of one of the subsects of the Yabunouchi school of tea. It was destroyed by fire in 1864 and rebuilt three years later. The 'crawl-in entrance' (*nijiriguchi*) is at the southeast corner, under eaves over an earthen floor. A three-mat guest area is bracketed by the host's mat by an area for retainers. This area for retainers, separated from the guest area by two sliding doors, is a unique feature of this tea room and represents a layout favoured by the samurai class.

25 Bruno Taut (1880-1938), the German expressionist architect, moved to Japan in 1933. He extolled what he called 'emperor art', by which he meant Katsura Detached Palace and Ise Shrine, as opposed to 'shogun art', referring to the Toshogu shrine at Nikko. His writings include the book *Nippon*. Taut left Japan in 1936 to teach in Istanbul. The German architect Walter Gropius (1883-1969), began with industrial architecture based on the techniques of modern industry, and, while advocating progressive and rational architecture, sought a

unification of the hand crafts and the industrial arts. While director of the Bauhaus, he assembled many creative personalities, such as Wassily Kandinsky, Oskar Schlemmer, Paul Klee and Laszlo Moholy-Nagy, and sought to create a unified design for Modern architectural space. He and his writings form one of the bases of the Modern Movement.

The Katsura Detached Palace was originally a seventeenth-century country villa of the Hachijo no Miya family. There are four sections to the main house, and four pavilions, several belvederes and a Buddhist chapel arranged throughout the gardens. A combination of *shoin* (palatial) and *sukiya* styles, it is regarded by many as the finest example of residential architecture in Japan.

26 The Grand Ise Shrine is located at Ise in Mie Prefecture and is one of the two or three most important shrines in Japan. It is associated with the imperial deity, the Sun Goddess Amaterasu. Made of unpainted Japanese cypress wood, it has a bold and simple design suggestive of South Pacific architecture. Ise Shrine is dismantled and rebuilt every twenty-one years, always following the same special Shinto architectural style, though some changes have crept in over the centuries.

27 The Toshogu Shrine at Nikko serves as the mausoleum of Tokugawa Ieyasu, the founder of the Tokugawa shogunate, who ruled Japan from 1600 to 1868. It was completed in 1636, and the shrine buildings and gateways are highly decorative and ornate.

28 Okamoto Taro (b 1911) is a painter, sculptor and designer of monuments. Born into an artistic family, he spent his youth in Paris, studying at the Sorbonne. After his return to Japan he fought in the Second World War in China, and when the war was over became active not only in the art world but in politics and as a writer and critic. His sculptures include the *Tower of the Sun* at the Osaka Expo and the sculptures decorating the

Children's Castle in Aoyama, Tokyo. His writings include *Nihon Saihakken (Rediscovering Japan)* and *Wasurareta Nihon: Okinawa Bunka Ron (Forgotten Japan: A Theory of Okinawan Culture)*.

29 The Jomon period, from about 10,000BC to 300BC, (Japan's Neolithic period), is characterised by the dynamic and dramatic clay figurines and pottery that have been discovered dating from that time. 'Jomon' means rope patterns, which are one of the commonly found decorative techniques on pottery dating from this period. The following Yayoi period, from about 300BC to 300AD, was when rice production was first introduced to Japan. Its pottery is much simpler and more austere and delicate.

30 Toshodaiji was founded in 759 in the western sector of Nara by the Chinese monk Jianzhen, and Todaiji was built between 710 and 784 in the eastern sector of the same city by Emperor Shomu.

Chapter VI
Rikyu Grey and the Art of Ambiguity

1 Earl Miner, *An Introduction to Japanese Court Poetry*, Stanford, Stanford University Press, 1968, p104.

2 *Ibid,* p25.

3 Translation from Ryusaku Tsunoda, et al, eds, *Sources of Japanese Tradition*, New York, Columbia University Press, 1964), Vol 1, p285.

4 William Empson, *Seven Types of Ambiguity*, New York, Penguin Books. Reprint 1977, pp5-6.

Chapter VIII
Intermediary Space

1 This international magazine was founded by the Greek
   planner CA Doxiadis. The term *ekistics*, which he coined,
   means the study of human settlements and their problems
   from an interdisciplinary approach.

Chapter IX
The Philosophy of Consciousness Only and Symbiosis

1 This is articulated in the Upanishads, a group of sacred texts
   that have been appended to the Vedas, the ancient texts of the
   Brahman religion in India. One of the most striking teachings
   of the Upanishads is that each human being possesses an
   absolute self (*atman*) identical to the great universal self
   (*Brahma*), and that the two can be unified through religious
   practice. The Upanishads are also the first Indian texts to offer
   a theory of *karma*, or deeds and their results.

2 The *alaya* was conceived of as a stream of continuity, but in
   orthodox Buddhist philosophy it is said to be 'empty' – that is,
   have no substantial existence. The concept of the *alaya* is a
   recognition of process apart from substance.

3 Nagarjuna lived in the second century in southern India. Of
   Brahman birth, he converted to Mahayana Buddhism. The
   central concepts of Nagarjuna's writings are the 'mean' and
   emptiness. Emptiness means that no phenomenon has substantial existence; and the mean refers to the Middle Way
   between all dualistic extremes, such as illusion and enlightenment, or non-existence and existence.

4 Maitreya (not to be confused with the Boddhisattva of that
   name) was a Buddhist scholar of fourth-century India.
   Asanga, his pupil, also lived in the fourth century, and taught

that the stream of the *alaya* consciousness could be purified, transforming our consciousness into enlightenment itself. Asanga's brother Vasubhandhu was the most prolific writer of the three and with him the philosophy of Consciousness Only reached its completion. His doctrinal innovations included distinguishing the sense of self from the *alaya* consciousness and his encyclopaedic listing of the afflictions that pollute the human mind.

Chapter X
The Symbiosis of Man and Nature

1   Yoshida Kenko, *Essays in Idleness*, Donald Keene (translation), Columbia University Press, New York, 1967, p10. Kenko (c1283-1352) first served Emperor Gonijo as a poet and in various official posts, but at about thirty he retired from secular life to become a monk. In his forties he composed *Essays in Idleness*, in which he ably expressed the essence of the Japanese aesthetic. Kenko had a broad range of acquaintances, aristocratic and common, religious and lay, and including members of the rising samurai class. While his work laments the passing of courtly values, it also portends the changes that were soon to occur in Japanese society. The sensibility that Kenko formulates in *Essays in Idleness* combines the quiet splendour of court life depicted in *The Pillow Book of Sei Shonagon* with the strongly Buddhist colouring of *A Tale of a Ten-Foot-Square Hut* to define the aesthetic consciousness of the new age.

2   Noboru Kawazoe (b 1926) is an architectural critic and the director of the Kawazoe Research Institute. His main writings include *Tami to Kami no Sumai* (*The Dwellings of the People and the Gods*), *Kenchiku to Dento* (*Architecture and Tradition*), *Seikatsugaku no Teisho* (*A Proposal for a Science of Lifestyle*), and *Toshi Kukan no Bunka* (*The Culture of City Space*).

Chapter XI
The Philosophy of the Karakuri

1   Dr K Atsumi, 'New Concept – BIOMATION – Its Revolutionary
    Impact on Industry and Society', *Proceedings of Discoveries
    International Symposium*, OSU, 1982.

Chapter XII
From Post-Modernism to Symbiosis

1   Jean-François Lyotard *The Post-Modern Condition: A Report on
    Knowledge*, Geoff Bennington and Brian Massumi (transla-
    tion), University of Minnesota Press, Minneapolis, 1984. Lyotard
    (b 1924) is a French philosopher, a professor at Paris Uni-
    versity and Director of the International Institute of Philosophy.

2   Michel Foucault (1926-64) was a French philosopher, the
    author of such works as *The Order of Things* and *The
    Archaeology of Knowledge*. He was preoccupied with identi-
    fying the forces that underlie human institutions, and carried
    out studies on the treatment of the insane, criminals, and the
    history of human sexuality. In *The Archaeology of Knowledge*
    he suggests that different ages recognised different styles of
    knowledge.

3   Giambattista Piranesi (1720-78), the Italian architect and
    engraver, was active mostly in Rome and produced many
    views of that city, but he is best known for *Imaginary Prisons*,
    with its fantastic and macabre variations on Roman architecture.
        Antonio Sant'Elia (1888-1916) argued for a new architec-
    ture free from all past conventions, and exhibited his ideas as
    sketches in the 1914 Nuove Tendenze group exhibition under
    the title *New City*. His concepts were visionary, and though his
    work had few links to contemporary modern architecture,
    many of his ideas uncannily were realised decades later. He
    died in the First World War at the age of twenty-eight.

4   Ludwig Mies van der Rohe (1886-1969), the German-born architect and leader of the purist school of Modern architecture, succeeded Walter Gropius as director of the Bauhaus, was a pioneer of furniture design. In 1937 he emigrated to the United States and became a leading exponent of geometrical, abstract Modern architecture.

5   Roger Caillois, *Man and the Sacred*, Meyer Barash (translation), Greenwood, 1980.

6   Gilles Deleuze and Felix Guattari, *A Thousand Plateaus*, Brian Massumi (translation), Athlone, London, 1988, p25.

7   François Marie Charles Fourier (1772-1837) was a French social reformer and economist whose vision of a new society exercised considerable influence on later anarchists such as Kropotkin. In Fourier's ideal society, the central government merely facilitated transactions involving goods, and people were organised into mostly agricultural co-operatives called phalanxes. Each phalanx consisted of about 1,600 people, who lived in common buildings called phalansteries.

8   Edward Robert de Zurko, the American architect active in the 1950s, was professor in the Department of Architecture at the Rice Institute, University of Texas.
      Little is known of Vitruvius except that he is the author of the celebrated treatise *De Architectura*, (before 27BC). In that work, Vitruvius reveals himself as strongly Hellenistic and it was closely studied by Renaissance architects such as Bramante, Michelangelo and Vignola.
      Leon Battista Alberti (1404-72), the Italian humanist and architect, was active in the early Renaissance. His theories, set forth in the work *De Re Aedificatoria*, were quite influential, and his church of San Francesco at Rimini is based on them.
      Andrea Palladio (1508-80), the Italian architect who gave his name to the neoclassical Palladian style, was, with Vignola, one of the most important theorists of his time. His

love of Roman architecture and strongly classicist styles are reflected in the church of San Giorgio Maggiore and the magnificent Sta Maria della Salute in Venice.

9   Claude-Nicolas Ledoux (1736-1806) was a French architect active during and after the reign of Louis XVI. His designs are original and sometimes fantastic, based on simple geometrical forms.

Karl Friedrich Schinkel (1781-1841) was a German architect who revived Greek architecture in the early modern age. He was also a stage director and a fine painter of Romantic landscapes.

Horatio Greenough (1805-52) was an American neoclassical sculptor and architectural theorist, whose ideas presaged the development of functionalism.

10 Jean Baudrillard proclaimed in his *Consumer Society* that Capitalism had reached a dead end and we were entering an age in which symbols will be exchanged instead of goods. In subsequent works he has emphasised that we have reached the end of the age where symbols and their content are regarded as of equal value, and entered one of simulation, where symbols without content will be the medium of exchange. Baudrillard's conclusion is that views of economy and government based on production and labour will collapse, to be replaced by views of society based on consumption.

11 Yoshimitsu Morita (b 1950) is one of the leaders of Japan's 'New Wave' cinema. He first attracted wide attention with *No yo na Mono*, and went on to work in a variety of genres with great success. His next major work was *Kazoku Geemu*, followed by a film version of Natsume Soseki's novel *Sorekara*.

12 Ferdinand de Saussure (1857-1913) was a Swiss linguist who has had a fundamental influence on modern thought. In his incomplete *Research on Anagrams*, begun in his last years, de Saussure began to move from the study of the common code

that has been the object of linguistic study so far (*langue*) to 'speech as action' (*parole*).

13 Keigo Okonogi (b 1930) is a psychiatrist at Keio University Medical School. *Moratortiamu Ningen* earned him popular recognition, and he has written several other books on topics of wide interest, including *Katei no nai Kazoku no Jidai* (*The Age of Families Without Homes*) and *Jikoai Ningen* (*Self Love*).

14 Gaston Bachelard, *The New Scientific Spirit*, Arthur Goldhammer (translation), Beacon Press, 1985. The English translation is based on the Japanese edition of the book.

Chapter XIII
The Symbiosis of Redevelopment and Restoration

1 *Asahi Shimbun*, 6 Jan, 1987; 9 Jan, 1987; 16 Jan, 1987; 15 March, 1987.

2 New Tokyo Plan, 2025. The City of Symbiosis.

Chapter XIV
Towards the Evocation of Meaning

1 English version based on the Japanese translation by Yasuo Kobayashi

Epilogue
Liberation from Craving and Ignorance

1 Noboru Kawazoe, see note 2, Chapter X.
Masato Otaka (b 1923) is an architect and the director of the Otaka Kenchiku Sekkei firm. His main works include the redevelopment of Sakaide City in Kagawa Prefecture, the

Bunka Kaikan in Chiba Prefecture, the Prefectural Government Building in Tochigi Prefecture, the Gumma Prefectural Museum of History, the Fukushima Prefectural Museum of Art, and the redevelopment of Motomachi in Hiroshima City.

Fumihiko Maki (b 1929) is an architect and the director of the Maki and Associates firm. A graduate of Tokyo University, his main works are the Toyota Memorial Lecture Hall at Nagoya University, the Kumatani campus of Rissho University, the Daikanyama Housing Complex, the library of the Hiyoshi Campus of Keio University, the Spiral Building, and the Kyoto National Museum of Modern Art.

Kiyofumi Kikutake (b 1928) is an architect and director of the Kikutake Kiyofumi Kenchiku Sekkei firm. His main works include the Izumo Taisha building, the Kyoto Community Bank, Aquapolis, the Tanabe Art Museum, and the Karuizawa Takanawa Art Museum.

Kiyoshi Awazu (b 1929) is a graphic designer and the director of the Awazu Design Institute. He is a professor at Musashino College of Art and a member of the planning committee for the National Ethnological Museum in Osaka. His writings include: *Dezain ni nani ga Dekiru ka? (What Can Design Do?)*, *Gaudí Sanka (A Tribute to Gaudí)*, and a collection of his works.

Kenji Ekuan (b 1929) is an industrial designer and the president of the GK Industrial Design Institute and the head of the Kuwasawa Research Institute. He was a special consultant for the design of the exhibits at the Tsukuba International Science Fair and the producer for the Japan IBM exhibit. His major writings include *Dogu Ko (On Tools)*, *Indasutoriaru Dezain (Industrial Design)*, *Makunouchi Bento no Bigakau (The Aesthetics of the Box Lunch)*, and *Dogu no Shiso (The Philosophy of Tools)*.

Shomei Tomatsu (b 1930) is a photographer. In the sixties, his work focused on street scenes in Tokyo and he is regarded as the founder of that genre in Japan. He received the Ministry of Education special prize for his work, including *Tuiyo no Empitsu (The Sun's Pencil)* and *11:02 Nagasaki*.